TABLE OF CONTENTS

Building Your *Next* Model Railroad

GOALS (It's more fun to get there when you know where you're going):

BUILD IT:

Production Editor: Cathy Slegl, **Typography:** Typetronics, Inc. Published by Eastwood Publishing Company, 2901 Blake St., Denver, CO 80205. Printed in the U.S.A. Library of Congress Card No. 85-082068. ISBN number: 0-9612692-2-7.

ALL THIS ACTION ON JUST ONE 2 x 8 FOOT LAYOUT

Thomasville, Colorado, Circa 1907 on the Colorado Midland.

Thomasville, Maryland, Circa 1925 on the Maryland & Pennsylvania.

Number on PHOTO	Description of model (Subject of article)	Issue of Model Railroading that includes model
1	Freight station (Pola kit-conversion)	Fall 1979
3	Frameless tank cars (MDC kit-conversion)	Spring 1980
9	Frameless tank car (Life-Like conversion)	Fall 1981
10	Sage-trunk trees (Walthers tree kits)	Winter 1982
11	Warehouse kit-conversion (Bachmann kits)	Spring 1982
12	36′ iron frame box cars (MDC conversion)	Summer 1982
12A	Wood grain elevator (Campbell conversion)	Summer 1982
13A	36′ wood gondola (MDC kit-conversion)	Vol. 13, No. 1
14	38′ PS&N and CGW reefers (MDC conversion)	Vol. 13, No. 2
15	36′ MDC stock car (straw & hay techniques)	Vol. 13, No. 3
17A	Section house (scratchbuilding/styrene)	Nov/Dec 83
17B	Open platform baggage (MDC conversion)	Nov/Dec 83
19A	Empty "Scene Site" (milk depot scenes)	March/April 84
19B	Open platform coach (scratch sides/MDC)	March/April 84
20	Open platform combine/RPO (MDC/ Scratch)	May/June 84
22	Scene Site (Time machine/diorama build)	Sept/Oct 84
24A	Loading dock (scratchbuilding/time machine)	Jan/Feb 85
24B	PFM brass 2-8-0 (MDC kit-conversion)	Jan/Feb 85
26	40′ gondola (MDC kit-conversion)	May/June 85
28	C&S standard cattle pen (scratchbuilding)	Sept/Oct 85
29	Timber section & farm houses (scratchbuilding)	Nov/Dec 85
30	Thomasville station (scratchbuilding)	Jan/Feb 86
30A	Crossing signs (scratchbuilding)	Jan/Feb 86
31A	Log bridge (scratchbuilding)	March/April 86

The Maryland & Pennsylvania caboose and locomotives are PFM brass imports custom painted by John Linssens, 13404 Virgo Dr., Dept. MRG, Littleton, CO 80124. The Colorado Midland locomotives are MEW brass imports custom painted for Little Town Hobbies in Littleton, Colorado. The Colorado Midland caboose is an MDC conversion described in THE MODELERS MANUAL, a hardback published by Chilton and available through hobby dealers. The white school is a slightly modified AHM plastic church kit. The box cars are Labelle, MDC and out-of-production Central Valley kits. Everything else in the scene is in the HOW TO BUILD YOUR NEXT *MODEL RAIL ROAD* book.

Number on PHOTO	Description of model (Subject of article)	Issue of Model Railroading that includes model
1	Athearn GP9 diesel (Diesel Detail Close-Up)	Fall 1979
2	SD38-2 diesels (Athearn/Life-Like conversion)	Winter 1980
5	Ice house & platform (Pola kit-conversion)	Spring 1980
5A	72′ TOFC flat & 35′ trailer (Conversion)	Spring 1980
8	Athearn flat cars (tractor & grader loads)	Summer 1981
10	Sage-trunk trees (Walthers tree kits)	Winter 1982
10A	Milk Depot (Life-Like kit-conversion)	Winter 1982
11	Warehouse (Bachmann kit-conversion)	Spring 1982
13	3-story foundry (Pola kit-conversion)	Vol. 13, No. 1
14A	B&O wagontop box car (Cannonball kit)	Vol. 13, No. 2
15A	Train Miniatures/Walthers reefer (weather)	Vol. 13, No. 3
16	Outhouse (styrene scratchbuilding)	Vol. 13, No. 4
17A	Section house (styrene scratchbuilding)	Nov/Dec 83
18	Concrete tilt-up warehouse (Yorke kits)	Jan/Feb 84
19A	Scene site (with milk depot — diorama)	March/April 84
21A	MDC Railbox (weathering modern cars)	July/Aug 84
22A	40′ AAR box car (MDC & Athearn detailing)	Sept/Oct 84
23	ATSF SD40-2 Athearn (Diesel Detail Close-Up)	Nov/Dec 84
24C	100T covered hopper (Athearn conversion)	Jan/Feb 85
26	Erie 44′ gondola (Mantua kit-upgrade)	May/June 85
30	Thomasville station (scratchbuilding)	Jan/Feb 86
30A	Crossing signs (scratchbuilding)	Jan/Feb 86
31	Modern-era structures (kit conversions)	March/April 86

The Baltimore & Ohio diesels are Athearn GP9 and SD9 models painted by James Loveless. The B&O caboose is a brass import from Pro-Custom Hobbies, 742 Frederick Rd., Dept. MRG, Baltimore, MD 21228. The semi-truck and trailer to the left is a Herpa model, the one in the center is from Lima. The pickup truck is a Life-Like model.

continued on page 19

Thomasville, Ohio, Circa 1953 on the Baltimore & Ohio.

Thomasville, California, Circa 1979 on the Santa Fe.

Build-A-Layout, step-by-step Part I: A Track Plan You Can Live With

The core of this model railroad is a 2 x 8-foot shelf full of potential for the future with plenty of operating action and construction right now.

There are a variety of ways to begin the construction of a model railroad. The range includes everything from finding a place for the snap track layout you played with on the carpet, to building the hills first and adding the track and right of way later. The modeler who has tried both extremes (or either extreme, for that matter) often decides to do it something like the way we're going to illustrate. There certainly are "other" ways, to build a model railroad — we're going to try to show the painless way that will offer the most pleasure during both construction and when the layout is "finished".

MODULES: PRO AND CON

There have been dozens of articles in **Model Railroading** magazine describing various modular types of model railroads. The subject is covered, in greater depth, in the BEST OF MODEL RAILROADING TRACK PLANS book and it takes 26-pages to tell part of the story. Briefly, the most popular size of module is 2 x 4-feet. Each of these modules is designed to be a self-contained scene unto itself. Some modules or groups of modules (what I call "multi-module sets") are even self-contained operational layouts with a yard, industrial area or branchline wandering off from the standard (for HO scale modules) two-track mainline. The mainline itself is used only for long trains when the module (or multi-module set) is joined to matching modules that belong to other members of some modular model railroad club. That's the prime advantage of the module; it offers both small space-limited operations (at home) and mainline action (when connected to other matching modules at club get-togethers in shopping malls or at conventions).

The disadvantage of the module is obvious in nearly every photo and plan; it is boring with a capital B. Given the design parameters of 2 x 4-feet and the need to interface the two-track mainline at both ends, there isn't much you can do with just a single module to make it look much different from any other 2 x 4-foot module. It is possible to overcome much of that disadvantage by building a pair of modules (like the plans on these pages) as multi-module set to overcome the boring part. There's a "Catch 22" to the multi-module set, however; it is easy enough to blend a single 2 x 4-foot module into a permanent home layout but very difficult to include a 2 x 8-foot set in a plan. That is precisely what you see on these pages; a pair of 2 x 4-foot modules joined (but separable for transporting them) into a 2 x 8-foot multi-module set. Said pair of modules is incorporated into TWO trackplans; one occupies 10-foot 4-inches x 19-feet of space and the other requires a minimum of 6-feet by 20-feet 9-inches. Those two layouts can also be built in slightly less space by using a few tighter-radii curves or in a lot less space by settling for just one loop and altering the full-train operating patterns. The layouts illustrate how that pair of modules can become part of a larger layout so the boring appearance of the module is lost.

PORTABLE VS. MODULAR LAYOUTS

The purpose of this model railroad is NOT, necessarily, to show you how to build a model railroad that can be joined to the modules of a model railroad club's layout. That is just an incidental benefit of the particular 2 x 8-foot plan. What this model railroad does provide is a "core" layout that you can build right NOW and know that you can use it later if you have more space, more time, more money, more interest or anything else that would make you want and need more than 2 x 8-feet of model railroad. This is also not (necessarily) a layout intended for beginners, although the 2 x 8-foot size is a lot more practical than the 4 x 8-foot size many newcomers choose (because plywood comes in that size) for their first layout.

You certainly can build the "No Frills" 2 x 8 plan on a half of a 4 x 8-sheet of ½-inch thick plywood using snap-together train set-type track. The layout you'll see being built, however, is more complex than that bare sheet of plywood. We'll show you how to build a PORTABLE model railroad that can (if you wish) also be a module. The portable concept will make it possible for you to move the layout if and when you move yourself to a new home. The techniques we'll use to build that layout are as advanced as the "Loads-in/Empties-out" operating scheme depicted as part of the 6-foot x 20-foot 9-inch plan to keep the most experienced modeler satisfied. If the complexities cause you to be ucomfortable, skip them and build the No Frills version on that half sheet of 4 x 8-foot plywood. You can apply your own experience, ranging all the way from the no frills approach of the rank beginner to the complexities that please the expert, to every phase of this layout's construction.

IS THE TIMESAVER A TOY?

There's an extensive article on the "Timesaver" switching game that the late John Allen devised in the BEST OF MODEL RAILROADING TRACK PLANS BOOK as well. Many modelers have seen these Timesaver games in operation at conventions and at club shows and, as a model railroad, they appear to be at least as boring as the modular layout. The switching action of the Timesaver is interesting enough, but the shape of the layouts, often made with snap-together track on bare 1 x 12 planks, is

Reprinted from November/December 1984 issue

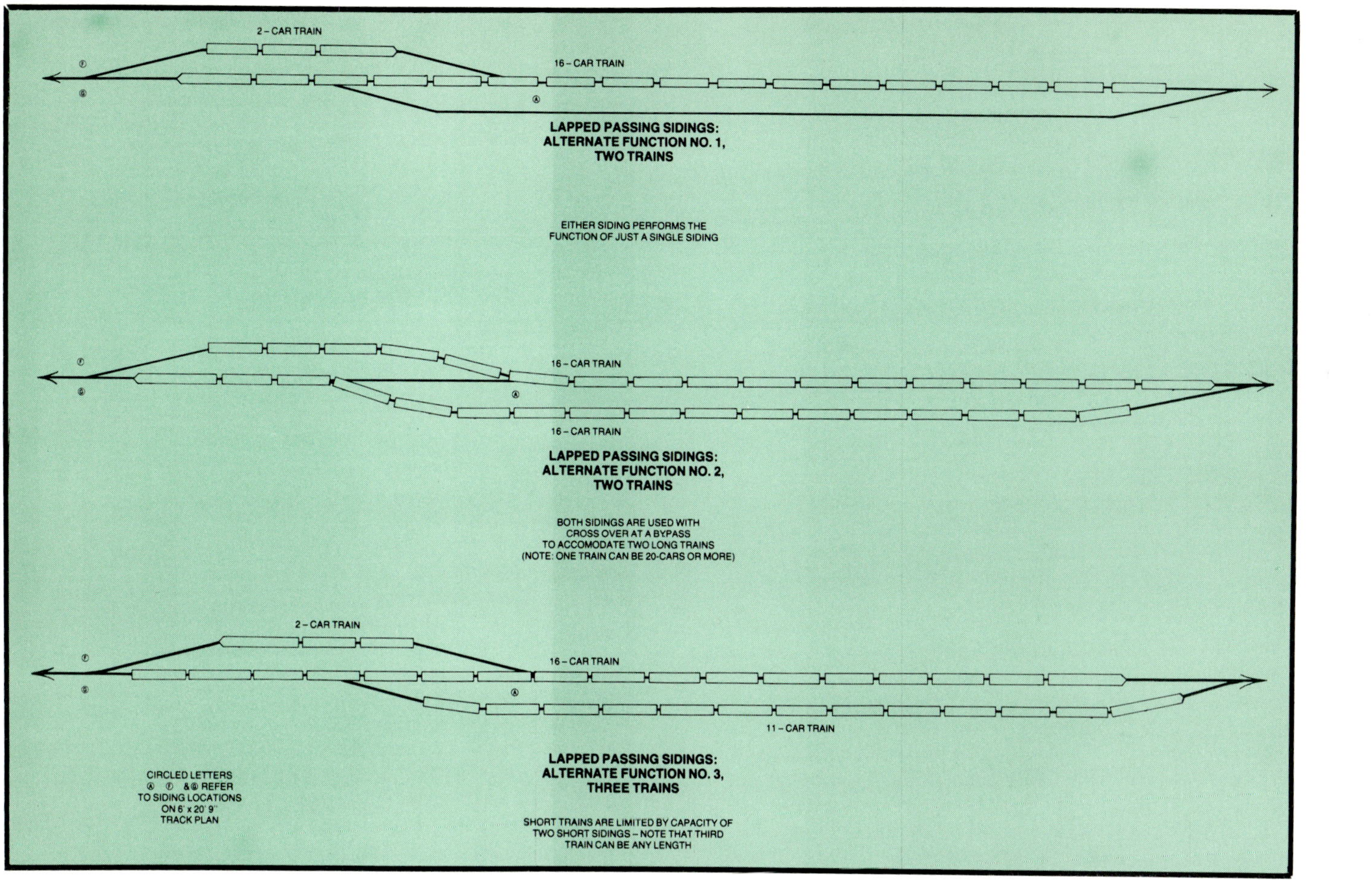

simply not what most of us have imagined as the fulfillment of our dream model railroad. The 2 x 8-foot track plan on these pages incorporates the Timesaver switching game's turnout locations and siding lengths so you can play-the-game if and when you wish. The Timesaver has been extended, particularly on the plan shown in color, to bring more elements of both realistic appearance and real railroad operations to the model railroad.

First, all the stubby sidings on the basic Timesaver have been bent enough to give them visual interest and most have been extended to avoid the stubby look. If you play the game, simply limit the siding lengths (with a nail in the ties or a parked freight car) so that siding C will hold only one car, so sidings A, D and E will hold only 2 cars and so sidings B and F will hold just 3 cars. Uncoupling ramps must also be located as indicated by the letters K (or you can simply uncouple the cars manually, lifting the cars at one end to uncouple them).

The Timesaver game is played by placing as few as three cars parked at A, B, D, E, or F with a locomotive and two more cars on either of the legs of the short passing siding midway between A and E. The player decides to pickup any 2 of the 3 cars on the sidings. The two cars behind his locomotive are to be spotted (placed) at the siding appropriate to the car type. A stock car, for example, belongs at a cattle dock. For purposes of playing the game, most folks simply make cardboard industry tags with the words box car on one, the words stock car on another, flat car on a third, tank car on a fourth, reefer on a fifth and so on up to 9 different tags. The "winner" of the game is the one who can move the two cars out and the two cars in using the least amount of time. With practice, you can even beat your own best time.

When you think you understand the game, add another car or two — it takes real skill to maneuver the cars when there are 8 or 9 of them. The locomotive speed can be set to a slow 7 scale miles an hour so you can control the locomotive with a reversing switch on the control panel. If you opt for that method however, you should replace the reversing switch with one that has a center off position so you don't throw the locomotive directly from forward to reverse — that action can damage both the motor and the gears. Alternatively, always stop the locomotive with the separate on-off switch on the power pack before throwing the reversing switch.

The Timesaver layouts used at most model railroad conventions are rather specialized devices with turnouts that automatically control the flow of power into the siding they reach (described in the Summer 1981 issue of **Model Railroading** magazine — the turnouts on this "project" layout are the "live-frog" type — shown in Fall 1981 — electrical power-routing trackwork). The Timesaver car quantity is sometimes changed to present a variation on the game for those who attend many such events. The modeler can create his own version, at home, by substituting new rules that might make, for example, the fewest number of moves to spot those four cars the criteria for winning. Remember, that "Timesaver" is simply built-into this track plan; you can choose to ignore the game and operate with a system more like that used by the real railroads.

LAPPED PASSING SIDINGS

You might consider the lapped passing siding as an example of the "end justifying the means". Here, we've taken the toy-like "Timesaver" track configuration and made it more like the real railroads' track patterns. That short Timesaver passing siding is of little value for two trains to pass each other because it is only long enough for a short steam locomotive or a single unit diesel and two cars — most modelers prefer trains of 5 cars or more on the average. The two large plans provide 9-foot passing sidings, in fact; long enough for 16-car trains to pass. The portion of these plans that includes the 2 x 8-foot pair of modules and the Timesaver, has the Timesaver 2-car train passing siding built into the 16-car siding with the results you can see in the diagrams. First, the mere existence of a 16-car siding does not imply that all of your trains be that long. Most trains will likely be shorter with only a rare "through freight" pre-planned (by your operating sequence and rules) longer than 16-cars. Obviously, ALL other trains must pull into sidings so that longer trains can stay on the mainline. The "Alternate Function No. 3. . ." diagram shows how a train of 16-cars (or even longer) can pass one or two shorter trains thanks to the use of the lapped passing siding. What is not obvious from the diagrams, is how the lapped passing siding can allow a freight train to be broken-down, at this "town" with fewer switching moves. The two sidings allow the "engineer", for example, to remove cars from the middle of the train if he uncouples so half the train is on either side of the pair of switches at "A". The sidings can also make it simpler to switch cars in and out of switchback track configurations (to get cars in and out of track "C", for example).

LOADS-IN/EMPTIES-OUT OPERATIONS

The reason why real railroads move cars in front of industries is so that the contents of that car can be unloaded or, if the car is empty it can be loaded. That seems obvious enough. It's far too obvious when you push a loaded hopper car beneath a coal tipple or pull a loaded car of lumber from a lumberyard — you can plainly see that these cars have not been loaded (or unloaded) by the "crew" at those industries. The need to load and unload those open-top cars prompted modelers like John Armstrong to devise the "Loads-in/Empties-out" system.

You will need a duplicate pair of cars, one with a load, the other empty. "Duplicate" can range all the way from the precise car number and shade of weathering to simply a pair of black hoppers with similar markings. The basic operating concept also needs an industry loading/unloading area that is covered or, at least, hidden from the view of the operators. The system also needs a turnout hidden at that same point so that there is an "invisible" second siding in that loading/unloading area. The "loaded" hopper car is pushed into one siding and a "day" later a second "unloaded" car is pulled from that second siding. How does that second car get there? You have two choices: connect the two loading/unloading sidings to a matched industry (via a tunnel) elsewhere on the layout, or simply move the cars on and off by hand. The 6-foot x 20-foot 9-inch plan as the "paired industry/two sidings/two turnouts" systems. Here, the cars of limestone (from the kilns) are used by the plaster plant to make plaster. Look closely and you'll see that a pair of parallel tracks lead beneath the scenery, from the kilns to the plaster plant. You can probably guess at the rest; loaded gondolas of limestone are pushed into the plaster plant and right on through to the mouth of the tunnel (hidden by a roofed unloading platform) at the kilns. Conversely, the second hidden track is used when EMPTY gondolas are pushed into the kilns to be filled with the heated limestone. Those empties are pushed on through to the inside of the plaster plant. The next switching crew then has a loaded gondola of limestone to pickup where it had left an empty one at the kiln. At the plaster plant, the loaded gondola left "the day before" is now empty. On this particular layout, the limestone is loaded into the kilns from trucks or wagons that reach it via a dirt road. The system will work with any set of paired industries like a coal mine/power plant, sawmill/lumber yard, etc. .

LOADS AND EMPTIES FROM THE OUTSIDE WORLD

Remember, I suggested there was enough "advanced" operating action on this plan to keep the experienced modeler busy? Here comes part of it: there is another loads-in/empties-out operation at the quarry. I envision that quarry to produce the red-colored building stone once popular for foundations and for what were called "flagstone" sidewalks. The stone from the quarry is shipped far from this town, over several other imagined railroads. The paired industries are quarry/outside world or, if you prefer, quarry/interchange. That hidden track should be visible (either by standing on a stool to look over the top of open-top hills or by a pair of mirrors, periscope-style) from below the layout. Loaded flat cars of stone are picked up by freights on the visible portion of the layout and pushed back into the quarry via the hidden turnouts at the rear of the layout. Conversely, the empty flats pushed into the quarry are picked up by freights via hidden turnouts at the back of the layout.

If you like things self-contained, you could make the quarry a limestone quarry and use similar operations to get the cars (gondolas in this case) in and out of the kilns. All these variations utilizing building stone, limestone, plaster and "the outside world" actually existed along a 10-mile stretch of the Roaring Fork River on the real Colorado Midland Railroad. We'll describe the more common operations on the layout (and on the real world prototype) in a later installment of this series.

FIDDLE YARDS & 0-5-0 SWITCHERS

You can, as I suggested, use the loads-in/empties-out operating concept even if you only have space for the 2 x 8-foot version of Thomasville. You may not need the extra turnouts to provide a pair of sidings for the smaller version but I'd suggest you include them so the layout is ready to expand if you find the space. If you're building just 2 x 8-feet worth of layout, then locate rerailing ramps at the locations marked "R" on the 6-foot x 20-foot 9-inch plan. The ramps on visible tracks can be disguised as road crossings (as Atlas and others do with their sectional track). Those ramps will make it easier to lift cars on and off the layout. That's where the 0-5-0 switcher (your five-fingered hand) is used — to manually lift loads and empty cars, and to lift cars destined for off-the-layout and onto the layout. The modelers in England often build entire hidden yards where they can rearrange the consists of 20-car trains using their hands to perform the switching maneuvers — the British modelers coined the term "Fiddle Yard" to describe such unprototypical actions.

OPERATIONS IN 2 x 8-FEET

There are at least three operating variations possible with this track plan: the Timesaver switching game, local or peddlar freight switching and industrial switching. The last two can be performed by two locomotives and two operators at once if you like excitement. The "pedlar" freight is a train passing through the town with a few cars to be dropped off and/or a few more to be picked up — you'll have to make-up and break-down that train, using cars stored on shelves near the layout, on either of the long

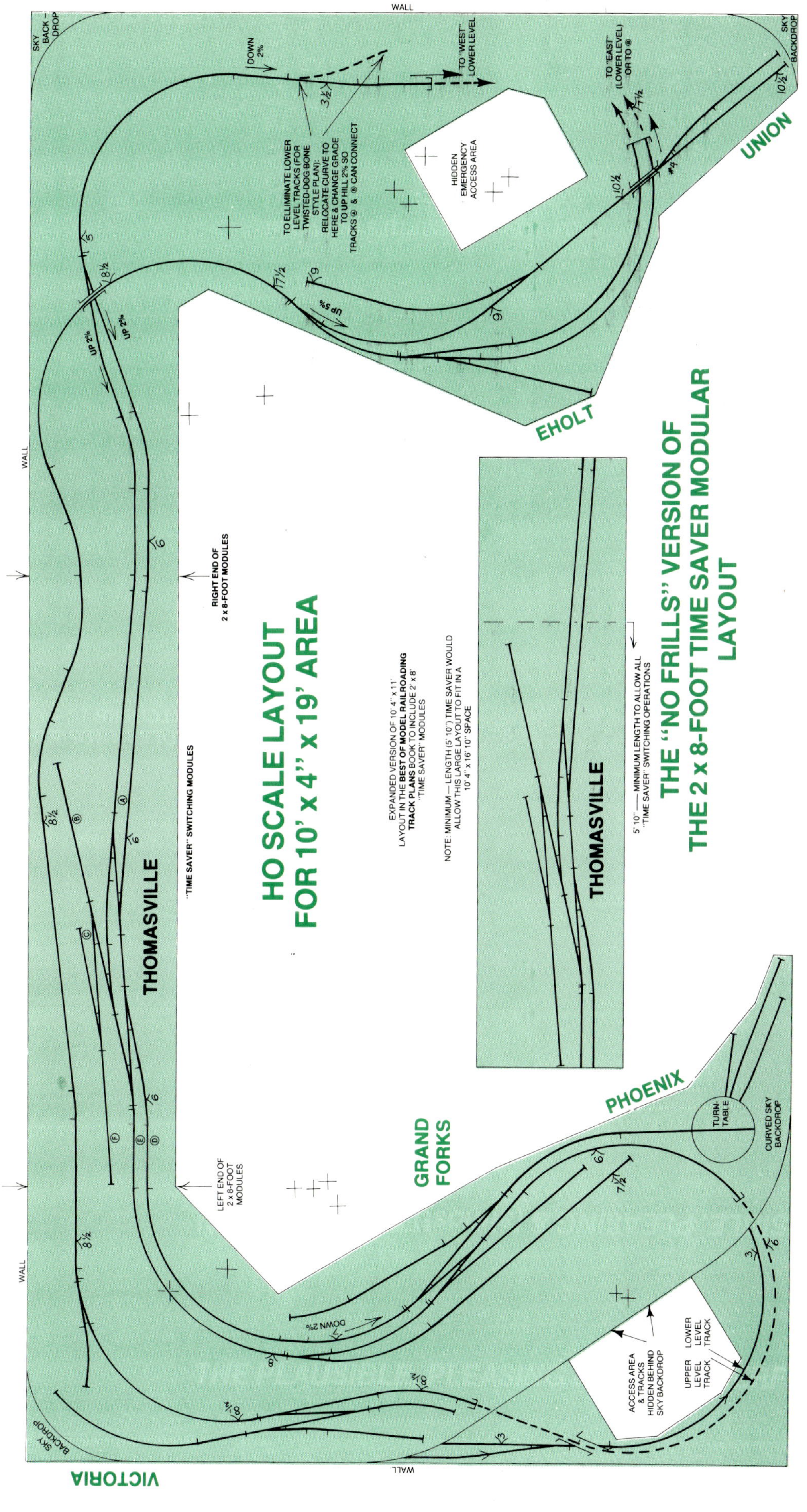
HO SCALE LAYOUT
FOR 10' x 4" x 19' AREA
EXPANDED VERSION OF 10' 4" x 11' LAYOUT IN THE BEST OF MODEL RAILROADING TRACK PLANS BOOK TO INCLUDE 2' x 8' "TIME SAVER" MODULES
NOTE: MINIMUM — LENGTH (5' 10") TIME SAVER WOULD ALLOW THIS LARGE LAYOUT TO FIT IN A 10' 4" x 16' 10" SPACE
THE "NO FRILLS" VERSION OF THE 2 x 8-FOOT TIME SAVER MODULAR LAYOUT
5' 10" — MINIMUM LENGTH TO ALLOW ALL "TIME SAVER" SWITCHING OPERATIONS
THOMASVILLE
THOMASVILLE
"TIME SAVER" SWITCHING MODULES
RIGHT END OF 2 x 8-FOOT MODULES
LEFT END OF 2 x 8-FOOT MODULES
TO ELIMINATE LOWER LEVEL TRACKS (FOR TWISTED-DOG BONE STYLE PLAN): RELOCATE CURVE TO HERE & CHANGE GRADE TO UP HILL 2% SO TRACKS Ⓐ & Ⓑ CAN CONNECT
HIDDEN EMERGENCY ACCESS AREA
TO "WEST" LOWER LEVEL
TO "EAST" (LOWER LEVEL) OR TO Ⓐ
DOWN 2%
UP 2%
UP 5%
DOWN 2%
UNION
EHOLT
GRAND FORKS
PHOENIX
TURNTABLE
CURVED SKY BACKDROP
ACCESS AREA & TRACKS HIDDEN BEHIND SKY BACKDROP
UPPER LEVEL TRACK
LOWER LEVEL TRACK
SKY BACKDROP
WALL
VICTORIA

parallel tracks to the lower right. The "Industrial" switcher would be a small steam or diesel engine that was assigned to Thomasville simply to move cars in and out of the various industries so they would be ready for either the "Pedlar" freight or for an imagined "third" freight train to pickup on its way through town. If you want to operate both pedlar and industrial switching, assign some outbound cars for on-the-railroad locations (to be switched by the pedlar) and others for more distant cities off-the-layout (to be switched by the industrial switching crew). If you only have 2 x 8-feet of layout, the cars left by the industrial crew will have to be carried off the layout by hand and others returned using the same means.

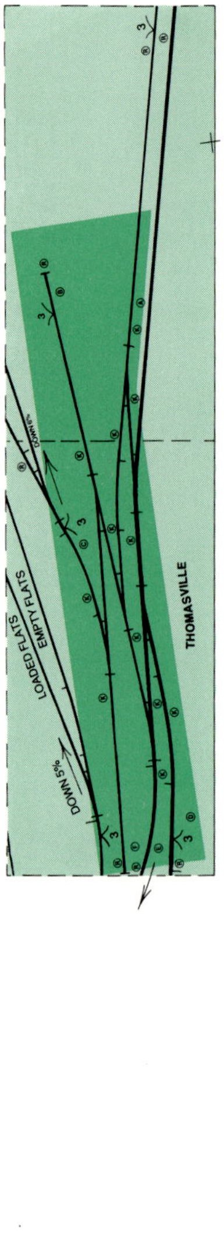

MAKING THE 2 x 8-FOOTER FIT YOUR SPACE

Let's hope that you like the Thomasville layout, but you have enough space for more than just 2 x 8-feet of layout. You can expand the Thomasville plan by simply making it one side of a double-track oval but, given 24-inch minimum radius curves, that layout would occupy 6′ 2″ x 14′ 2″ of space as an island which means that, given access aisles around three sides, it would fill a 10 x 16-foot room. If you want that simple a layout, you could wack off the right end of the 8-feet to squeeze it down to the no-frills 2′ x 5′ 10″ size and jam the oval into 10 x about 14-feet. There's a much better way; the 10′ 4″ x 19′ plan can be recreated in that size (as shown) or squeezed down to as little as 10′ 4″ x 16′ 10″ using the 2′ x 5′ 10″ version of the plan on these pages. That plan itself is an extension (extended by adding the 2 x 8 Thomasville plan) of a layout described in the BEST OF MODEL RAILROADING TRACK PLANS book. That layout has a lower (hidden) level that can add full-train operations that duplicate the actions of entire trains traveling "off-the-layout" via connections at A and B in the lower right. You can also connect A and B directly to one another for a simple oval-style operation.

The 6-foot x 20-foot 9-inch plan is a variation of the layout I am building for myself. You may find that your garage or basement has a wall long enough to accommodate that length (as I have). You can reduce the parallel

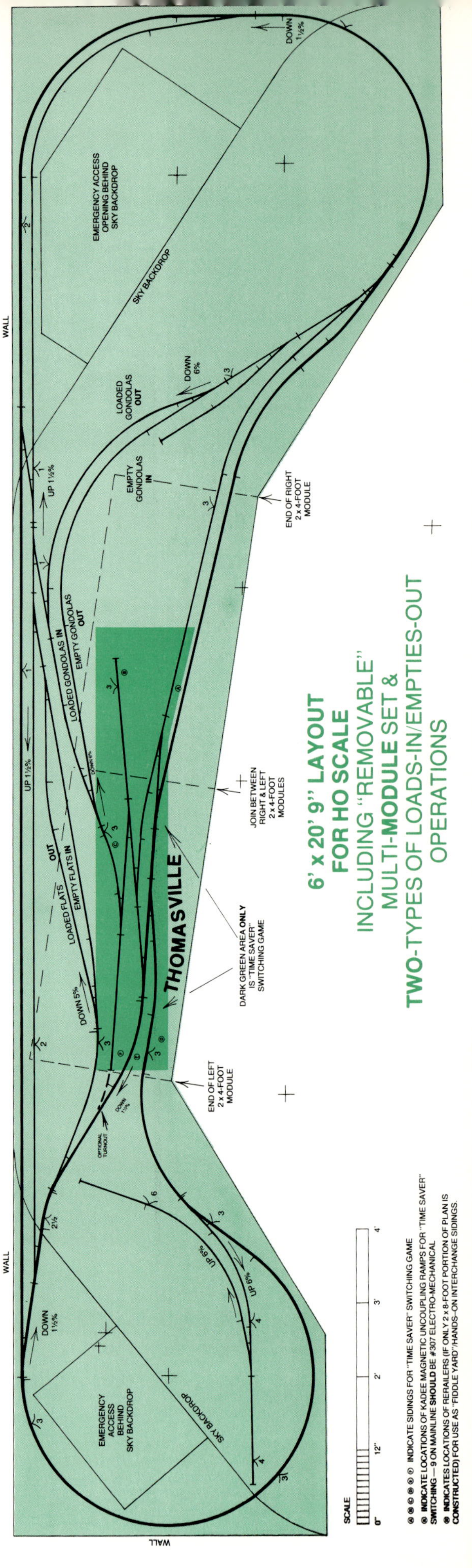

curve track 34 and 36-inch radius leading to the right from Thomasville down to 24 and 26-inches and save about 6-inches of length, but this is still a 20-foot long plan — if you have less space, opt for the 10′ 4″ x 16′ 11″ plan. This layout provides enough hidden trackage so you can actually operate both styles of loads-in/empties-out systems described earlier as well as using whole trains for pedlar freight and "off-the-layout" through freights. Passenger trains and other express freight and passenger trains would circulate around the oval-style tracks using track D at Thomasville. The shorter passing siding (part of the Timesaver) could be envisioned as serving a branchline that departs the scene as track E. Track E also allows trains to reverse direction with backing up, but there is no way to re-reverse them with the plan as drawn. If you feel you must reverse full trains from operations in either direction, the track at F could be extended a few inches to the left to a turnout to an additional turnout (marked "optional"). That connection would allow you to use the tracks leading to the plaster plant as a second reversing loop. If you wish, you can also skip the second sidings and the hidden turnouts for the various loads-in/empties-out operations (to make Thomasville's track look much like the "No Frills" portion of the 10′ 4″ x 19′ layout).

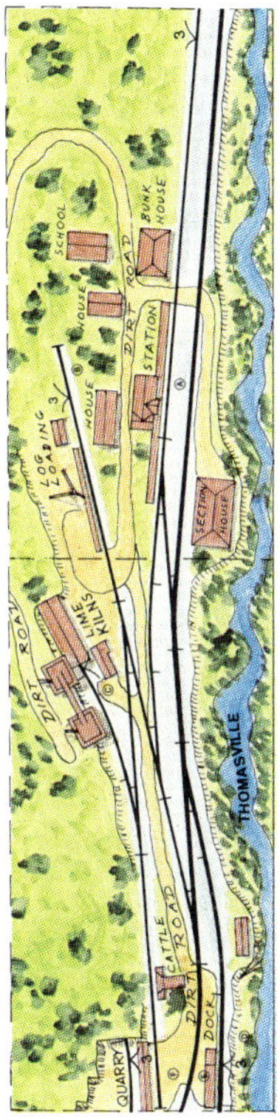

DECISIONS, DECISIONS

The track plans on these pages are certainly not the only ways you can build the Thomasville shelf layout into a room-size track plan. There are more ideas for it's use (as a substitute for any other pair of modules) in the BEST OF MODEL RAILROADING TRACK PLANS book. If you like the Thomasville town itself, it could certainly be used as a town to replace existing towns on a variety of other track plans using the "Scene Module" method also described in the . . . TRACK PLAN book. Thomasville is as versatile a plan for a small town's railroad tracks as you could wish for — in later installments we'll show you even more of that versatility, including alternate industries and the use of the "Time Machine" concept to provide even more value-per-square-foot of layout space.

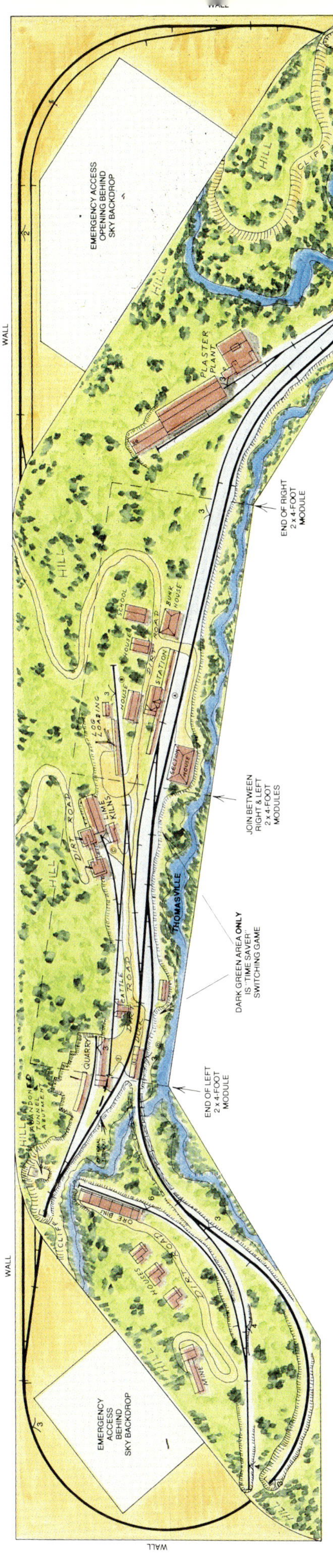

6′ x 20′ 9″ LAYOUT FOR HO SCALE

TO READER

Ⓐ Ⓑ Ⓒ Ⓓ Ⓔ Ⓕ INDICATE SIDINGS FOR "TIME SAVER" SWITCHING GAME

Ⓚ INDICATE LOCATIONS OF KADEE MAGNETIC UNCOUPLING RAMPS FOR "TIME SAVER" SWITCHING — 9 ON MAINLINE **SHOULD** BE #307 ELECTRO-MECHANICAL

Ⓡ INDICATES LOCATIONS OF RERAILERS (IF ONLY 2 x 8-FOOT PORTION OF PLAN IS CONSTRUCTED) FOR USE AS "FIDDLE YARD" HANDS-ON INTERCHANGE SIDINGS.

More Modeling in the Same Space with the Time Machine concept

A combination of state-of-the-art techniques, including lift-out dioramas or "scene sites", a change in backdrop and wholesale substitution of one era's railroad equipment for that of another era, create the "Time Machine". With it, you can literally have three true-to-prototype model railroads in the space of one. It's the no compromise method of modeling ALL the real railroads you want with historical accuracy.

CIRCA 1925

Somewhere in the "Woods" geography of North America. Judging by the equipment, we're somewhere north of Baltimore on the Maryland & Pennsylvania. Wooden grain elevators would soon disappear from the east (as would the wood outhouses) but the brick factory would remain. The locomotives were painted and weathered by John Linssens, 13404 Virgo Dr., Dept. MRG, Littleton, CO 80124.

CIRCA 1959

Somewhere in the "Farmland" of North America. There are farms in the background. The rock cliffs suggest we're along a river valley and, of course, on the Union Pacific. Those metal grain elvators are probably still there, but the Geeps and RS2 are long gone. The Athearn GP9 models were painted, detailed and weathered by commercial painter John Linssens.

Reprinted from November/December 1985 issue

CIRCA 1979

More "farmland", but this time it's along the Burlington's old route now worked by the green and black BN power. The round grain silos are now a more common sight than the old rectangular grain elevators. Box cars no longer haul the grain, now it's covered hoppers and airslide cars.

The construction techniques to build these "Scene Sites" appears on pages 33, 34, 61 and 65.

The use of "Scene Sites" is further explained on pages 86, 87, 88, 89, 24 and 25.

There are more photos of the "Time Machine" concept in action on pages 2, 4, 5, 19, 20, 21, 23 and 90.

Note: There is only one grain elevator in any of these photos. What appears to be a second grain elevator is really a reflection of the first in a 2 x 2 foot square mirror across the left end of the layout. The mirror is a permanent part of the layout to visually double its size. The photos on page 88 show the mirror for what it really is, a "scenic" devise.

CIRCA 1979

The concept of pooled power seems to create an ebb and flow of "foreign" locomotives. You're likely to see a Family Lines GP40-2 in the midwest and just as likely to see a BN diesel in the southeast. That Athearn GP40-2 was detailed with scale-size handrails in the January/February 1984 issue; the PS waffle box appears in the November/December 1985 issue. The blue L&N flat roof waffle box is a weathered MDC out-of-the-box kit.

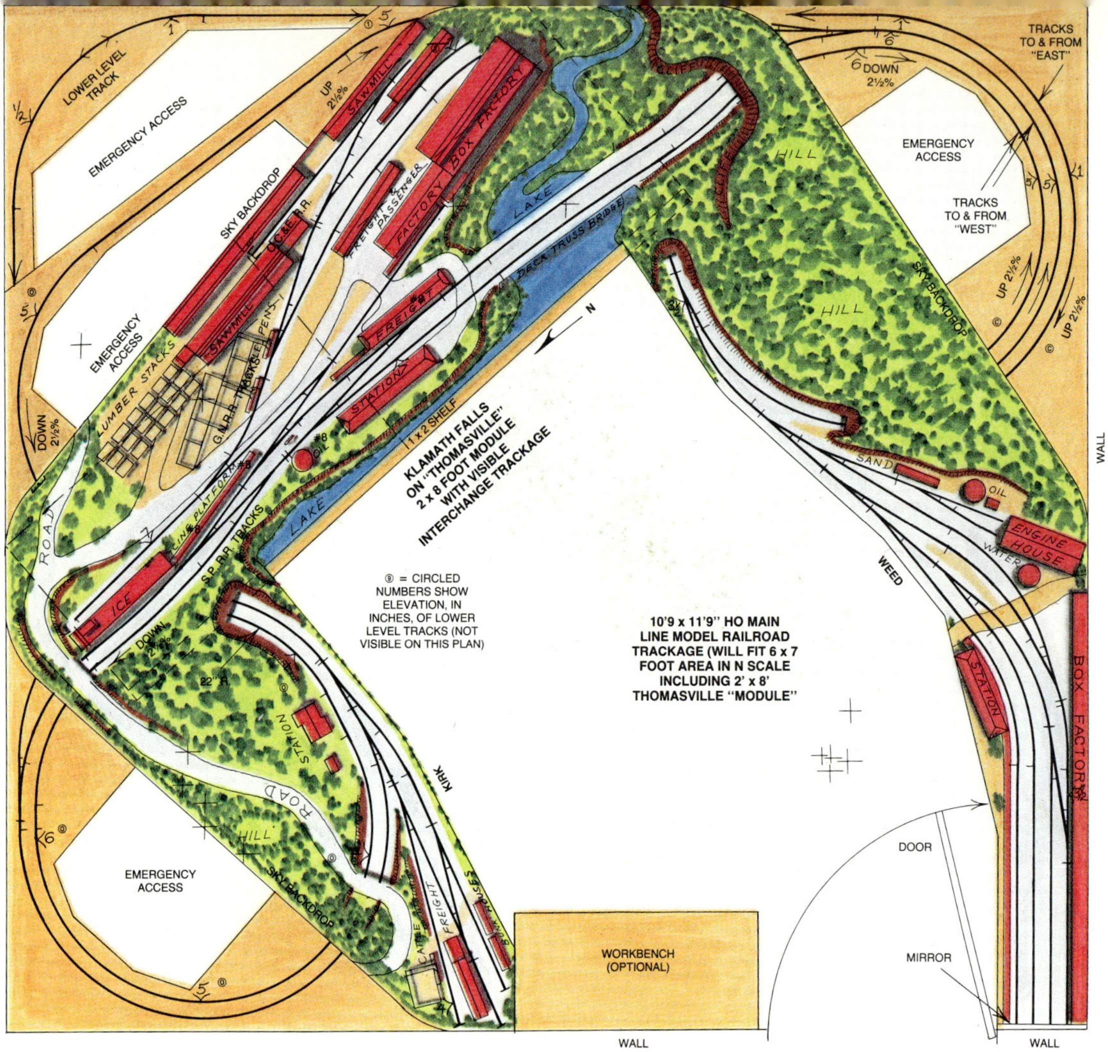

OUTER TRACK TO LOWER LEVEL

ALTERNATIVE (to Thomasville) SCENERY & STRUCTURE TREATMENTS & "VISIBLE INTERCHANGE" OPERATIONS FOR THE 2 x 8 FOOT LAYOUT AS PART OF 10' 9" x 11' 9" and 8' 9" x 9' ROOM-SIZE PLANS

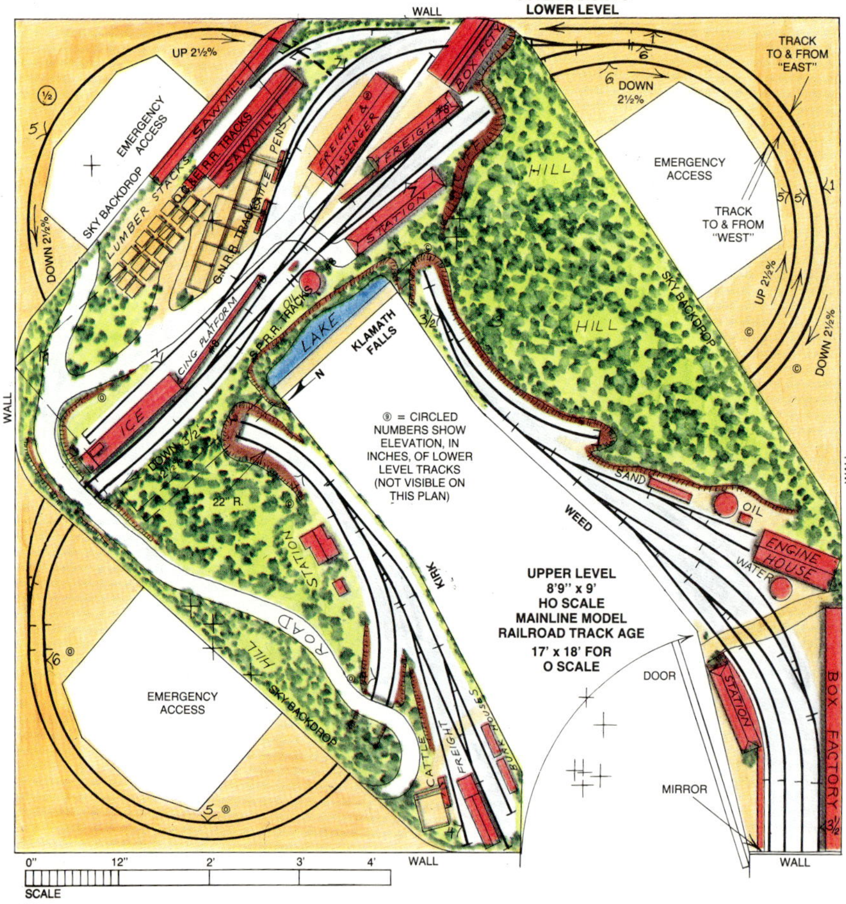

Track Plan: HO Mainline in 8′ 9″ x 9′ (with 10′ 9″ x 11′9″ option)

N scale mainline in 6 x 7 feet
O scale mainline in 17 x 18 feet

Expanding the 2 x 8 "Thomasville" module into a room-size railroad.

The Thomasville module that appears in the BUILDING YOUR *NEXT* MODEL RAILROAD book is a versatile piece of model railroad. That plan has plenty of self-contained operation in just 2 x 8 feet but it is also designed for those that can, someday, have an entire room devoted to a model railroad. The plans on these pages offer two such options; one for an 8 foot 9 inch by 9 foot room (that really only has space for one of the two 2 x 4 foot tables — but most of the Thomasville trackage). The second plan includes the entire 2 x 8 foot segment (plus backside extension) for a 10 foot 9 inch by 11 foot 9 inch room. Both plans are designed for relatively long trains to take maximum advantage of the lapped siding feature of Thomasville's plan.

If you prefer to build your models in the larger O scale or smaller N scale, these two plans will work for you, too. The 8′9″ x 9′ plan squeezes an incredible amount of operation in what would be about 17 x 18 feet in O scale. Any two car garage has that much space as do some spare rooms and, of course, basements. Usually, HO scale plans cannot be adapted directly to N scale by simply reducing the size. The 10′9″ x 11′9″ plan, however, has a wide enough entry aisle so you could reduce the plan to 6 x 7 feet for an N scale version and still have more than three feet of aisle width. The best possible N scale version of the plan, however, would be to build it in the 8′9″ x 9′ foot space but with the passing sidings merely spaced closer together than in the HO version. The large radius curves (the HO equivalent of a 24 inch radius N scale curve is a whopping 40 inches) would allow the operation of nearly scale-length N scale trains in this relatively small space.

There is almost as much hidden trackage as visible track

There's no doubt about it, this plan is complex. There is almost as much hidden trackage as visible track. Why? so you can route an endless number of complete trains through the visible portion of the layout from either "east" or "west". What you'll see is precisely what you would see in the real world; a parade of trains running just as though they really did come from somewhere (outside your modeled world) and going to some distant destination (also outside your modeled world). All that hidden trackage makes such operations possible by simply throwing a few remote controlled turnouts and a few block switches.

Holding or layover tracks

Modelers call those hidden tracks holding or layover tracks because those words best describe their function. The hidden tracks are places where trains headed off the layout are stopped ("holding" tracks) or held over ("layover") while other trains are routed OUT of the hidden tracks and onto the visible layout.

To match the prototype railroads, you'll want most of the trains that disappear towards the "east" to reappear, after being held or laid over, coming *from* the "east" (and, hence, "westbound"). That demands reversing loops and that routing is part of the hidden trackage. If, for example, the Amtrak westbound passes through Klamath Falls (the name we've given the Thomasville area on this plan) it will disappear from the layout on the inner of the three tracks in the upper right of the plans. That train will be traveling clockwise around the upper right curve to enter the reverse loop following the direction of the arrows on the hidden tracks. The train will be reversed to reappear on the middle track of the three in the upper right of the plans and reenter Klamath Falls (Thomasville) heading westbound.

That westbound Amtrak train passes first through Weed and then Kirk before disappearing from the layout into the tunnel at B near Weed. It will use the same reversing loop but retrace its path via C and B to appear (after a suitable layover on any unused part of the hidden trackage) as an eastbound train at Weed headed for Kirk and Klamath Falls (Thomasville).

In effect, that is an oval operation

Notice that the trains that disappear at B (headed "east") can run through the hidden reverse loop to reappear at A, still headed "East". In effect, that is an oval operation with the sides of the oval joined together (on the hidden trackage) at D — really a reverse loop (all the visible trackage) to reverse loop (the hidden one) operation. That path would be useful for trains that you want to always have heading eastbound with, say, loaded cars of coal. A second such "unit" train of empty coal cars could be set in operation heading perpetually westbound.

The layout can live

The plan is designed to squeeze as much mainline operation as possible in as small a space as possible. It also happens to utilize the Thomasville trackage; one way to insure that at least that part of the layout can live on even if you move to a smaller, or larger space. The various loops feed trains into the Thomasville area exactly like trains would be routed into such a town on a huge, club-size layout. That's also the way a real railroad site, like Thomasville, or Klamath Falls or wherever, appears as you watch the trains in action.

Trains 10½ feet long can pass one another

The towns of Weed and Kirk do not duplicate the prototype flow of trains the way that flow is duplicated at Klamath Falls. Trains 10½ feet long can pass one another, at both Kirk and Klamath Falls. The hidden holding/ layover siding on the reverse loops is also long enough to accomodate 10½ foot long trains. If you're modeling the fifties, where 40 foot cars were predominant, your train could still have two diesels (or a large steam

Reprinted from November/December 1985 issue

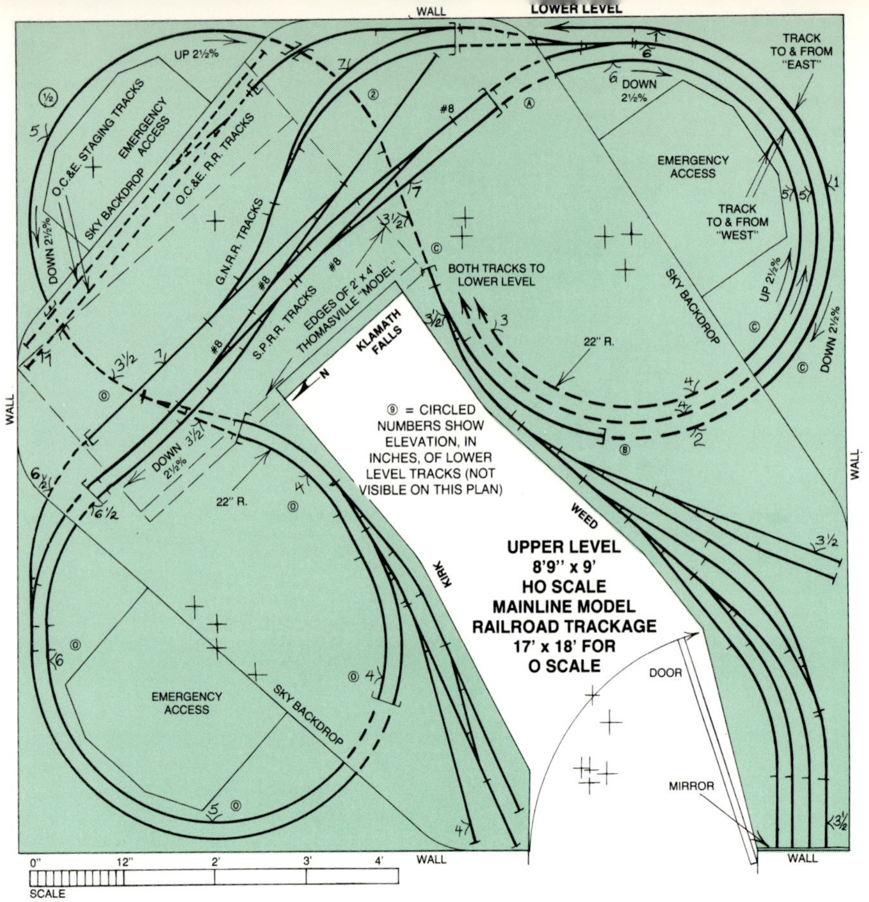

locomotive) and 21 cars. 1907 era trains could have double-headed steam locomotives and as many as 24 cars of an average 36 foot length.

Through trains actually pass right by

Only half of the trackage at Weed is actually on the plan — the other half is reflected in a mirror in the lower right corner of the plan. What's more, the through trains actually pass right by Weed; only trains that need to drop off or pick up cars head into (or back into) the trackage at Weed. On the 8'9" x 9' plan there's only room for a 24 INCH long passing siding at Weed. This is long enough for any locomotive to run around two or three cars so it can push those cars into any sidings or get behind them to make-up or break-down a local freight. Similar short sidings are the 15 inch siding at Klamath Falls and the 20 inch siding at Kirk; all allow local locomotives to perform their switching chores without tying up the mainline trackage or running through those 10½ foot long mainline passing sidings.

On the enlarged version of the plan, to fill a 10'9" x 11'9" area, a crossover has been added at Weed and the tracks extended to provide a second, 36 inch

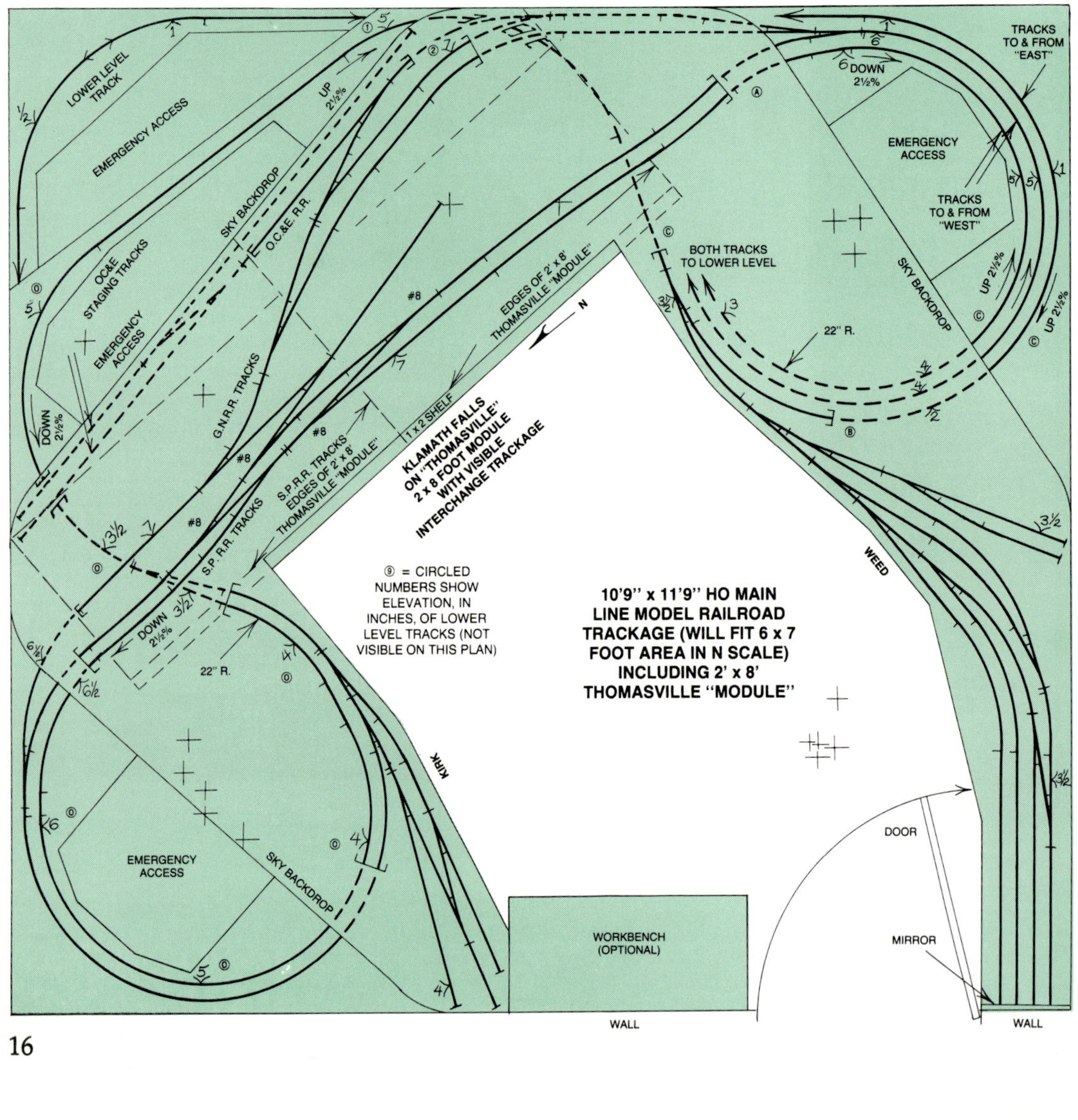

long, passing siding. The tracks at Kirk could be curved to flow above the workbench if you wanted more operations at that site.

The nominal minimum radius curve is 24 inches. That's actually the radius of only the outside curve between Kirk and Klamath Falls. The inner curves are 21½ inch radius on the hidden reverse loop; and in the upper right and lower left corners of the visible or upper level. You could make those inner curves 22 inch radius but long passenger cars and articulated steam locomotives and TOFC trailer-toting 89 foot flat cars could hit one another with only a two inch spacing on the curves. If you are certain you will only operate diesels and 50 foot or shorter cars, the inner radius in those three areas could be 22 inch.

All but the beginning and end of the grades are hidden

There are fairly stiff, 2½ percent grades on this layout, another compromise needed to squeeze mainline operations into such a small space. All but the beginning and end of the grades are hidden inside tunnels, except for the short stretch out of tunnel B near Weed. There is little visual lack of realism from the stiff

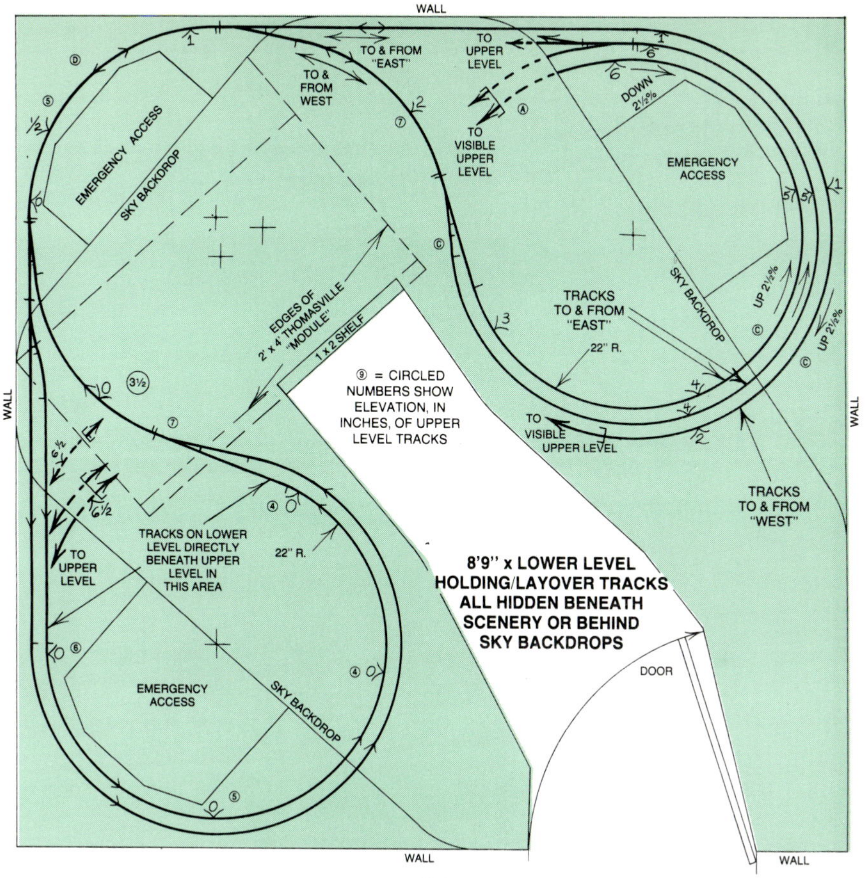

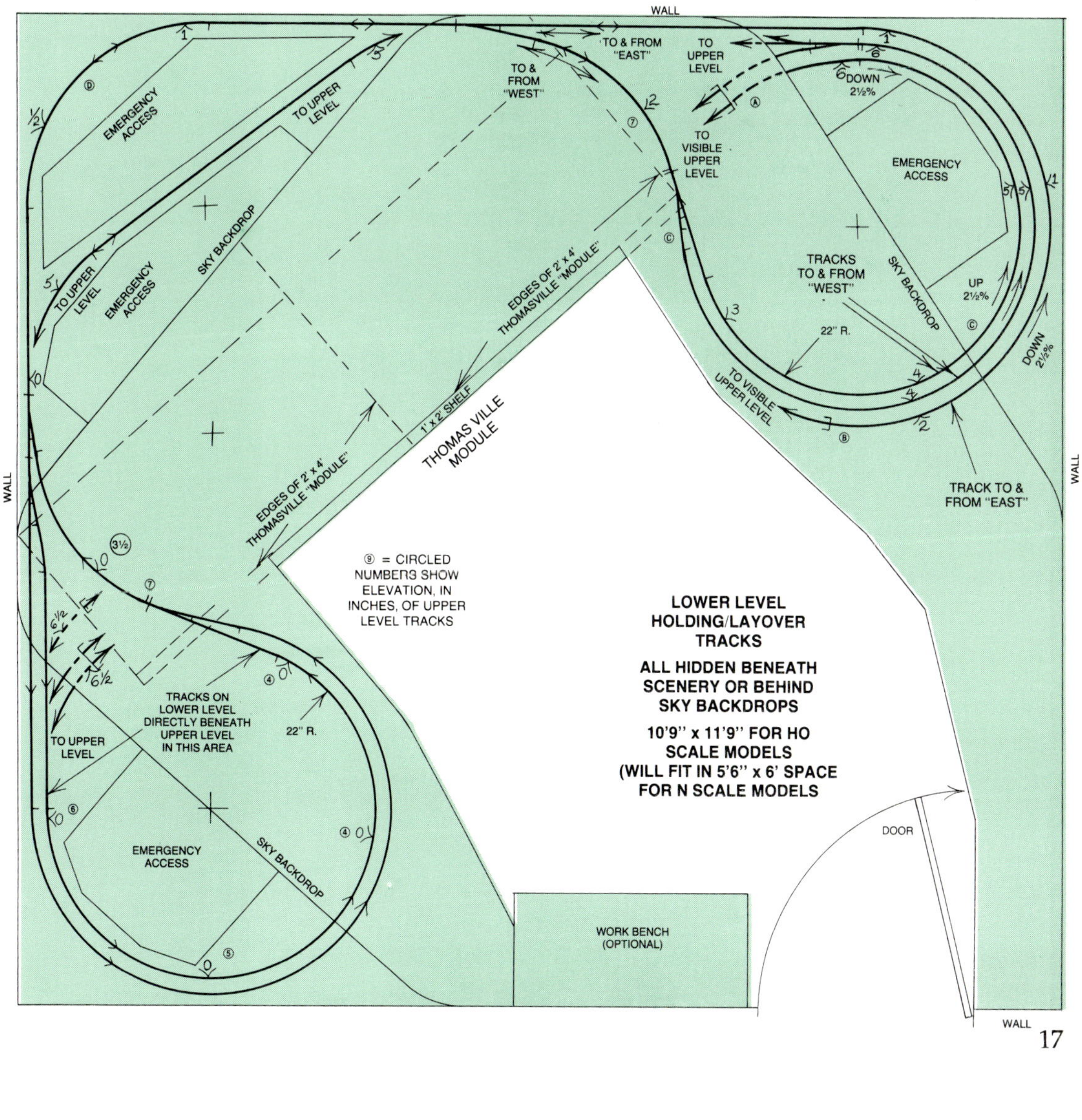

grades but they will effect how many cars some locomotives might be able to handle. If you do opt to build the 8'9" x 9' layout in N scale, the vertical separation between the tracks can be decreased from 3½ inches to 2 inches; that will allow you to decrease the grade to about 1½ percent.

It's wise to lay all the hidden track first

One of the confusing aspects of a plan that occurs when squeezing so much operation into such little space is the need for some tracks, particularly in the three corners opposite the doorway, to be placed directly above one another. If you use the open grid style of benchwork, 1 x 2 supports shaped like the goal posts on a football field can support the upper level plywood subroadbed and roadbed. It's wise to lay all the hidden track first, get it operating, wired and running reliably, then add the upper level plywood subroadbed and trackwork. With the open grid style of benchwork, you can reach those lower level tracks from beneath the layout. On this plan, there are three hidden access holes that will also make it easier to reach the lower level tracks because they will not be hidden by scenery.

The plan shows the sky backdrop curving in front of all three of those access areas. I would suggest you curve the sky backdrop around the corners of the room and extend the hills above eye level so just the tops of the hills hide the forward edges of the access holes. That's obviously a lot easier to accomplish if you are modeling the Rockies than if you are recreating Kansas.

OPERATING A VISIBLE INTERCHANGE AT THOMASVILLE

There have been three very different methods of setting the site for the trackage on the Thomasville 2 x 8 foot layout. The versatility of that plan is evident in the way the layout we actually built can be modified, very slightly, to represent virtually any geographic area from California to Colorado to Missouri to Maryland and any time period from 1907 to 1925 to 1953, 1959 or even the eighties.

The as-built version uses the track running diagonally toward the rear of the layout as a "loads-in/empties-out" siding serving an industry that consumes carloads of visible materials. As-built, that industry is a foundry or other consumer of scrap metal.

On the plan in the BUILDING YOUR NEXT MODEL RAILROAD book that actually depicts the real life Thomasville, (also published in the November/December 1984 issue), that track serves a lime kiln that would consume gondolas of limestone and ship boxcars of bulk or bagged lime. Again, it's a loads-in/empties-out operation. You can, however, use that track (and the hidden tracks beyond it) as a VISIBLE INTERCHANGE with another railroad. That is precisely what has been done by moving "Thomasville" and its trackwork to Klamath Falls on this track plan.

At the real Klamath Falls, the Great Northern (now Burlington Northern) and the Southern Pacific and the logging Oregon, California and Eastern railroads interchanged loaded and unloaded cars. Those are two of the most modeled mainlines in the world and the presence of a logging branchline makes the Klamath Falls site even more suitable for modelers. What's more, those operations began back in 1926 and continue today — pick your era and model it or select two or three eras as we have for "Thomasville" and model them all with a "library" of structures, scene sites, rolling stock and locomotives.

The operations at Klamath Falls are outlined, with some photographs, in John Signor's RAILS IN THE SHADOW OF MOUNT SHASTA ($27.95 from hobby dealers or Darwin Publications, 850 N. Hollywood Way, Dept. MRG, Burbank, CA 91505). On this plan the general scenery and structures of the Klamath Falls area, but none of the actual track configurations, are suggested to give a realistic background for the operation of Great Northern (or Burlington Northern), Southern Pacific and Oregon, California and Eastern equipment.

The OC&E tracks disappear to stub-ended staging sidings hidden behind piles of lumber and sawmill buildings in the upper left but accessible from the access area behind the sky backdrop. The Great Northern mainline joined the SP outside of Klamath Falls so the two railroads have separate lines through Klamath Falls on this model. The GN and SP have joint tracks, on the plan, through Kirk and Weed and they share all the hidden reverse loop and holding/layover tracks.

At least five different lumber company railroads joined the mainline tracks for interchange at Kirk during some time in history. The Weed Lumber Company Railroad also had major trackage at Weed. You have, then, a choice of the OC&E and a half-dozen other logging lines to add to the SP/GN/BN selection of equipment. In addition, the GN owned the Spokane, Portland & Seattle Railroad and, for whatever reason, you were as likely to see SP&S diesels in this area as GN power in the sixties. There were literally acres of sawmills and veneer plants and box factories in the area. A representative sample of these structures is included on the larger plan to feed traffic through Klamath Falls.

There was a Southern Pacific enginehouse at Weed right into the diesel age. You can use that enginehouse for SP power or designate it as a Weed Lumber Company Railroad facility to add a fourth railroad to the plan. Weed would be operated as a small yard with its own locomotive for switching, just as it was in the real world. The plan suggests only a cattle pen and freight station at Kirk, typical of nearly any small town along the GN/SP trackage. You could expand Kirk to provide an enginehouse for yet another logging line if you wish. With two mainline railroads and two or three branchlines, there's a wide spectrum of operations possible in what is a very small layout space.

VARIATION ON THE THOMASVILLE THEME "2 x 8" MODULE WITH VISIBLE REAR INTERCHANGE TRACKAGE

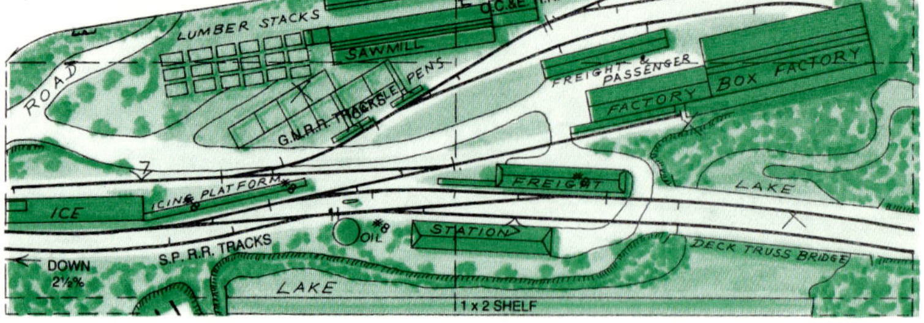

The Whole Scene

Most of the locomotives, rolling stock and structures in these scenes on the Thomasville layout have been assembled following information published in past issues of **Model Railroading** magazine.

continued from page 5

Number on PHOTO	Description of model (Subject of article)	Issue of Model Railroading that includes model
4	Varney/Life-Like tank cars (weathering)	Summer 1980
4A	Athearn GP9 by John Linssens (Diesel Detail)	Summer 1980
8	Athearn flat cars (tractor & grader loads)	Summer 1981
10	Sage-trunk trees (Walthers tree kits)	Winter 1982
11	Warehouse kit-conversion (Bachmann kits)	Spring 1982
13	3-Story Foundry kit-conversion (Pola kits)	Vol. 13, No. 1
17	47′ covered hopper (MDC kit-conversion)	Nov/Dec 83
17A	Section house (scratchbuilding/styrene)	Nov/Dec 83
19	Alco RS2 Diesel (Hobbytown/Diesel Detail)	March/April 84
21	Metal grain elevator (scratchbuilding)	July/Aug 84
22	Scene Site (Time Machine/diorama-build)	Sept/Oct 84
22A	40′ AAR box car (Athearn & MDC detailing)	Sept/Oct 84
24	AAR tank cars (Gould & Mantua detailing)	Jan/Feb 85
24A	Loading dock (scratchbuilding/Time machine)	Jan/Feb 85
25	40′ AAR box car (McKean/Athearn conversion)	March/April 85
26	40′ gondolas (MDC kits/Freight Cars Fifties)	May/June 85
29	GP9 and GP9B diesels (Diesel Details)	Nov/Dec 85

NOTE: All back issues are available. Use envelope in this issue to order any copies, freight prepaid.

Additional stock kits include the Alloy Forms trucks and automobiles, a Walthers/Ulrich Pennsylvania 35 foot highway trailer, and (out-of-production) Rio Grande GS gondola and an Athearn Conoco tank car. The switch stands are Sequoia (ex-Apag) and Utah Pacific. The small shed is a kit-bashed Life-Like kit.

Operations on the Thomasville Layout

There's room on this 8 foot shelf-size layout for the same type of operations possible on much larger, room-size, model railroads.

The track arrangements, structure locations and scenery suggested on the track plans utilizing the "Thomasville" 2 x 8 foot layout are designed to make the layout as interesting to operate as it is to see. It looks real and, with some planned operations, it runs real.

"LOADS-IN/EMPTIES-OUT" OPERATIONS

The 2 x 8 foot segment of the layout has been expanded into four different track plans. The two that are featured on the "Thomasville" plan on pages 9 and 11 treat the siding at Ⓒ as another industrial siding (like Ⓐ, Ⓑ, Ⓓ, Ⓔ and Ⓕ). Siding Ⓒ leads through an industrial building to a hidden pair of sidings to allow you to simulate the unloading of open-top cars, like gondolas or hoppers. That "Loads-in/Eempties-out" operation is explained in the next article.

THREE RAILROADS ON JUST 8 FEET

Two more plans are included in this book, "Klamath Falls", p. 14-18, they treat siding Ⓒ as merely another segment of visible trackage that leads to another real railroad. Similarly, all the trackage to the rear of the layout, beyond siding Ⓒ and including the track marked "L/O", is visible on these plans. Here, "Thomasville" has been relocated to Klamath Falls, Oregon to simulating a real town served by three real railroads. The "mainline" tracks on the plan simulate the Southern Pacific's route, the tracks running, left to right, from siding Ⓕ through siding Ⓒ to the two 30-inch radius curves simulate the Great Northern tracks. The two tracks and the two crossovers at the rear simulate the trackage of the third railroad to serve Klamath Falls; the Oregon, California and Eastern Railroad's logging line. Three railroads on just 8 feet of model railroad.

WHICH TYPE OF OPERATIONS?

You can simulate either the one railroad and Loads-in/Empties-out operations at Thomasville or the three railroad interchange at Klamath Falls utilizing this same track plan. The scenery and structures must, of course, be installed when you build

PHOTO I. *Thomasville, Circa 1979 with the geographic scene set in the arid southwest somewhere on the Santa Fe. The westbound local is powered by an SD40-2. With modern 50 foot cars like these, there's only room for four cars with the locomotive stopped on the turnout in front of the two metal structures.*

Reprinted from November/December 1985 issue

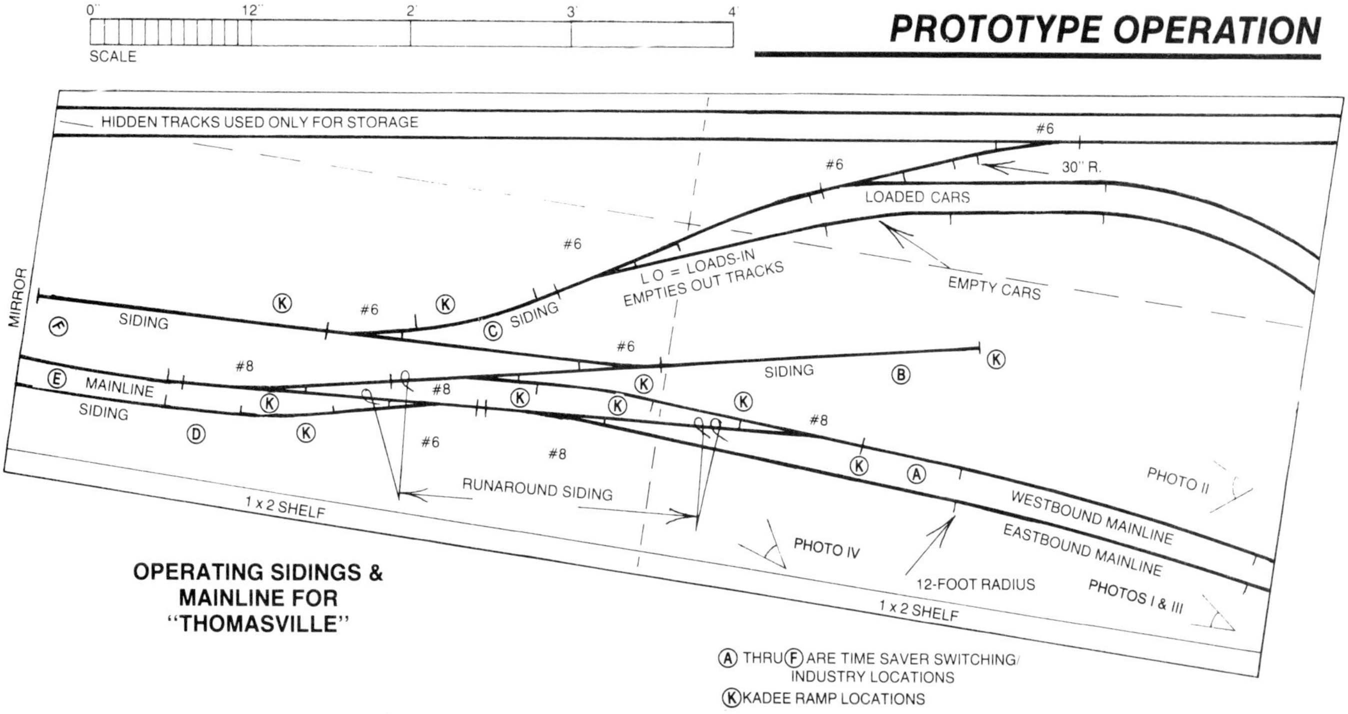

PHOTO III. *Thomasville, Circa 1953. This time, the hillsides are covered with more trees and lush green shrubs to set the geographic scene in the east, somewhere on one of the Baltimore & Ohio Railroad's branchlines. With the 40 foot cars that were the average in this era, the "Eastbound Local" can just squeeze five cars and clear the switch points in front of the station. The GP9 has spotted the caboose on the westbound track and is about to couple onto the remaining four cars of the train (the fourth car is out of the photo in the lower right). An SD9 is assigned to switching duties at Thomasville.*

PHOTO IV. *You don't need to date the layout as far back as 1907 to include passenger switching operations. Most real railroads set out and picked up baggage, express, reefers, RPO cars and diners at small towns like Thomasville (see page 63 of the Sept/Oct 1985* Model Railroading *for more about these "head end" operations). On the full-size Colorado Midland, Thomasville was the place where the diner on eastbound Train 6 was dropped off after serving dinner in the evening to be picked up by westbound Train 3 to serve breakfast the next morning. The action was common from 1907 to about 1914 when the railroad added more diners and simply left them in the consist.*

the layout because half the trackage is hidden on the "Thomasville" version, while nearly all but the track against the back wall is visible on the "Klamath Falls" version. It's the Thomasville version that appears in ALL of these photos. The buildings and some of the scenery have been changed to alter the era and geography but the operations are the same. You must, then, decide which type of operations you want before you install the building sites or start the scenery.

The article on the Thomasville plans explains how the railroad would be operated if you have either a 6' x 20'9" space or a 10'4" x 19' foot area (or larger). That article also explains how the short "runaround" siding can be extended to form a lapped passing siding.

THREE-RAILROAD INTERCHANGE OPERATIONS

That lapped siding also appears on the Klamath Falls version of the plan first published in the November/December 1985 issue. The three-railroad interchange operations at Klamath Falls are part of both the 8'9" x 9' and the 11'9" x 12'9" layouts. A chart of 8 additional 3-railroad interchange operations (and another 3-railroad plan) appears on page 45 of the July/August 1985 **Model Railroading.**

STUB-ENDED STAGING TRACKS

You can duplicate all of the operations of any of those room-size layouts on just this 8-foot segment of the plans. The train lengths will be much shorter, of course. One of the few disadvantages of a small shelf layout is that you must carry the equipment on and off the layout by hand. On a larger layout, you can run entire trains into the hidden holding/layover tracks. There are many experienced modelers whe prefer to make-up the trains by hand on tracks called "staging tracks". The operations on stub-ended staging tracks are described in the July/August 1985 and the September/October 1985 issues of **Model Railroading.** The concept can certainly be applied to this 8 foot long layout.

THREE-TRAIN OPERATION AT THOMASVILLE – USING *VISIBLE* STAGING TRACKS

Use the staging track operating principle to place three trains on the Thomasville layout to start an operating session:

Train No. 1, the *Westbound Local* freight would be placed on the track marked "Westbound Mainline". There is about 28 inches of track to the right of the number 8 turnouts points, enough for four or five freight cars, depending on their length. The locomotive can rest on the turnout itself. Photos I and III show Westbound Local freights in action.

Train No. 2, the *Eastbound Local* freight would be placed on the "Eastbound Mainline". Here, you have the choice of placing the locomotive on the track in the far lower right corner of the plan or of imagining that the locomotive has already runaround its train (on trackage — not modeled — to the right of the plan) to couple to the caboose for some switching operations. There's about 43 inches of track with the far left car clear of the runaround siding; six to eight cars if you don't include the locomotive. Photo II shows an 8 car 1907 era freight in this location.

Train No. 3, the *Thomasville Turn* freight would simulate a freight train that would be stationed at the next town up the line from Thomasville. This train would really be just a locomotive and (optional) a caboose. The train would spend most of its days just switching cars in and out of the sidings at Thomasville. A few cars headed ONLY for the next town would be moved by this locomotive. It might also "arrive" at the beginning of an operating session with a car or two from that next town bound for industries at Thomasville. It is the switching engine and crew.

The *Industrial Capacity* of Thomasville, for our operating-a-model railroad purposes, is limited by how many cars can be stored at the various industrial sidings. Sidings B and D are about 24 inches long — four or five cars each. Siding F is about 21 inches long — three or four cars. Siding C will hold one car outside the Loads-in/Empties-out structure. Inside that L/O structure, each of the two curved sidings is about 36 inches long — five to seven cars each. We won't use the two storage tracks or the crossover leading to one of them with this type of operation. The total "industrial capacity" of Thomasville, then, is between 22 and 29 cars. The difference depends on car length; it takes more of the 28- to 36-foot cars of the 1907 era to fill a siding than the 40-footers of the fifties or the 50-footers of the most modern eras. To start an operating session, fill about half those siding lengths with freight cars.

You would then have three locomotives and a total of 21 or more cars, all waiting some attention from the various switching crews. How you handle the operations from there on is up to you. One possibility would be to allow the locomotives of Train 1 to pick up any cars bound for the west and to leave any cars for Thomasville on siding B. Train no. 2 would pick up any eastbound cars and leave any of its Thomasville-bound cars on siding D. Train no. 3, the switcher, would spot any outbound cars routed west on siding B and any outbound cars for the east on siding B to await the crews of trains 1 and 2. The switcher would, of course, handle all the switching in the sidings at Thomasville. You could certainly perform all these operations with just one local switching train; designating it as "eastbound" (and heading it in the proper direction, of course) at one operating session and designating it "westbound" for the next operating session.

You can make the operations of a small layout like this even more interesting by using a card type of operating system like that described in the Volume 13, No. I issue of **Model Railroading** magazine. Even the computer operations in the January/February 1985 issue and the "Assigned Service" operations described in the March/April 1985 issue can be used effectively on this layout.

If you want to hone your skills as a switching "crew", you can play the "Timesaver" switching game. That game is described in THE BEST OF **MODEL RAILROADING** TRACK PLANS book. Essentially, two to six cars are spotted at sidings A, B, C, D, E and F while a train arrives with two to six more cars to replace those already spotted. The game is played against the clock with the locomotive's speed set at just a crawl. The quickest time to swap, say, "loaded" cars at A and F for two "empty" cars in the train, wins. The more cars used, the more complex the game.

You certainly do not have to duplicate all of the construction techniques that built Thomasville. Nor, for that matter, are those techniques limited to just Thomasville. You can recreate the plan on a sheet of ½ inch plywood and use Atlas Snap-Track and cork roadbed if you wish — the operations will be just as exciting. The operating reliability, no stall performance, and the realism of the layout should certainly be better if you follow the suggested construction methods. Have fun.

PHOTO II. *The piñon pines on the hills, the snow-capped mountains and sage set this geographic scene in the Rockies. The time is about 1907 on the Colorado Midland. Train no. 2, the Eastbound Local, is at the lower left — its locomotive is switching a string of tank cars to set out a tank with a hot box (a truck journal bearing that's worn too far to continue). Here, the Eastbound train is a passenger with a baggage, a Railway Post Office combine and two coaches. The baggage has been spotted behind the station to be loaded with some express to await the next passenger train east. The shorter cars of this era allow you to use about 25 percent more equipment for trains with more cars and sidings with more "Industrial Capacity" (see text).*

REAL RAILROAD ACTION AT THOMASVILLE

Thomasville, Colorado was one of hundreds of small communities served by the mountain railroads. For those of us who want the scenic grandeur of a mountain railroad but the operating excitement of the city lines, this is one possible prototype town; a very busy place indeed.

Morris Cafky's long out-of-print COLORADO MIDLAND lists the shipments made from Thomasville in 1907:

No. of Carloads	Commodity	Probable Type of Car
153	lime	box car (assigned service)
12	lime rock	gondola
210	logs	flats and gondolas
20	lumber	Box cars (with small end doors), flats or gondolas
25	hay	Box cars or stock cars
7	cattle	stock cars
1	potatoes	Box car or reefer

PREVIOUS ARTICLES IN THIS SERIES:

Overview: "Modeling the Gold Hill Mining District" Sept/Oct 84

Part I: "Operations on the Narrow Gauge: Rosters" Nov/Dec 84

Part II: "Freight Car Routing *via* Assigned Service" March/April 85

Part III: "Freight Car Movement at Mines and Mills" July/Aug 85

Real Loads/Real Empties really ! ! ! !

A "Modeler's Trick" applied to operations.

John Armstrong, the dean of model railroad track planners, was the first to publicize the concept of what he called "Loads-in/Empties-out" back in the sixties. Briefly, the scheme is a way to make it appear that open-top cars are actually unloaded at an appropriate industry. We all strive for realism in our railroads and in the way we run them. That effect is strained, however, when we shove a loaded gondola into, say, a scrapyard and later pick up that same loaded car claiming it to be "empty". This concept avoids that glitch.

"IT REALLY IS EMPTY"

The action that you see on your model railroad is that of a locomotive pushing a loaded gondola into an industry. A "day" or so later, after allowing time for that car to be unloaded, the car is pulled from the industry and it really is empty.

"MAGIC"

The "magic" is accomplished with the use of TWO gondolas; one empty and the other full. Inside that industrial building (actually, beneath the mountains behind that industry) there are also TWO tracks; one to hold empty gondolas and the second to hold loaded gondolas. The locomotive simply pushes the loaded cars into the appropriate track (after you throw the hidden turnout, of course). Later, the locomotive is routed, *via* the hidden turnout, to the second track to couple onto one of the empty cars.

On this small "Thomasville" shelf layout, the loaded and empty cars are moved on and off the tracks by hand. You reach in through the rectangular hole in the right end of the layout to remove any excess numbers of loaded cars or to place additional empties on their track to await the arrival of the local switch engine during the operating session.

"INTERCHANGE OPERATIONS"

This same type of hand-carry operation would also be used, incidentally, to recreate interchange operations if you elect to make the track visible (rather than burying it beneath the hills). That two (or three) railroad interchange operation is the type suggested if the layout is operated like Klamath Falls, Oregon where the Great Northern, Southern Pacific and Oregon, California and Eastern interchanged cars. With two (or three) railroad interchange operations, entire cars, not just "loads", would "disappear" off the layout. You would, of course, carry the outbound cars off by hand and replace them with inbound cars.

"MATCHING PAIR OF INDUSTRIES"

If you have room to extend the layout for about 8 feet or more to the right of the "Loads-in/Empties-out" tracks, you can model the matching industry that would receive the loads from the first industry. That type of a matching pair of industries is

In this Circa 1925 scene, on the Maryland & Pennsylvania Railroad, the foundry is about to receive a Big Four gondola load of coal. The local switch engine is just pulling the empty, that was spotted as full car yesterday, from the industry. The foundry would also receive gondolas loaded with scrap.

Reprinted from November/December 1985 issue

The foundry is still in operation, in this Circa 1979 scene on the Burlington Northern. The main structure is stone, painted to match the new ribbed-metal annex (beside the Railbox car). The empty gon has just been pulled from the building and is being replaced by another load. The third car, with its load, will be spotted beside the annex to wait for the first car to be unloaded. The text explains how those loads of coal or scrap really are "unloaded".

illustrated on the 6′ x 20′9″ version of the Thomasville plan. On that plan, lime kilns at Thomasville *receive* empty gondola cars and the kilns *ship* loaded gondola cars full of white lime.

On the right of that 6′ x 20′9″ plan, a plaster plant *receives* the loaded gondolas and *ships* empty gondolas. It would, of course, ship plaster in bulk or in bags in box cars.

The loaded gondolas are simply pushed (right-to-left) through the mountain (on their "Loaded Cars" track) from the plaster plant to the kilns on the left. Empty cars are pushed (left-to-right) into their "Empty Cars" track as they disappear beneath the shed at the kiln to reappear at the plaster plant.

"PUSH THE CARS ON THROUGH"

There's about 6 feet of track between the kiln and the plaster plant. If you have the dozen or so loaded gondolas and another dozen or so empties, you can merely push the cars on through. With fewer cars, the locomotive itself would have to disappear into the kiln shed to extract loaded gondolas or into the plaster plant to extract empties. On the real railroads, it is unusual for the locomotive to actually enter the building.

You can certainly push the empty cars closer to the plaster plant by hand and the loaded cars closer to the kiln (between operating sessions) to avoid the need for the locomotive to enter the industry.

"THAT HAND-SHOVELING OPERATION"

The lime kilns, that will someday occupy the center of the Thomasville layout, have not yet been modeled. The kilns themselves were loaded and unloaded by hand. Wagons carried the raw lime rock to the top where it was shoveled into the kiln. At the bottom, it was shoveled into box cars or gondolas. We cannot recreate that hand-shoveling operation, so the loading dock will be covered with a shed (as it might well have been in the rugged weather conditions of the mountains). The shed will hide the lack of workers to shovel the lime and provide a hidden "portal" to the tunnel that hides the loaded and empty car tracks.

"A SMALL FOUNDRY"

The photos of the models show a three story brick structure at the mouth of that loads-in/empties-out tunnel in the Circa 1925, 1953 and 1959 scenes. That structure is supposed to simulate a small foundry that consumes loads of scrap metal and an occasional load of coal. In the circa 1979 scenes, the foundry is a slightly more modern stone structure with a most modern steel annex (a Pike Stuff brand "Prefab Warehouse" plastic kit).

"SCRAP METAL DEALER"

If you elect to replace the lime kilns with a foundry, as the industry that consumes the loads, then you might want to replace the plaster plant with a scrap metal dealer. The scrap metal dealer would ship loaded gondolas full of scrap metal. Again, a shed would be needed to simulate the loading area at the scrap metal dealer. The shed would hide the lack of loose scrap and cover the right entrance to the tunnel that houses the "Loads-in/Empties-out" pair of tracks.

THE MODEL RAILROADING HANDBOOK, Volume III, published by Chilton Book Co., is available from hobby dealers. It lists more than a dozen "pairs" of industries that would ship open top loads and/or consume the loads from open top cars.

You certainly do not need to limit the switching action at these industries to just the loaded and empty gondolas. The lime kilns probably shipped as much lime in box cars as they did in gondolas. The plaster plant shipped most of its plaster in box cars. The foundry would ship most of its castings in box cars with, perhaps, some huge castings in gondolas or flat cars. You could easily arrange to push empty flat cars into the foundry and pull out duplicate cars with loads of crates for a second pair of "Loads-in/Empties-out" moves (actually, empties-in/loads-out with the crates of foundry castings or forgings). You'll have to pick your own third industry to receive those crates of castings. That type of three-industry loads-in/empties-out operation is also described in Volume III of THE MODEL RAILROADING HANDBOOK.

Modeling The Action Of Mountain Railroading Part IV: Lime Kiln Operations (Part 1)

A rarely-modeled mountain industry.

Jim Cassidy

The track plan, first published in the November/December 1984 issue, that is the basis for the "Build-A-Layout. . ." series included four small structures that were labeled "Lime Kilns". We've received more mail asking about them than we would have expected. They do exist. Sometime next year we intend to show you how to model them. In the meantime, though, we thought you'd like to know a bit more about them in case you want to include such a scene on your own mountain-based model railroad.

These particular kilns were built right at the turn of the century along the Frying Pan River about 50 miles over the mountains from Aspen, Colorado. The kilns baked or roasted limestone from quarries just up the valley. That limestone (actually, calcium carbonate) yields (more or less) pure lime (calcium oxide) when burned. Lime was used for a number of manufacturing processes including the making of plaster. There also happened to be just such a plaster mill just a few miles downriver from these kilns. The kilns were near Merdith, (2 miles east of Thomasville) the limestone quarries at Lime Spur (a half mile east of Thomasville) and the plaster mill was at Ruedi (4 miles east of Thomasville) all on the Colorado Midland and all gone by 1921.

These limestone kilns still stand along the Frying Pan River in Colorado. These types of kilns were once a major shipping and receiving industry in the mountains; a prime source of operating traffic for a model railroad.

Lime kilns operated in dozens of locations during the 1900-1920 era but they were replaced by kilns right at the plaster plant. The plaster plants were located nearer the major cities.

It would appear that the gondola loads of limestone were carried up a road to be dumped into the tops of the stone kilns by wagons or horse-drawn two-wheeled carts. No photographs of these kilns in operation are known to exist, although the kilns are still standing. The lime was then shoveled out the arched doors into waiting box cars (or gondolas) for shipment to the plaster mills. The lime was also used in the processing of sugar beets and in smelting operations. A list of a number of shippers and receivers of lime rock apears in the March/April 1985 issue of **Model Railroading.** Box cars used for lime shipments were marked for that use alone ("assigned service") because the highly corrosive lime contaminated the interior of the car to make it unsuitable for other commodities.

PREVIOUS ARTICLES IN THIS SERIES:

Reprinted from November/December 1985 issue

Build-A-Railroad, step-by-step

Part II: Taking any trackplan from Model Railroading pages to the three-dimensions of benchwork, roadbed, track location *plus* Modeler's Tricks for building up and down grades

This trackplan, like every plan in **Model Railroading** magazine and in THE BEST OF MODEL RAILROADING . . . TRACK PLANS book, has all the markings and dimensions you need to locate the tracks on the bench work — here's how to do it, one step at a time . . .

The benchwork for a model railroad serves far more functions than to merely support the track like the frame of a kitchen table. The tracks are only part of what makes a model railroad; the benchwork also supports the scenery and must allow access to the bottom of the roadbed for wiring and to any hidden tracks. That term "access" is what made open grid style benchwork popular back in the very beginning of model railroading. The open grids provide the support and stability for the roadbed — it's the strength of the framework, then, not the strength of the tabletop (roadbed) that supports the track and scenery.

There's another factor you should consider when you build your open grid benchwork; how are you going to get the layout out of the basement (or spare room) when you move to another home? You do not need to make your benchwork quite as strong as the modular segments shown on these pages — 1 x 2 lumber could be substituted for the 1 x 4 outer

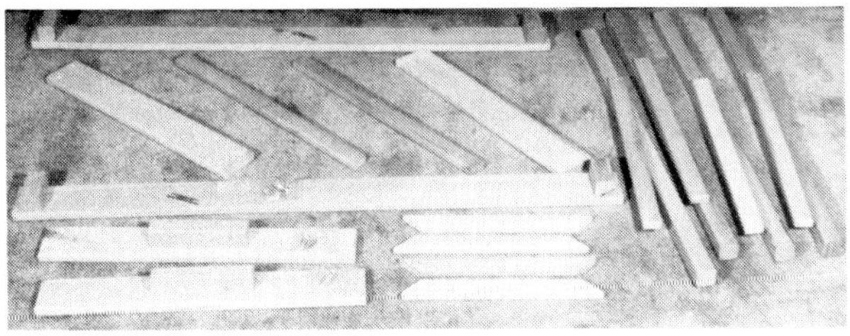

You can cut the benchwork yourself from 1 x 2, 1 x 4 and 2 x 2 fir to match the benchwork plan Figure 1 or you can buy a kit from Proto Power West. One of their 2 x 4 benchwork kits and two of their pairs of leg kits are shown.

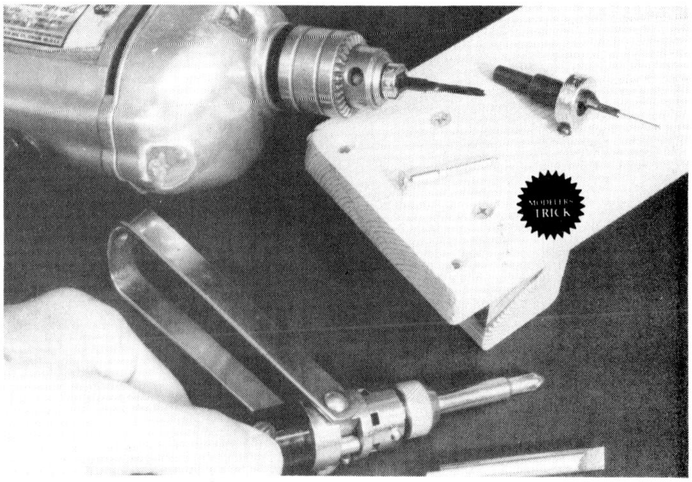

Buy a wood screw hole-drilling bit for your electric drill. You can buy adjustable-depth bits (right) or standard size bits like the one in the drill. You'll need a number 8 x 1¼ and 8 x 1¾ to install the risers and roadbed even if you purchase pre-drilled benchwork kits.

Buy wood screws with Phillips heads; the standard screwdriver bits slip out of slotted head screws too easily.

Also, buy either a Yankee-brand push-style automatic screwdriver, a ratchet-style screwdriver like this one or a variable speed electric drill and bits — there are over 200 screws in this 8-foot long layout.

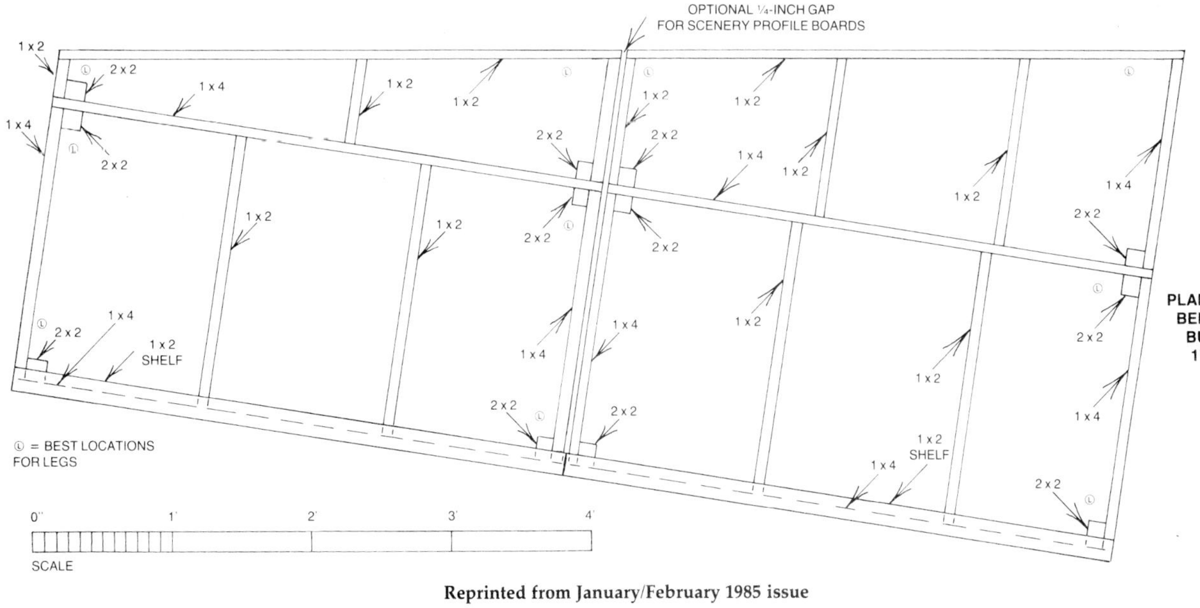

FIG. 1
PLAN FOR OPEN-GRID BENCH WORK WITH BUILT-IN PAIR OF 1' x 4' MODULES

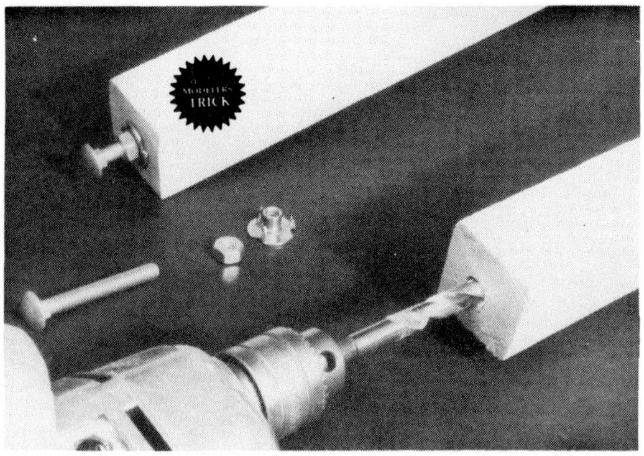

Drill a 5/16-inch hole about 2-inches into the bottom of every leg. Insert a Tee-nut for a ¼-inch bolt into the hole, then thread-in a carriage bolt and nut. The bolt allows you to adjust the length of the leg to conform to the nearly always-unlevel floors so the top of the benchwork can be perfectly level.

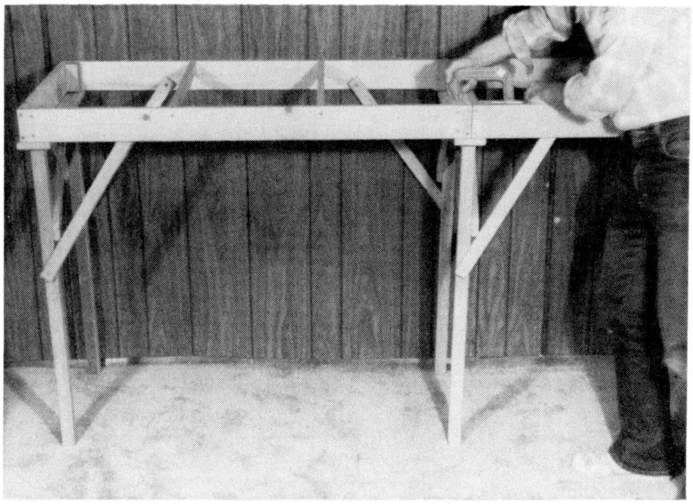

Use at least two screws on every joint in the main benchwork. I've attached the 1 x 4 horizontal member of the Proto Power West leg unit with a pair of screws. You can install the legs on the first module and use it to support adjacent modules. I inserted two pieces of ⅛-inch plywood between the modules — later, scenery profile boards will be cut to fit between the two modules.

A pair of 6-inch C-clamps are a big help in keeping things aligned while you drill holes and insert and tighten screws. Here, they're holding the two modules together while I drill two ¼-inch holes to accept 2-inch x ¼-inch carriage bolts, nuts and flat washers to clamp the two modules together.

framework if your layout is only going to be portable (moved, hopefully, once or twice in your lifetime) as opposed to modular (moved once a month or more). With that one change, consider the benchwork plan to be the minimum use of lumber. Even that third lengthwise (8-foot) center brace is worthwhile whether you opt for the modular idea or not.

You will see that two 2 x 4-foot modular sections of a layout have been built-into this layout. The sections have been moved, effectively, forward 1¾-inches to provide space for a 1 x 2 sill that is the place where visitors and operators will lean their elbows when viewing your layout. Skip that sill and they'll rest on your scenery. At the rear, the layout has been extended and angled to get further away from the boring parallel track and table edge sight of many modular layouts. The use of two modules allows the tracks between the ends of the modules to swing in large-radius ess bends (5-foot radius through the number 8 crossovers and a whopping 12-foot radius to the left) for a visually pleasing layout. Some modular clubs will allow you to use this layout as-is, other groups will demand a sky backdrop just 24-inches from the rear of that arm rest — if you plan on operating mostly with a modular club, skip that rear angle extension.

The benchwork for these modules came from a kit — five kits, actually — from Proto Power West, 3432 Lucero Ave, Dept. MRG, La Verne, CA 91750. The kits build 2 x 4-foot modules that are accepted by most modular clubs in both HO and N scale (assuming you locate the tracks at each end to match the club's specifications). Proto Power has a leg system that provides a horizontal 1 x 4 on top of the legs to support the joints between two modules — it saves the need for legs on adjoining modules and the only attachment points are the diagonal 1 x 2 braces — the weight of the layout is usually enough to keep the legs in place vertically. The prices of lumber vary almost daily, so send a stamped, self-addressed envelope to Proto Power West for their current price list; the 2 x 4 benchwork kit complete with screws and pre-drilled holes, is about $30 and each pair of legs (we used four pair) is about $16 including postage. You might also want to contact Sievers Industries, Jackson Harbor Rd., Dept. MRG, Washington Island, WI 54246 and Modular Layout Systems, 3780 W. Delhi Rd., Dept. MRG, Ann Arbor, MI 48103 for prices on their ready-to-assemble modular benchwork kits. If you want to build your own benchwork, use the plan on these pages and substitute 2 x 2 or 2 x 4 legs for the Proto Power West units at the points marked L on the plan.

The plywood sub roadbed and Homosote roadbed are part of the benchwork but you will not find any plan for them or for the vertical supports to hold them above the benchwork. Those parts of the benchwork must be located to match the trackplan and to provide support for any structures adjacent to the tracks. The photographs and captions show you how to make those parts of the benchwork. The height of the risers, above the benchwork, will be determined by the depth of any valleys you want below track level. I planned a relatively shallow valley along the front of the benchwork and another near the right end; my tracks are located 4-inches above the benchwork. If you are planning on operating with a modular group, you may need to place the roadbed right on the benchwork so the ends will clamp to the next modules beyond the right and left of your layout. In that instance, valleys will need to be cut into the crossmembers or new crossmembers cut from ¾-inch plywood to allow the valleys to hang below the top of the benchwork. If you elevate the tracks as shown in the photographs, there will be no way to clamp your modules to others.

If you are going to use your layout as part of a modular club layout, you will need to make the legs the length to match your layout height to the club's. The Proto Power West legs elevate the top of the benchwork to 40-inches. If you opt for the ⅜-inch plywood subroadbed and ½-inch Homosote roadbed that will raise the track level another ⅞-inches. Those risers elevate it, in this case, another 4-inches. Frankly, I'd like it about 10-inches higher but, for photography purposes, the current 44-inch height is just fine. On this layout, the tracks across the rear will, eventually, joint with more segments of the railroad. The hidden tracks needed to be two-inches lower than the visible tracks, so that meant that the benchwork needed to be at least two inches lower than those double-track mainline tracks. For a home layout, you can build segments of the benchwork with different heights to make the lowest track level with top of the benchwork or you can select a "zero" elevation for the top of all segments of the benchwork. More reasons why it pays to plan on paper with pencil before you start sawing wood.

FIG. 2
CUT LINES FOR PLYWOOD & HOMOSOTE FOR LAYOUT ROADBED

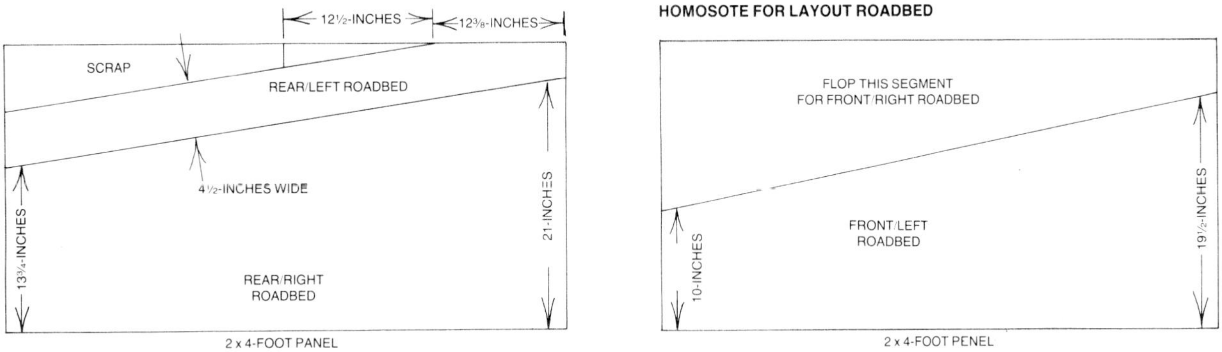

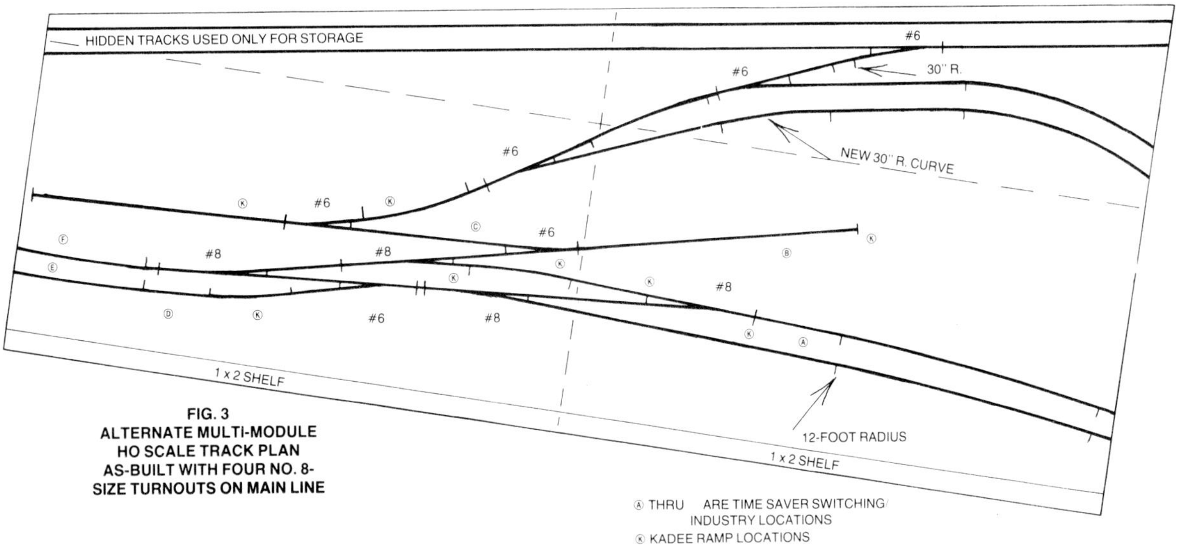

FIG. 3
ALTERNATE MULTI-MODULE HO SCALE TRACK PLAN AS-BUILT WITH FOUR NO. 8-SIZE TURNOUTS ON MAIN LINE

I disassembled the legs to install the rear extensions of 1 x 2 benchwork on the two modules. Notice that each joining corner is supported by a 2 x 2 attached with those number 8 x 2-inch woodscrews. If you are building portable (as opposed to modular) benchwork, you can use 1 x 2 (and 2 x 2) lumber for all the benchwork.

It is absolutely essential that the benchwork be perfectly level if you are going to attach the subroadbed (plywood) and Homosote roadbed directly to the top. If you are elevating the road-bed, however, it's really only the roadbed itself that must be level — still, level benchwork makes it easier to judge grades and alignment. I added a fourth pair of Proto Power West legs to the right rear corner to support that extension, with a 1 x 2 diagonal to support the center, rear extension.

To transfer the trackplan from the printed page (or from your own scale drawing) to the benchwork, start with more complex groups of turnouts. The process is easier if you can cover the entire benchwork with solid sheets of plywood and Homosote but the material is expensive. I cut the plywood and Homosote to match the patterns in Figure 2, leaving the forward edge open (it will be a river) and part of the rear open (to be buried beneath mountains).

Locate the straight portions of the turnouts, first, by measuring how far each is from the forward edge and ends of the benchwork. That 1 x 2 is a sill, on this layout; the actual trackplan begins on the backside of it. Draw the straight lines using a yardstick or longer piece of straight 1 x 2 to guide the pencil. Next, locate the points of the turnouts (the points and frog are indicated on the trackplans published in Model Railroading *magazine as well as in the... TRACK PLAN book). The scale on the plans can be used, with a compass (or a pair of dividers) to determine the dimensions needed.*

Make a trammel (a large compass) by driving a nail into a yardstick at the one inch mark. Use the nail as the pivot while you swing the yardstick through the curve with a pencil held at the desired radius (plus that inch for the pivot). Again, the curve centers are shown (as X marks) on our plans. Here, I'm marking the two hidden curves at the upper right of the plan.

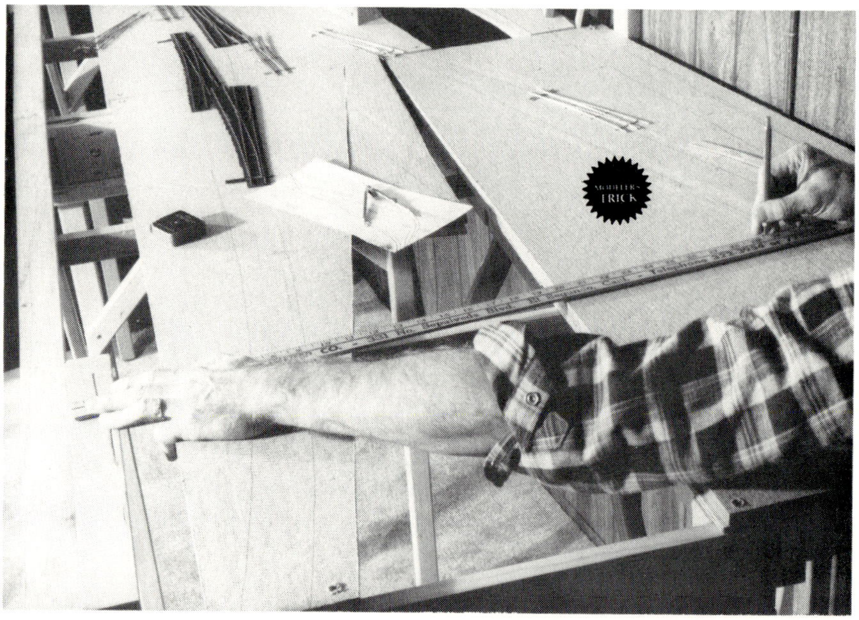

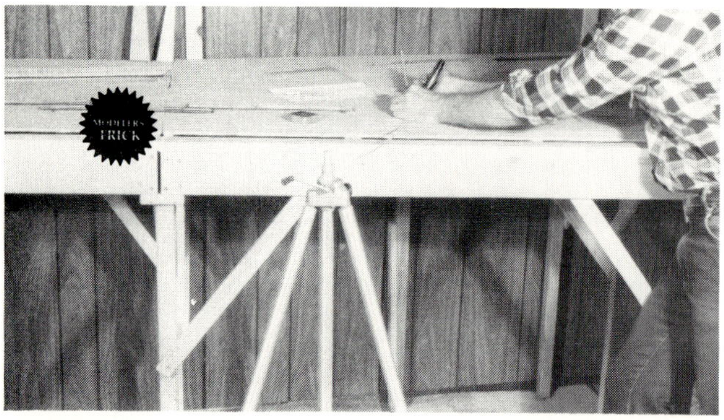

When the X mark for the curve center is not on the benchwork, you'll need to improvise. You can elevate a curve center on a pile of boxes or use any kind of tripod. I started with a 4-foot radius for the mainline curve on the lower left of the plan but found that a whopping (and realistic) 12-foot radius would fit. The two tracks are spaced 2³/₈-inches apart at the crossover — the curve center was moved so that both curves are 12 foot radii that moves the tracks closer at the far left (to a 2-inch spacing). I replaced the four number 6 turnouts at the crossovers with number 8 turnouts for a smoother transition through these ess-bends as shown in the plan figure 3.

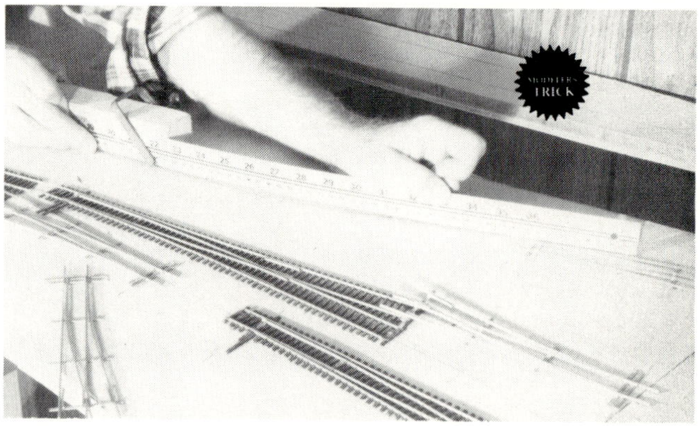

The transition from straight track to curve should be a spiral with ever-decreasing radii from straight to the nominal curve. On most plans, you will need to adjust the curve radius down an inch (and move the curve center. Draw that smaller curve, then connect it to the straight by making your own spiral/transition curve "tool"; simply clamp a steel ruler to a length of 2 x 2 as shown. Hold the 2 x 2 parallel with the straight and bend the ruler so it corresponds to the radius of the curve about 12 to 18-inches from the straight. Trace that bend onto the roadbed as shown.

This is the most important alignment technique of all; sighting down the track centerlines (and, in this case, through the straight portions of the turnouts) so be sure there are no sudden kinks or bends. That centerline is what will determine the smoothness of your track so get it perfect and erase any errors with an eraser so only a single and accurate pencil line marks the track centerline. Be sure to mark all the switch point locations, too, so you can get the turnouts installed where you want them.

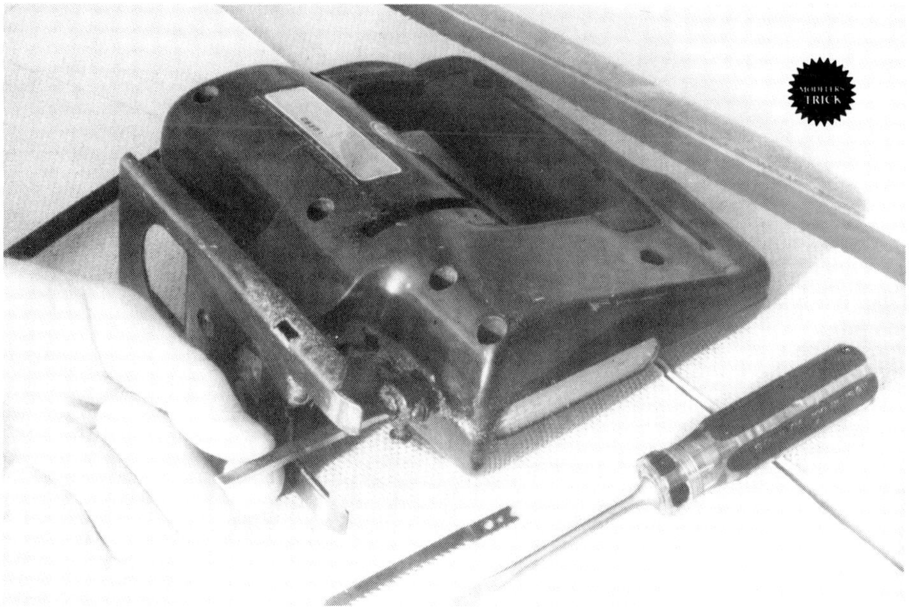

I use a electric saber saw to cut the plywood and the Homosote. Sears number 2876 blade makes the smoothest cuts in plywood. Their number 2873 blade is really a knife that cuts 1/2" Homosote wallboard or 1/4" Upsom board (both materials available from lumberyards) without much dust or fuzz.

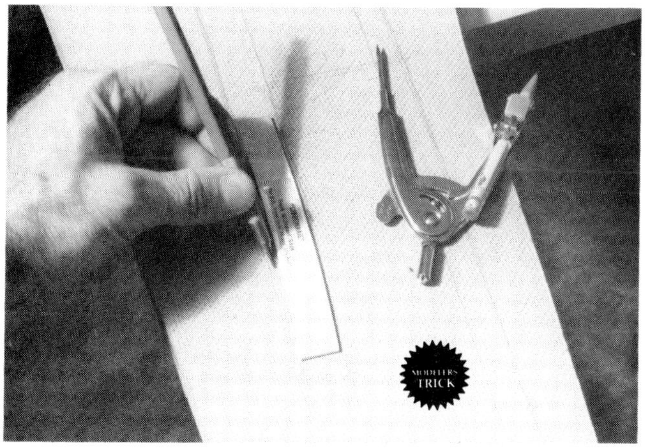

I use the Baumgarten track radius gauges to be sure the track is curved and even for plotting short curves, The gauges are available from Wallace Metal Products, Box 421, RD No.2, Dept. MRG, Parksburg, PA 19365. They have another use when marking track roadbed edges on the Homosote: the (approximately) 5/8-inch width of the gauge is about half the width of most real ballast shoulders. I cut the Homosote even with the ballast shoulder and shape the shoulder with plaster when the scenery is installed.

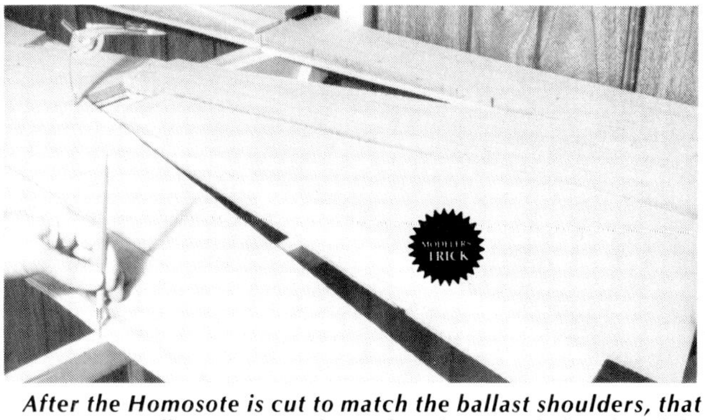

After the Homosote is cut to match the ballast shoulders, that Baumgarten/Wallace gauge can be used, again, to mark the edge of the earth fills — they happen to be about the same distance as the gauge width from the ballast shoulders on real railroads — cut the plywood there and you'll be likely to get a more realistic roadbed and fill shape on the finished layout. In tunnels, however, both the plywood and the Homosote should be twice the width of the gauge (about 1 1/4-inches) from the track centerline to provide support for short walls to keep derailed cars (and locomotives) from falling through the benchwork's open grids to the floor! After the plywood is cut, position it and the Homosote on the benchwork and mark where the edges cross the grids as shown.

Short pieces of 1 x 2 or 1 x 4 (with the grain placed vertically) can be used to support single or double track roadbed. For areas with more than two tracks and where buildings are beside the track, you'll want to make U-shaped risers from 1 x 2 lumber the width of the roadbed. Place a riser beneath the plywood subroadbed at every point where the plywood passes over the open grid benchwork members. The relatively thin 3/8-inch plywood must be supported every 18-inches so you may need to add additional crossmembers to some open grid designs.

Use an adjustable tee square with built-in bubble level to position the risers. The ruler will provide the proper height measurement while the bubble keeps the tops level. Clamp the riser down, then drill the pilot hole for the number 8 x 1 1/4-inch wood screw. Remember to deduct the thickness of the roadbed and subroadbed from the height of the riser. Also, find a 4-foot length of perfectly straight 2 x 2 to use as a straight edge to be sure a series of three or more risers are all precisely the same height. I used an additional layer of 1/2-inch plywood as a gusset beneath the 3/8-inch plywood subroadbed where the 3/8 material crossed the joint between the two modules. One of those pieces of plywood is shown laid (temporarily) across the tops of two U-shaped risers at the left. Notice that risers must be placed on both sides of any joints in the benchwork (like the joints between these two modules). With the U-shaped risers, the crossmember can overhang to align with the ends of the modules. The C-clamp holds the two risers together until they are attached to the benchwork with the 8 x 1 3/4-inch wood screws.

All the risers are in place except for two where the downgrade to the hidden trackage crosses the joint between the modules — those risers will be added after the plywood and Homosote are in place. Three pieces of 1 x 2 have been installed at the rear to support a 1/8-inch tempered Masonite sky backdrop be fitted after the trackwork is complete.

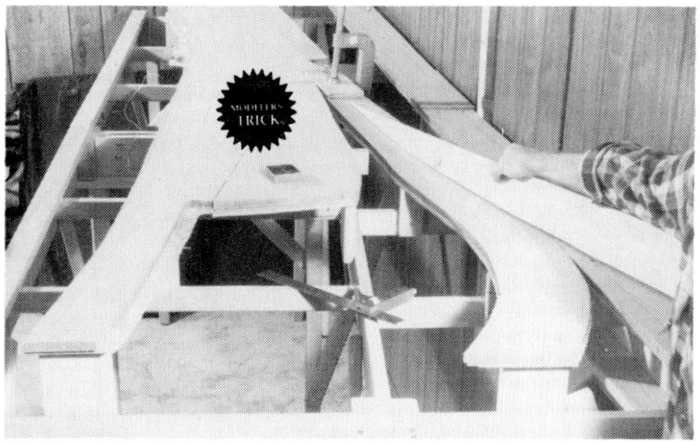

Attach the roadbed to the rear risers first so you can stand inside the open grid benchwork to reach the rear roadbed. A pair of old irons are used as weights to keep the Homosote down on the plywood. Drill number 8 x 2-inch pilot holes for number 8 x 2-inch woodscrews right through the Homosote, 3/8-inch plywood and into the risers, then use the wood screws to attach the assembly. It's wise, to apply white glue or resin cement between the plywood and Homosote so the two form a more rigid structure.

The transitions between upgrades and level or downhill track must be a 6-foot vertical radius or more to keep long cars from uncoupling as they move from level to downhill (or uphill) track. Use a tape measure to make a plywood template (as shown) with a 6-foot radius in both convex and concave shapes (to check, respectively, bottom-of-grade and top-of-grade vertical curves). You can usually adjust the roadbed by removing the screws that hold the risers to the open grid benchwork so both riser and roadbed can be moved up or down. Clamp the riser to the benchwork when you have the roadbed where you want it, and install new woodscrews to hold the riser in place.

I saved the joint where the roadbed crosses the joint between the two modules for last. A gusset of 1/2-inch plywood is placed between the riser and the bottom of the 3/8-inch subroadbed. A layer of white or resin glue is applied between the two layers of plywood (and between the Homosote and the 3/8-inch plywood). A pair of C-clamps holds the three layers tightly and in vertical alignment while the glue sets for 48-hours. The risers to support this segment of roadbed are inserted from below until they are 1/16-inch away from touching the bottom surface of the plywood. The risers are then attached to the benchwork with woodscrews. That 1/16-inch clearance provides the room to bring the roadbed down, if needed, to produce a smooth roadbed. Finally, attach the roadbed, 3/8-inch plywood and 1/2-inch plywood gusset to the risers with the number 8 x 2-inch wood screws.

Build-A-Railroad, step-by-step

Part III: What To Do Before You Lay Track:

1. Setting sites for structures
2. Building the gaps to be bridged
3. Installing hidden Kadee uncoupling ramps
4. Laying the turnouts and track

This is **probably** your second layout, so you are **probably** wise enough to know that there are many projects that precede any type of actual track-laying.

The structures from your first (or second or. . .) layout can certainly be used on this one. If you don't have the actual buildings, use the plans from the kits. If you lack the kits, look in Walthers catalog for the dimensions of the kits you intend to buy or at kits for similar-size structures. All of these buildings have appeared in previous articles in Model Railroading *magazine. Most structures will need a flat platform or foundation and this exercise will show you where the flat tabletop needs to be extended (or, as we'll see) where to fit "Scene Sites".*

The location of structures on a model railroad is more critical, to the realism and operating potential of the layout, than most newcomers realize. Use two of the freight cars that are typical of the most modern era you will model (36-footers for 1880-1910, 40-footers for 1910-1950 and 50-footers, like these for more modern eras). By moving the three-story structure back just an inch, we found room for a second car (the "We can. . ." box car) and a matching industry. Use a couple of NMRA gauges (lower, right) to determine how far from the previously-marked track centerlines to place each structure.

There haven't been many model railroads constructed for any magazine that are intended to be the type of layout a more experienced modeler might want. It's relatively simple to build a model railroad on a flat sheet of 4 x 8-foot plywood even if you do cut a few holes for bridges and valleys. It's also relatively simple to create a nicely-landscaped layout, maybe even one set in the mountains (and, maybe, even with HOn3 trackwork) if that layout is meant more to look at (and to be photographed) than to operate. This seemingly simple 2 x 8-foot layout, though, is one that is meant to be operated in every conceivable meaning of the term; from simulated through freights, to Loads-in/Empties-out, to "Timesaver"-style switching. The only thing small about this project is the size of the layout. All of which is an apology, of sorts, for the number of

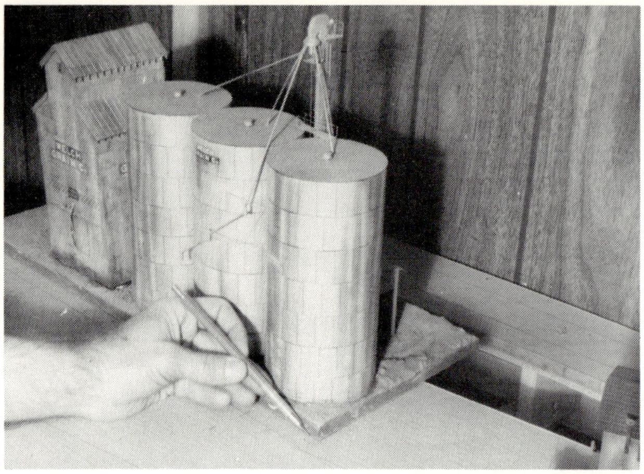

This grain elevator is one of three structures from the "Scene Site" article that appeared in the September/October 1984 issue of **Model Railroading.** *This circa 1972 grain elevator (and its circa 1952 and circa 1907 counterpart scene sites) are on permanent loan from Albin Burroughs for this layout. For most structures, it's wise to make a separate base or scene site like this. The edge of the base can rest against the roadbed at the end of the ties so the tie ends can help disguise the seam between the building's base (the scene site) and the rest of the roadbed. There's a second article on the "Scene Site" concept in the March/April 1984* **Model Railroading** *that further explains the incredible space-expanding value of the system. For now, what you need are flat segments of ½" thick roadbed just a fraction larger than the structures you will use on the layout. Since the roadbed is in place, here, we'll mark the location of the scene site for the grain elevator so we can remove that portion of the roadbed.*

With the exception of the three-story brick structure (built from an article in Vol. 13, No. 1 issue of **Model Railroading**) *all six major buildings at Thomasville will be built on removable bases or Scene Sites. Cut those bases from either ½-inch thick Homosote or lightweight foam core board like Gatorfoam. Mark the outline of each Scene Site (this is the station's site) so you can remove the portion of Homosote roadbed from beneath the Scene Site. It would have been wiser to have done this BEFORE gluing the Homosote to the plywood, but it is difficult, indeed, to plan that far ahead and still obtain visually-pleasing results — you really SHOULD do some of the layout planning with the actual structures you will use as we have in these photos.*

If the Homosote is glued down (like this) you'll have to cut through it to the plywood with a heavy-duty industrial knife (hardware stores sell them from Stanley and others). Be sure to guide the knife with a steel ruler. Make a dozen relatively light cuts, then pry-out the Homosote with a screwdriver. Test-fit the Scene Site in its place — you may need to cement some scraps of cardboard on the plywood to elevate the Scene Site to the top of the roadbed. Do not, for goodness sake, glue the Scene Site in place now or forevermore — leave it removable so you can add details to the structure (or so you can build or mount the completed structure) and so you can change eras in the Time Machine/Scene Site system.

pages and photographs and words it has required to bring the model railroad this far.

If you are the modeler this series is designed to reach, you have already built at least one model railroad. One of the major lessons that first layout can teach you is patience. The more work you can complete before you actually lay the track, the less track you will have to rip up. Even more important, the more pre-planning and pre-track-laying work you can do, the less the chance that you'll have the railroad complete when you realize that you did something radically wrong back in the beginning. You can carry this type of thing to extremes, starting way back at the track plan stage: don't be affraid to modify the original track plan when you transfer it to the tabletop (as we did in fitting four number 8 turnouts in place of four number 6 turnouts). One of the things you may notice, about each of the major projects or steps we document on this layout, is that there will nearly always be a change made in the previous work. No, we don't want it to be that way, but we know, from our own experience, that you'll build a better model railroad if you are flexible enough to admit you made a mistake as early in the game as you discover it and fix it right then. This time around, we discovered that one of the sidings (to the log-loading ramp, siding Ⓑ) should be moved or pivoted about an inch to the rear to provide more clearance for a structure. That siding would accomodate another whole car if it were also lengthened an inch: Progress.

BRIDGE-BUILDING, FROM THE ROADBED UP

One of the many reasons why it's smarter to work from a track plan than to just lay track as you go, is the selection of bridge sites. If you are wise enough to plan the sites and the bridges in advance, you can do the sawing and cutting BEFORE the track is laid. It's easier this way and it doesn't give the saw the chance to loosen and ruin the track you've laid. Be sure the cut is perfectly square (at a 90 degree angle) to the track centerlines and make the cut at least 1/8 inch away from the bridge to give a bit of room for adjustment — the scenery can fill in that 1/8 inch gap on each end of the bridge abutments.

The bridges to fill this gap are shown in a how-YOU-can-do-it chapter on pages 81-85.

This bridge is just 10 scale feet high, a single span wood pile trestle. A pair of scraps of 3/8 inch plywood space the floor of the valley far enough below the roadbed. Just clamp the spacers and another scrap of 3/8 inch plywood (for what will be the valley floor) to the roadbed and glue them. For longer and/or taller bridges you may need to add a vertical 1 x 4 beneath the roadbed at each end of the bridge (like the one at the left).

I added about six 2 inch long number 8 Phillips headed wood screws to the bridge area to be sure the opening was at least as strong as the rest of the roadbed. Add the screws while the wood glue is still wet.

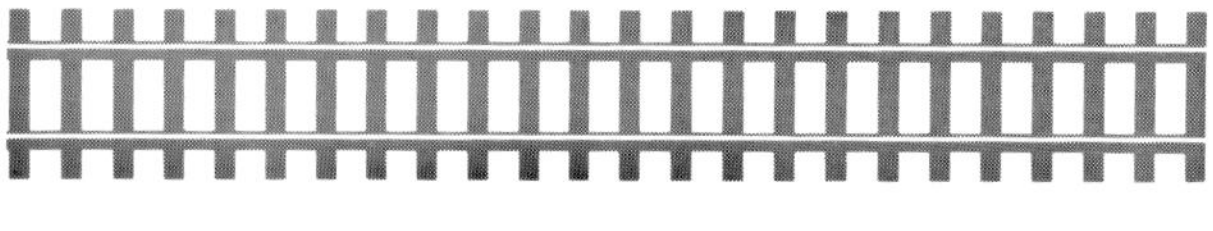

INSTALLING KADEE'S ELECTRO-MAGNETIC RAMPS

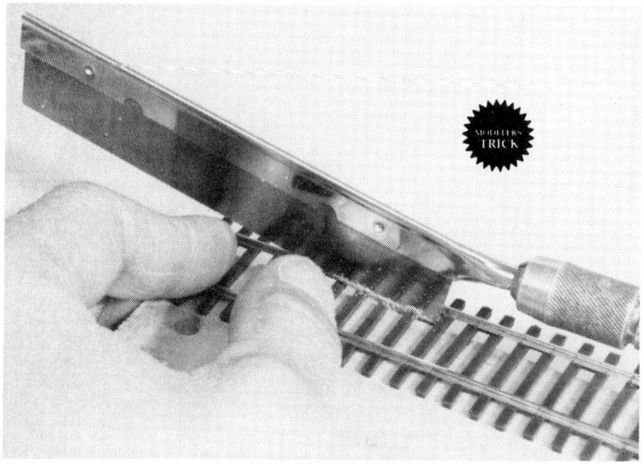

Most modelers seem to have the best results with uncoupling Kadee couplers if the center of the ramp is placed at the foul point of two adjacent tracks (where the cars on the two tracks just clear each other — see earlier photograph for positioning structures and scene sites for maximum siding capacity). Here, we're going to install ONLY the Kadee number 307 "Magne-Electric" electrical uncoupling ramps. These ramps only operate when you push a button to energize them and they are ONLY needed on mainline tracks where trains could accidentally uncouple when passing over the Kadee permanent magnet ramps — we'll install the permanent magnet ramps AFTER the track is in place. There appears to be a need for a total of four of the number 307 ramps on the mainline — remember that you'll need ramps to uncouple cars from the train as well as ramps to uncouple cars to leave them on the siding; hence, the need for at least a few ramps on the mainline. We're using more than absolutely necessary on this layout because the plan incorporates the "Timesaver" switching game — the extra ramps are the only drawback to our adapting that game plan to a segment of the mainline.

The ties must be cut from between the rails so the top ends of the steel magnet pieces can extend to within .010 inches of the bottoms of the rails. Use a razor saw to cut the ties just 1/32 inch in from the base of the rails. I used a cut off disc in a Dremel tool (the same shown for cutting the rail, later), but you must be extremely careful to not melt the ties. Experiment with both cutting methods on a scrap of track to see which one works best for you.

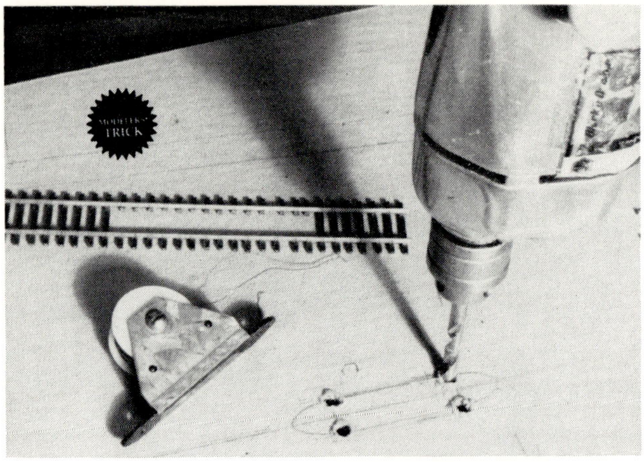

Mark the location of the Kadee number 307 ramp accurately. I did NOT follow Kadee's instructions because I found the ramp would function with this modified installation and operating method: First, the ramp needs a bit more power and that can be accomplished by using 12 volts of DC current (rather than the 16V of AC Kadee suggests) if you ALSO install a 2000 microfared 35 WVDC Filter Capacitor across the DC terminals of the power pack. I used a Radio Shack part number 272-1020 filter (electrolytic) capacitor. You must, of course, have a separate power pack just to actuate the Kadee ramps with this method but it does allow you to recess the ramps enough to hide them beneath some .010-inch "dummy" ties and ballast. The installation hole is $1\frac{1}{8}$ inches wide, centered precisely beneath the track (you already have a marked track centerline) and $3\frac{1}{2}$ inches long (centered over the foul point — precisely where you want the cars to uncouple). I drilled a $\frac{1}{4}$ inch hole in each corner of the ramp location.

Use a fine tooth blade in a saber saw to cut the straight portions of the ramp opening — the $\frac{1}{4}$ inch holes should be large enough to allow the blade to turn at a right angle for each of the four cuts. Slice any fuzz or slivers from the opening with a hardware knife.

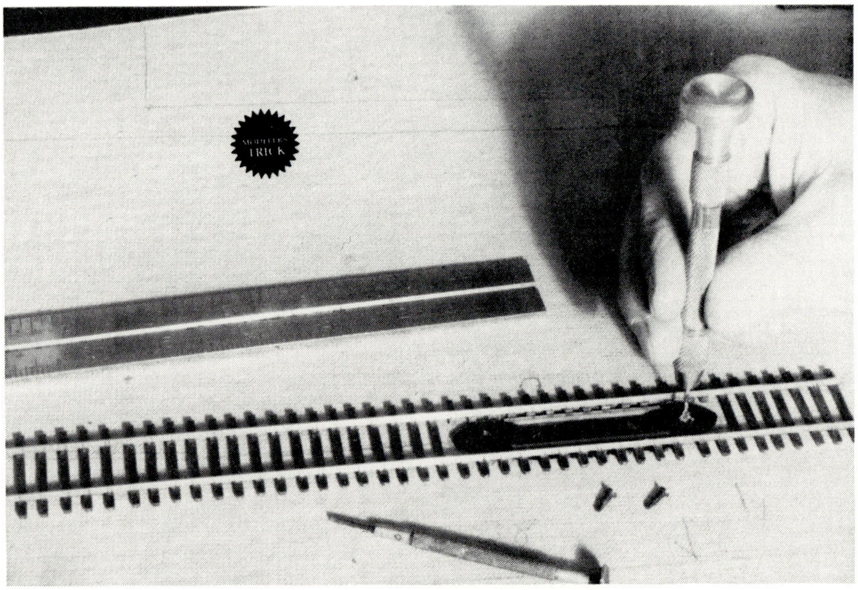

The ties on the Railcraft flex track just happen to be the same depth or height as the mounting bracket for the Kadee ramp. If your ties are thinner you may need to reduce the thickness of this ramp by filing across the bottom or by recessing it into the Homosote. If your ties are thicker, you'll need to add shims to bring the top of the ramp to within precisely .010 inches of the bottom of the code 70 rail (use a piece of .010 inch thick Evergreen styrene if you have no other means of measuring .010 inches). If you are using code 100 rail, the ramp will be higher than the tops of the ties (.020 inches ABOVE the bottom of the rail) and you will have to disguise the ramp as a road crossing like the Kadee number 312 between-the-ties ramps we'll be using for all other uncoupling locations.

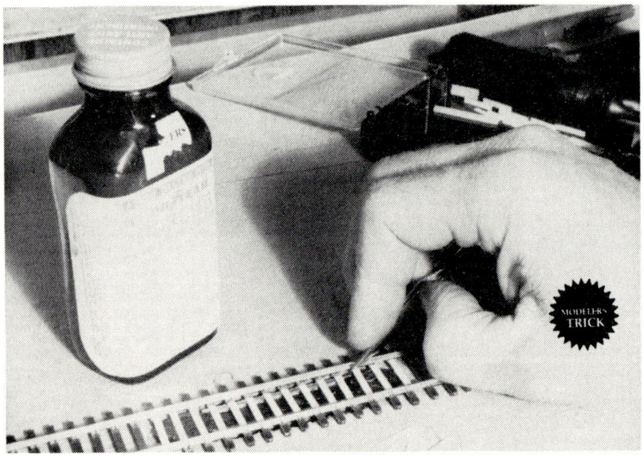

Cut fake ties from Evergreen HO scale 1 x 8 inch plastic. Scrape the plastic with the teeth of a razor saw, before you cut it, to simulate wood grain. Glue the ties to the Kadee ramp with Pliobond as shown. We'll paint the ties when we paint the Railcraft ties. The remaining visible portion of the ramps will be buried beneath the ballast. The screw and nut that hold the ramp's magnet are accessible from beneath the $\frac{3}{8}$ inch plywood so you can replace that part of the ramp (the only "working" part) without disturbing the track if the magnet accidentally overheats and shorts out from using too much current for too long. If you are using a subroadbed thicker than $\frac{3}{8}$ inch, you might want to saw notches beside the ramps (in the subroadbed) to leave room for a wrench and screwdriver to remove the magnet coil from below.

You'd think that a two-inch separation between tracks would be plenty with a 30 inch radius curve. Wrong. Read the NMRA number S8 Standard for curves and believe it — it takes more than 2½ inches of separation for the overhang of an HO scale Big Boy to clear the side of a streamlined passenger car. I needed to cut the Homosote roadbed along the 18 inches or so to the far left of the layout to move the tracks far enough apart and still have them resting on Homosote.

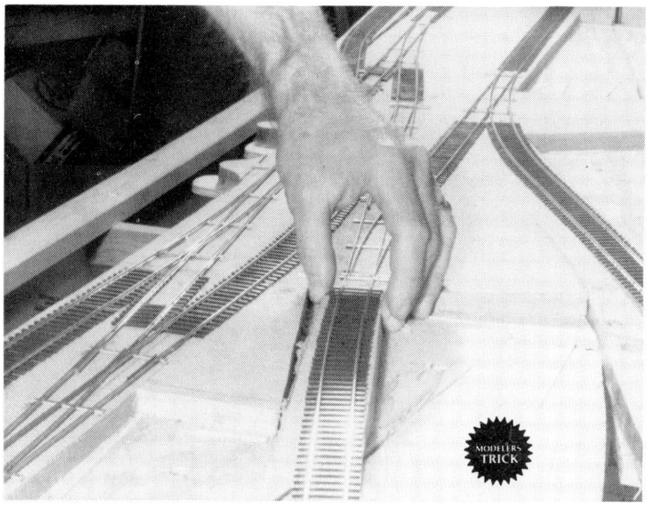

After I fitted all the rail joiners, I found that the switchback track to the right on the plan was almost a half-inch further towards the rear than it was when I cut the Homosote. The solution: move the roadbed, not the track.

A rule I admit I forgot: never, ever, put a turnout at the top or bottom of a change in grade. The coupler pins will catch on the turnout rails to derail the car. Check any doubtful locations by passing a couple of thicknesses of paper beneath a coupler pin you've checked to be at the proper height above the rails — this one did not clear.

Fix the problem during the construction stage, not the operation stage! To move the bottom of the grade away from the turnout, the roadbed was pried upward and the vertical 1 x 2 moved to a newly-drilled screw hole. A claw hammer helped to get the roadbed up (after the screws were out). The bottom of this downgrade is now on the plain flex track below the level at the lower left so coupler pins no longer catch on the turnout rails. At the top of this grade, I moved the hidden turnout about 6 inches downgrade to get it off the hump at the transition from the visible track to the downhill grade.

MORE DERAILMENT PREVENTION: *File only the very corners (about .010 to .015 inches of the corner) to a gentle radius at EVERY switchpoint to avoid the chance of wheel flanges picking the points. File the flange side of that radiused point to blend it smoothly into the stock rails when the points are against them.*

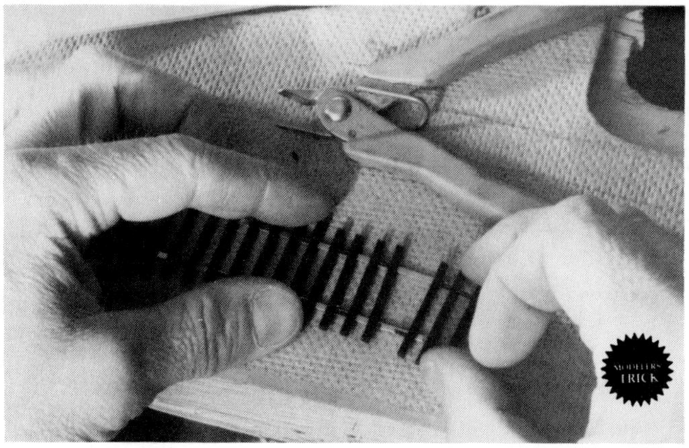

It's usually only necessary to remove one tie from the cut ends of the flex track to leave space for the rail joiner. In fact, the extreme ends of each piece of the Railcraft flex track have thinner ties (and no spikes) so those ties can stay. At the diverging (two-track) ends of every Railway Engineering turnout, however, at least three ties must be removed from the flex track to leave room for the prototype-style longer turnout ties. Remove the ties by simply cutting the plastic web beneath the rail with diagonal cutters.

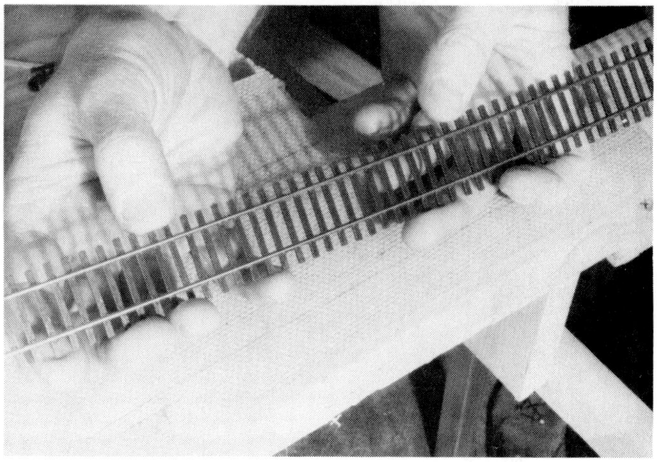

Work very carefully when you try to bend the Railcraft flex track into curves so you don't break the scale-size spikes. Walk the ties on the outside of the curve toward the extreme ends using two hands as shown. It may take as many as a dozen such "walks" to get the ties spread enough to bend the rail into 18 inch radius curves.

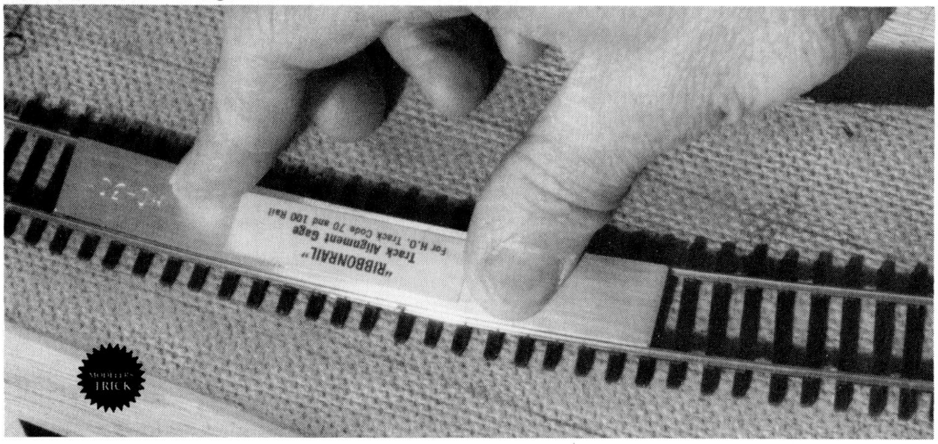

I find the aluminum track gauges from Wallace Metal Products, Box 521, RD2, Dept. MRG, Parkesburg, PA 19365 to be essential. They make curve gauges from 18 inches up to 48 inch radius. I also use a 44 and 48 inch to check the transition radius of curves (the gentle change from straight to curve over at least 12 inches of the "curve"). It is best to just lay one edge of the gauge into the track so you don't force the track to conform — when you remove the gauge the track won't spring back out of alignment.

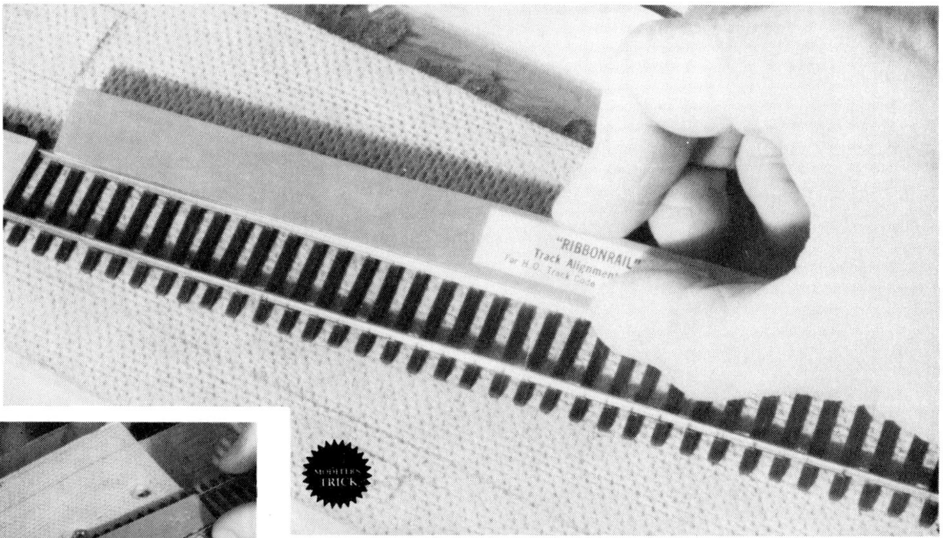

The Wallace gauges allow you to sight down the gap between gauge and rail to detect misalignment as small as a few thousandths of an inch. I even use their straight gauges to check straight track and to see where the curve really does start.

A trick for larger-radius curves: use a straight gauge (or steel ruler) and lay it as shown. Notice the gap between the rail and the center of the straight edge; that's the chord of the curve. If you bend the track so that gap is the same wherever you move the straight edge, you will have a constant-radius curve. On large radius curves (6 to 12 foot radii or more) it's the constant curve that matters more than the precise radius.

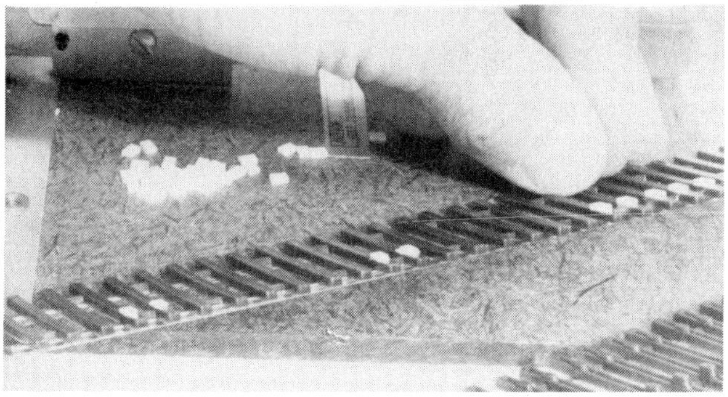

TRACK-LAYING: BUILDING-IN SUPERELEVATION

The real railroads build in banked corners on nearly every curve. That banking is about 6 to 8 inches, with the outer rail of the curve elevated above the inner rail. The Precision Scale "Top Track" brand flexible track is available wilth molded-in supports to provide .040 inches (about 5 inches, in HO scale) of banking or, as the real railroads call it, "superelevation". You can add those supports to any brand of flexible track by simply cutting some Evergreen brand HO scale 4 x 8 inch strips (to give 4 scale inches of superelevation) into 1/8 inch lengths in North West Short Line's "Chopper" (shown). The usual types of plastic cement will not stick to the plastic ties on most flex track so the superelevation blocks must be glued in place with Pliobond or contact cement. The up and downhill grades on that outer rail should also be built in by gluing some 1 x 8 HO scale strips about 8 ties apart as shown. Pile three blocks 8 ties from the 4 x 8s, pile two 1 x 8 blocks 8 ties away from the pile of three and glue a single block 8 ties in — that will give a lead-in grade of about 27 ties for a smooth transition into the banked curve. Later, the ballast will bury the blocks.

PBL makes diagonal cutters with jaws that make one side of the cut 90-degrees and the other sharply beveled. These types of cutters are called "flush cut" and Lambert as well as PBL and others distribute several types to hobby shops. For most cuts, an abrasive cut off disc in a motor tool like Dremel's is easier, but you must wear protective glasses to guard against a broken disc or metal debris. With either method, the cut should be filed smooth along the length of the rail to remove any burrs.

PREPARING THE READY-LAID TURNOUTS

The Railway Engineering turnouts are ready to use; the printed circuit board ties are soldered to the rails to provide all the rail-holding and alignment strength needed. If you are modeling an old yard or industrial area, you can bury the turnout's ties in ballast and dirt like the prototype. For most situations, though, you will want to add the "missing" ties to make it look like it has ties and spikes that hold the rails, not solder. It's easier to fit the ties if you first fit the turnouts that are directly adjacent to one another (with no short pieces of plain track between them). Next, fit the tracks leading to and from the turnouts so you can see precisely where the extra-long turnout ties should stop and the regular ties should begin. I found it helpful to solder complex sections of track, especially track with turnouts on each end, into a unit. The process made it easier to realign the tracks later.

You will eventually want to solder EVERY rail joiner to allow the operation of oversize wheel flanges (on your friend's Rivarossi, Model Power, Life-Like or such locomotives). We'll show you how to handle expansion joints and insulating gaps in the next installment. I use a large soldering gun with an acid flux and Ersin 5 core solder. Apply the solder ONLY to the outside of the rail joiner.

TRACK-LAYING — FITTING & RAIL ALIGNMENT

For most model railroads, track alignment is really more the alignment of turnouts (switches), especially so if you are using ready-laid switches rather than soldering your own together from rail. That process involves an even more delicate type of alignment. We're using ready-laid turnouts from Railway Engineering, 220 Olean Cr., Dept. MRG, Sparks, NV 89431 on this layout because their turnouts with code 70 rail allow operation of locomotives, like Rivarossi's, that have oversize wheel flanges. There's a full report on the use of these turnouts in the Spring 1982 issue of Model Railroading *but we're going to modify the tie-laying portion of that article and provide some ideas for superdetailing the turnouts.*

If possible, use a steel ruler to physically align one turnout to the next. When the turnouts are precisely where you want them (those track location centerlines we marked in a previous installment are absolutely essential to this process), lay the flex track beside the place where it will fit and mark where to cut the rails. You'll need a couple of track gauges (those are Kadee's in the lower, left). Save the end ties from the Railcraft flex track, by the way, because they're thin enough to clear the rail joiners. We used Railcraft's code 70 rail joiners, too.

There is no substitute for the best track alignment tool of all; your eye. We showed you how to sight down the track centerlines when you drew them in pencil. Now, it's necessary to sight down the track laid over those centerlines after the rail joiners are in place (but BEFORE you solder any joints). It may not be apparent in this photo, but there was a slight kink in the rails between these two switches that was corrected by shortening one of the rails on the flex track by about 1/64 inch. Erase any of the pencil centerlines that are now incorrect. Carefully mark the locations of all the turnouts' throw bars (the points).

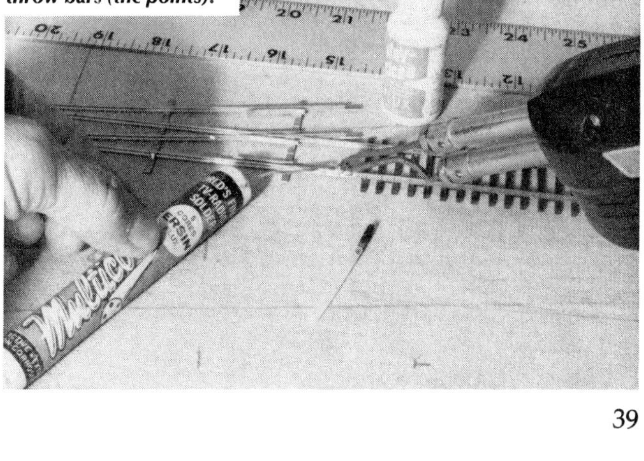

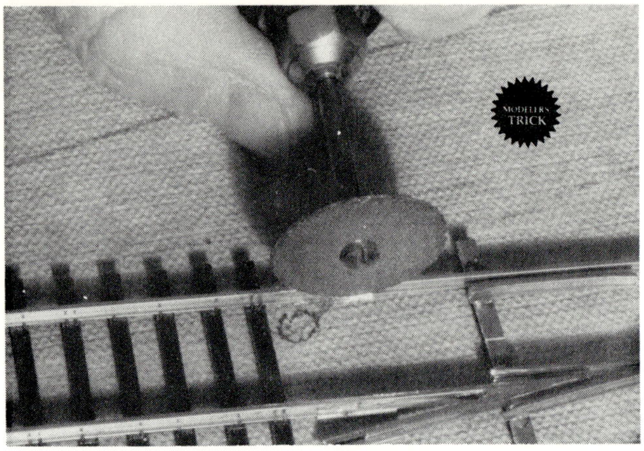

The only portions of the track that will foul the oversize flanges are the rail joiners. If you solder the joiners to the rail, you can use a cut off disc in a motor tool to slice off the rail joiner flanges from the inside of each rail as shown. The solder-reinforced rail joiner will hold the track securely and insure a positive flow of electrical current across the joint without the need for jumper wires — in other words, soldering the rail joiners is one way to insure performance even if you don't bother to cut off the inside joiner flanges.

For now, only solder the rail joiners that connect track in 12 to 24 inch long segments; leave the other joiners loose until after the track is glued permanently in place. The 12 to 24 inch sections can be lifted off the layout while you add the wood ties to the turnouts and paint the track as shown in the later steps.

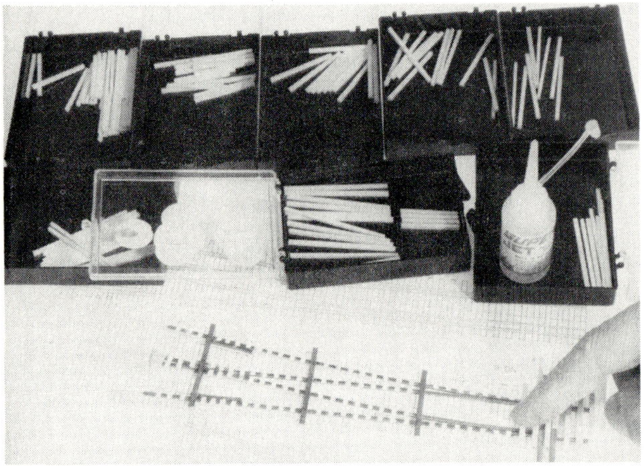

The Railway Engineering turnout is placed rails down (and printed circuit board ties up) over the tie template so the tie plates can be installed. You will have to adjust the tie spacing, as you lay those tie plates, to compensate for the printed circuit board ties' positions. The wood ties are glued to the tie plates. I use Super Jet thickened cyanoacyrlate cement to attach the ties to the tie plates.

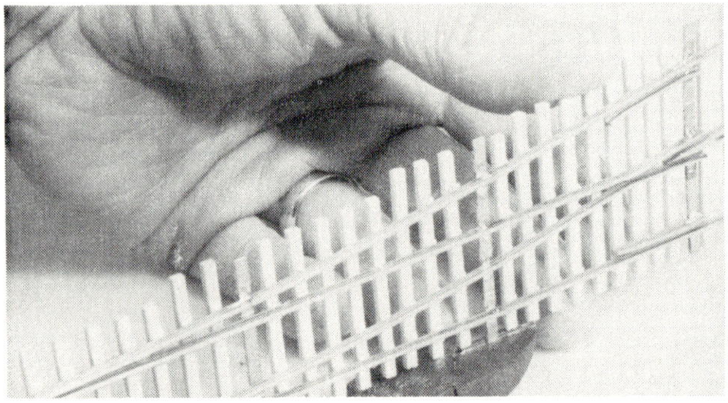

Let the Super Jet cement dry overnight. Lift the turnout from the template and use flush cut diagonal cutters (these are the type sold to dealers by Lambert) to trim the Railway Engineering printed circuit board ties to match the adjacent wood ties.

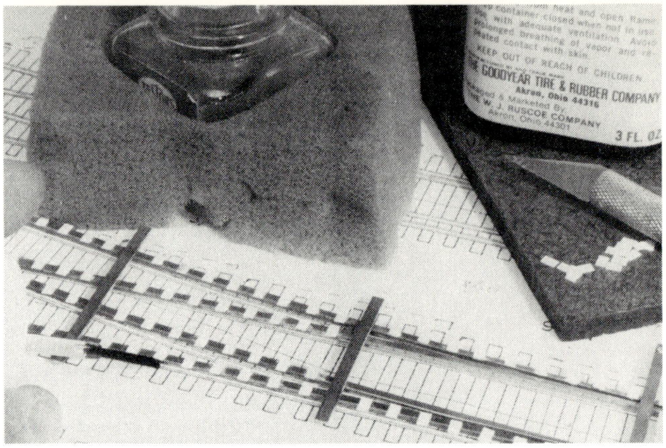

The wooden ties are strictly for looks, with these Railway Engineering turnouts. Since looks (or realism) is the object, we decided to go a few steps further and add some other details including simulated tie plates to match those on the Railcraft flex track. These tie plates, then, will determine where the wood ties fit so you must use a tie-placing template to position the tie plates properly. The tie plate installation is quick and easy if you follow these steps: Use a North West Short Line "Chopper" to cut the tie plates (and, later, the wood ties) quickly and to a perfect length. I used Evergreen HO scale 1 x 8 plastic strip cut to .100 lengths. Coat the bottoms of the rails (but NOT the moving switch points!) with Goodyear Pliobond or Walthers Goo and let it dry for a few minutes. Use Testors liquid cement for plastics to attach the tie plates. Dip the cement brush in the cement, touch the brush tip to a tie plate so the liquid picks up the tie plate. Drag the very tip of the brush over the Pliobond-coated rail to deposit a trace of cement (as shown) and to let the rail pull the tie plate off the tip of the brush. Install about 6 to 8 tie plates (until there's not enough cement left on the brush to pick up another tie plate). Use a hobby knife to align the tie plates (while the cement is still soft) so they are centered over the rails and across the tie marks on the template. At the frog and guard rail areas, I left the tie plates protruding only to the inside (the plates are not long enough to protrude out of both sides). The whole process is simple once you get the feel for dragging the brush across the rail with just enough pressure to leave both cement and a tie plate. The cement partially dissolves the Pliobond and bonds the plastic tie plate.

There are three sources for turnout tie templates: Campbell includes tie templates in their packages of wood switch ties. The National Model Railroad Association sells tie templates. Boyton & Associates, Inc. Dept MRG, Clifton House, Clifton, VA 22024-0026 sells packs of 72 templates for $2.95 plus 50¢ postage. I did not like the tie spacing on any of the three so I modified Boyton's. I wanted to simulate the types of switch ties that have obvious steps in their lengths; the templates are marked for ties that graduate, in length, in six inch increments. I remarked the tie ends to match the Baltimore & Ohio Railroad's (and others) standards with tie lengths graduating in 12 inch increments. These are the numbers and lengths of ties on the B&O's standard switch tie drawings:

Tie Lengths for No. 6 Turnouts		for No. 8 Turnouts	
qty.	Length (scale feet)	qty.	Length
8	9 feet	12*	9 feet
8	10 feet	9	10 feet
5	11 feet	7	11 feet
7	12 feet	7	12 feet (includes 2 12 footers for switch stand)
4	13 feet	4	13 feet
3	14 feet	4	14 feet
3	15 feet	5	15 feet
3	16 feet	4	16 feet
1	17 feet	2	17 feet

*With 8½ foot ties like those beneath the Railcraft track, no ties longer than 16 feet are really needed. The above lengths are the way the B&O did it. In fact, there is usually only enough length of rail, on the diverging end Railway of Engineering turnouts, for the 14 foot ties; the 15, 16 and 17 footers must be placed beneath the Railcraft flex track (after the plastic Railcraft ties are removed, of course). I cut all the ties from HO scale 6 x 8 lumber (Railway Engineering offers it in switch tie bundles). *Note: only four 9 foot ties are needed for the shorter Railway Engineering No. 8 turnouts.*

Drill a ³/₈ inch hole at the precise center of each turnout's throw bar. The wire linkage that moves the turnout's throw bar from either an electric switch machine or via manual linkage (we'll show you both in the next installment) will move in this hole. Use a hobby knife to scrape away any slivers and to cut any fuzz from the Homosote around the hole. This is one of the turnouts that will be hidden by scenery, so no "decorative" tie plates or ties were needed.

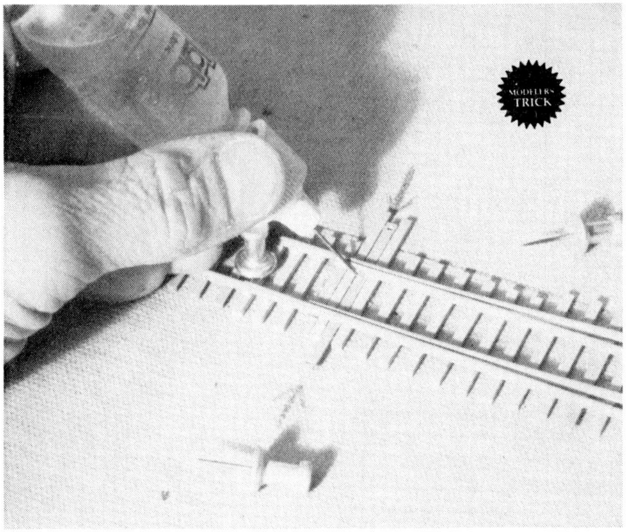

Apply a drop of LaBelle no. 106 plastic-compatible oil to the places where the turnout throw bar moves under the rails so no glue can stick to the turnout's moving parts. Be generous with the oil, touching a drop to any places where the points themselves move across the plastic tie plates — you don't want to take any chances of gluing the points to the ties.

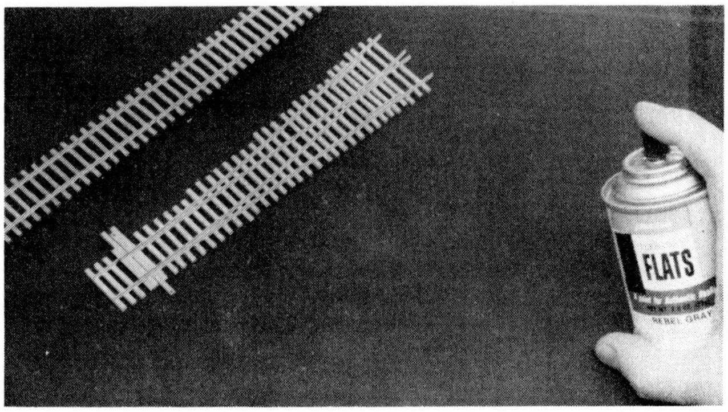

Mark the location of each piece of track with a piece of masking tape and a number or letter on the bottom of the ties. You can spray paint the track after it is glued in place, but you'll have to use water based paint unless you can work outdoors. For the basic color coat, I find Floquil or Pactra sticks best; the remaining weathering and shading colors can be water based. Carry the tracks outdoors or to a spray booth and spray them with Pactra's Camoflage or Rebel Grey. We'll cover most of that grey with stains for ties and rail after the track is laid and operating.

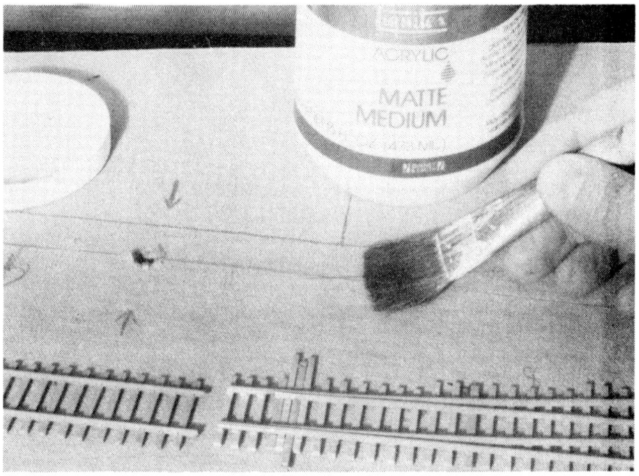

GLUING-DOWN THE TRACK

When you're using flexible track and ready-built turnouts, there's really no need to use scale spikes; you can literally glue the track in place. We'll use artist's matte medium (a cross between clear latex paint and white glue) because it dries more flexible than white glue so it makes it easier to pry-up the track if you need to relocate it. The flexing also helps to keep the track from telegraphing too much of the train's sounds. The first step is to temporarily move the track you just aligned to cover the Homosote with the matte medium to seal the surface but to leave the pencil alignment marks visible.

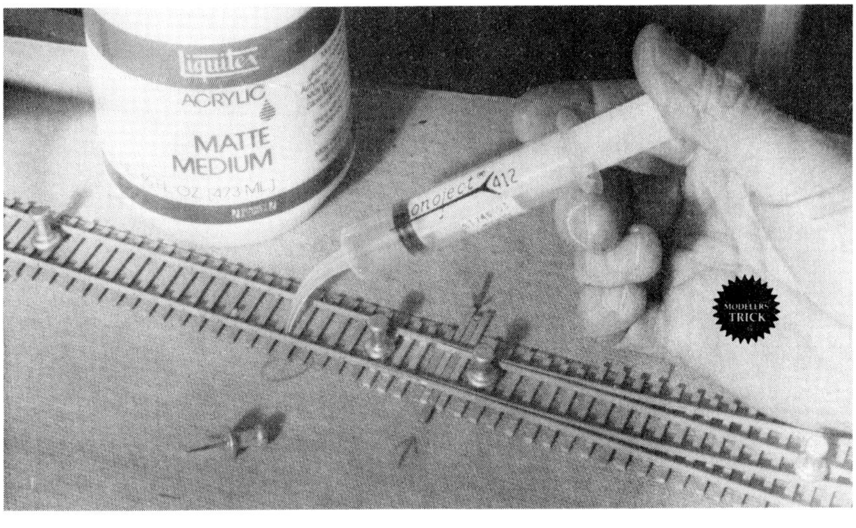

Replace the track after the matte medium dries and, for the third time, lay your head down to align the track by eye. When each section is perfect, hold it fast by pushing a metal map pin into the Homosote so the head of the pin pushes the track down. Be sure to use plenty of pins and sight down the track to be sure there are no up and down waves between the pins — in some areas, you may need to add more pins or even use a straight piece of wood to get the track to lay perfectly flat. Be sure to put plenty of pins at both ends of those uncoupling ramps and place track gauges across the rails until the matte medium dries.

Build-A-Railroad, step-by-step PART IV: Let's run some trains!!!!

Patience is one of the lessons most of us learned from the mistakes on that first model railroad. Since this is the second, we know (don't we?) it's best to get the Kadee ramps, rail gaps and DERAIL-PROOFING done *before* the trains roll . . .

Sometimes it's necessary to overstate the obvious: a model railroad is supposed to *operate*. Once you've built that first layout, you'll begin to understand why this, your second (or is it twenty-second?) is going to really run. State-of-the-art applies to operation and, simply translated, it means building a layout that *allows* you to route trains and locomotives in patterns and paths that duplicate the prototype.

It's nice to take a prototype track layout in your favorite town and translate it to scale. That is seldom satisfying enough for an active modeler unless your favorite town happens to be a busy place like the Baltimore wharves in the fifties or Durango in the teens. With this plan we've done what most experienced modelers found most successful; worked from both ends towards the middle.

We started with a real world site, Thomasville, Colorado on the Colorado Midland (a railroad that was abandoned over fifty years ago). From the model side, we started with the Timesaver switching game that the late John Allen developed (that has become a part of nearly every model railroad convention). At the conventions, you'll often see that layout on a piece of bare 1 x 12 lumber with plastic snap-track. There are, obviously, a lot of compromises between an abandoned prototype and a game-style track plan.

The first installment of this series explained how we worked the Timesaver into the plan using, among other things, the prototype railroad's practice of using lapped sidings. This time, we're ready to consider installing some permanent Kadee uncoupling ramps. I use the word "consider" because there are now two schools of thought on the installation of Kadee ramps; the old school thought is what you see in these pages; ramps where you need them to take advantage of the delayed feature of Kadee's couplers. The new school would likely avoid the use of ramps completely and settle for manual uncoupling using a small screwdriver to lever the couplers apart or the new magnetic uncoupling tool from Rix's. The Rix's tool (or that screwdriver) is "new school" because modelers who really do build walk around controls have realized that they are always very close to their trains. When you're that close, you can use manual control for the turnouts like our invisible Finger Flickn' system or any one of a dozen ground throw manual switch point controls.

Once you find that you really like throwing the turnouts at the turnout, rather than by remote control via an electric switch machine and push button, you may think about also operating the couplers manually. Those that really operate with Kadee couplers soon tire of the jockeying back and forth over the ramps that is neccessary about one time in five — the realism of the old school thought of "hands-off" operation disappears during the uncoupling process. Kadee couplers couple with about 99 percent reliability; it's the uncoupling that can drive you mad.

Okay, you've decided that this is the layout that will use manual uncoupling. Next decision: do you build-in the Kadee ramps or not? My advice: build them in. The installation of Kadee's eletro-magnetic (Magne-Electric) ramps is possible on a finished layout but the vibration from the saw alone is likely to act like a real world earthquake. It's not much more pleasant to saw through the ties to install the between-the-ties ramps. If you position the ramps properly, they won't interfere with your manual uncoupling but they'll be there if you tire of working couplers by hand.

POSITIONING KADEE RAMPS

If you happen to want to build this layout as a true set of modules, for operation with other modules in a club, you'd best check the club rules about Kadee ramps. Most clubs will not allow any type of Kadee ramp on the mainline except the Magne-Electric (electro-mechanical) type that is buried and actuated only when you push the button. Why? Because a train passing over the other styles of Kadee ramps can uncouple if there is the slightest surge or slack in the train. If the engineer accidentally nudges the throttle or the locomotive hits a dead spot twenty feet down the line, a pair of cars can part back there on your ramp. The electric ramps are a good idea on the mainline.

Why ramps on the mainline at all? Because you need to leave part of the train there while you switch the sidings. Hence, at least one mainline ramp is needed. On this layout, with its built-in Timesaver, we would have had as many as nine Kadee ramps on the mainline. I opted to pick one route as "mainline" to cut the number of Magne-Electric ramps from nine to four — if you're going to attend module club operations, you'll need all nine mainline ramps to be Magne-Electric.

The basic rules for location of ramps are simple: locate the ramps so the cars will uncouple, reliably, at the foul point between mainline and siding (see photo). Pencil-in a ramp at every stub or dead-end siding and on the exit end of every passing or through siding. Next, trace the operations of a switching crew as it spots cars on those sidings to see if the train passes over one ramp on its way to the second ramp near the siding. If so, that first ramp can probably do the work of two using the delayed action feature of the Kadee couplers; you'd simply disengage the couplers by pausing when over that first ramp to push the car into position beyond the penciled-in position of the second ramp.

On this particular layout, I installed ramps just where they are suggested for the Timesaver game; at every siding. For more normal (to modelers recreating the prototype), the ramps marked Q, T, U and Z on the diagram could be eliminated. If you do eventually add to the right end of the layout, the ramp at S should be moved to the far left end of the passing siding (or another ramp added at that point). The above the ties ramps are quite visible in the photos, but most will be hidden by highway (dirt roads, actually) crossings later.

Reprinted from May/June 1985 issue

The tight clearances at either end of the short passing siding forced me to file one of the Kadee no. 307 Magne-Electric ramps so its end would slide under one of the printed circuit board turnout ties. I also cut off both ends of the ramp marked "Q" on the plan.

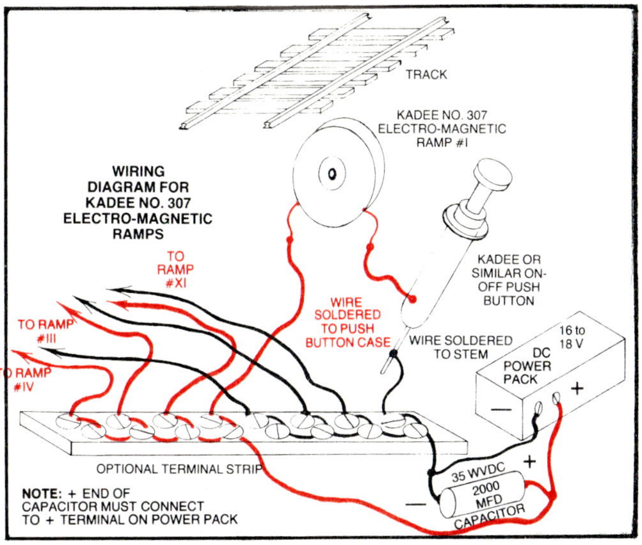

You'll want each siding to hold as many cars as possible which means that the Kadee ramps must be located so the cars will uncouple as close to the foul points as possible. To determine the foul points, simply place two of your widest cars side by side and roll them into the turnout to see when they hit each other — back them up enough so there is a scale foot (about 1/8 inch) between them (to allow for rocking cars that might roll by on the main line) — that's the foul point. Position the ramp so the center of the ramp is below the couplers when the cars are at the foul points when you can — ramp R (below the Express reefer) wouldn't fit beneath the turnout so it's a bit outside the foul point. We'll mark the foul points with scale size sign posts later.

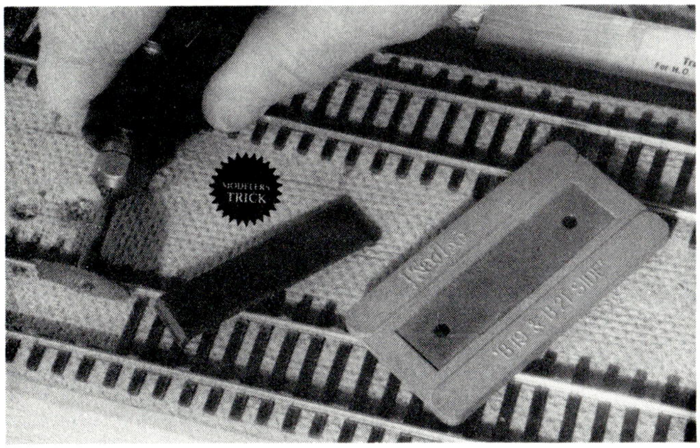

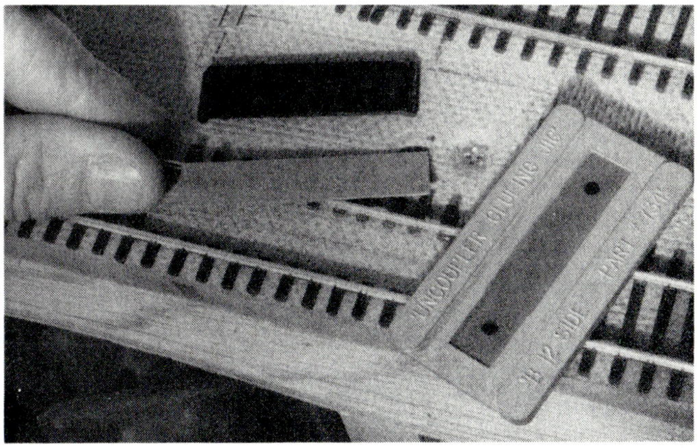

You must use a Kadee no. 334 Uncoupler Gluing Jig (far right) to hold the number 321 ramps (center) until the glue dries. The 334 jig holds the ramp just the right height above the rails for optimum uncoupling reliability. Cut the ties with a cut-off disc in a motor tool (wear eye protection). A shim of postcard or file card stock is usually needed to get the ramp elevated to the proper height. I used Matte Medium to glue the ramps because it's easier to pry loose if I located the ramp in the wrong place.

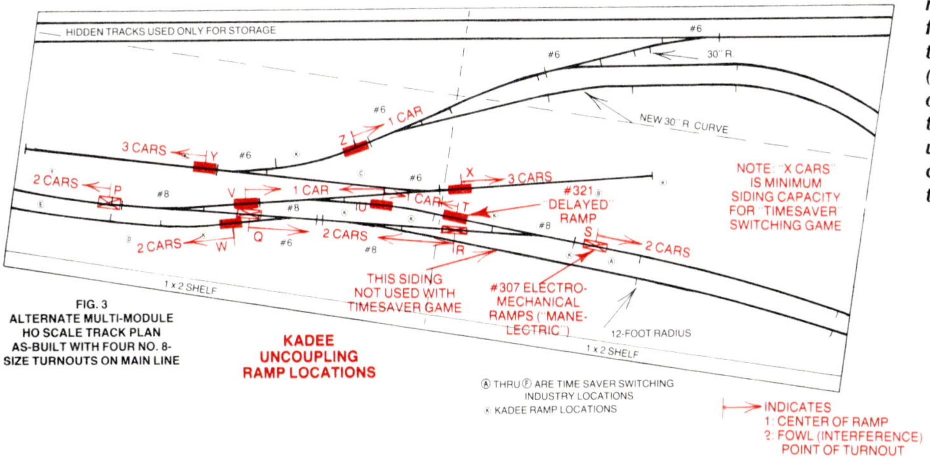

FIG. 3
ALTERNATE MULTI-MODULE HO SCALE TRACK PLAN AS-BUILT WITH FOUR NO. 8-SIZE TURNOUTS ON MAIN LINE

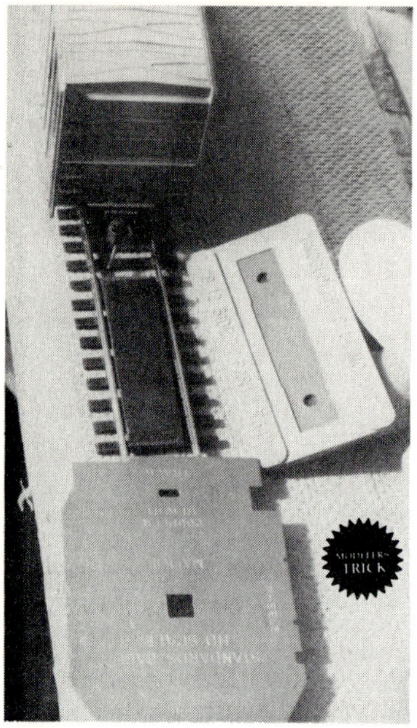

You are not supposed to try to uncouple cars on curves but the real world of modeling is seldom so simple. The ramps marked U, W and Z are all on (or near) curves. Position the ramps as far toward the outside of the curve (because that's where the couplers will be) as you can. Use an NMRA gauge (lower) to be sure the flangeways are wide enough between the ramp and rail.

It's possible to open (uncouple) Kadee couplers using a small screwdriver inserted between the knuckles. It's difficult to see where to insert the screwdriver (some modelers tape them to penlight flashlights). There's another way to manually operate Kadee couplers; using the Rix's uncoupling tool. The tool has two magnets that simply pull the coupler hoses apart when the tool is placed between the cars as shown. The tool is $2.50 plus $1.00 postage and handling, from Rix Products, 5221 Hogue Rd. Dept. MRG, Evansville, IN 47712.

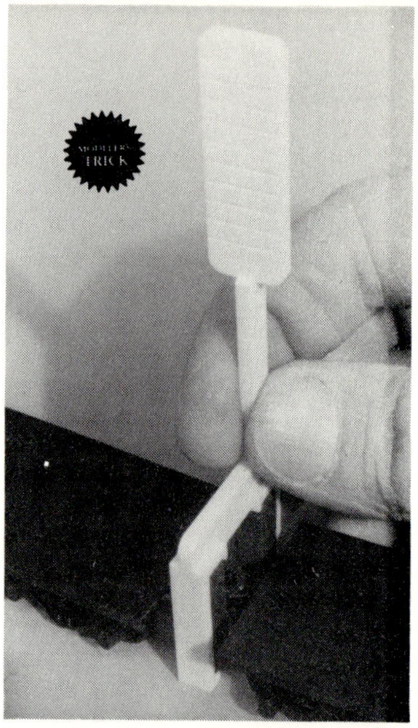

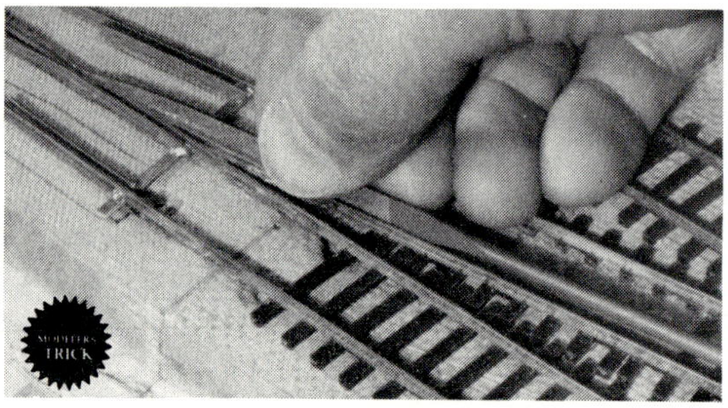

Smooth the frog area, as well as any gaps you may cut later, with a flat jewelers' file that is thin enough to clear the frog area.

DERAIL-PROOFING FOR OVERSIZE FLANGES: *I found that the Rivarossi flanges hit some solder in the bottom of the frog areas of the Railway Engineering turnouts. I'd recommend you use a jewelers' file but, if you're careful, you might be able to clean out the area with a cut-off disc in a motor tool as shown (again, wear eye protection). Don't hit the sides or tops of the rails!*

I checked every rail joint, every frog, every guard rail, every wire connection point and every rail gap for flaws by rolling a truck from a Rivarossi steam locomotive over the area. I also tried a Central Valley truck with precise wheel flange contours. Any slight clunk or hop was corrected by filing the rail smooth.

The visible turnouts were located in a compact enough area so I could solder ALL the joints in the rails that connected the turnout complex. The ties were then glued to the bottoms of the turnouts as shown before. I pressed a steel ruler down on the ties, while the glue was still wet, to force them into the cement to make the bottoms of the turnouts as smooth as possible. This entire complex of trackwork was then flipped over, the connecting tracks soldered in place and the whole pinned and cemented down with Matte Medium applied with a syringe.

It's a wise idea to sand all the surfaces of the Homosote smooth with a piece of fine grit sandpaper wrapped around a scrap of 1 x 4. Sand the surface before coating it with the sealing coat of Matte Medium and after that coat dries, then install the tracks.

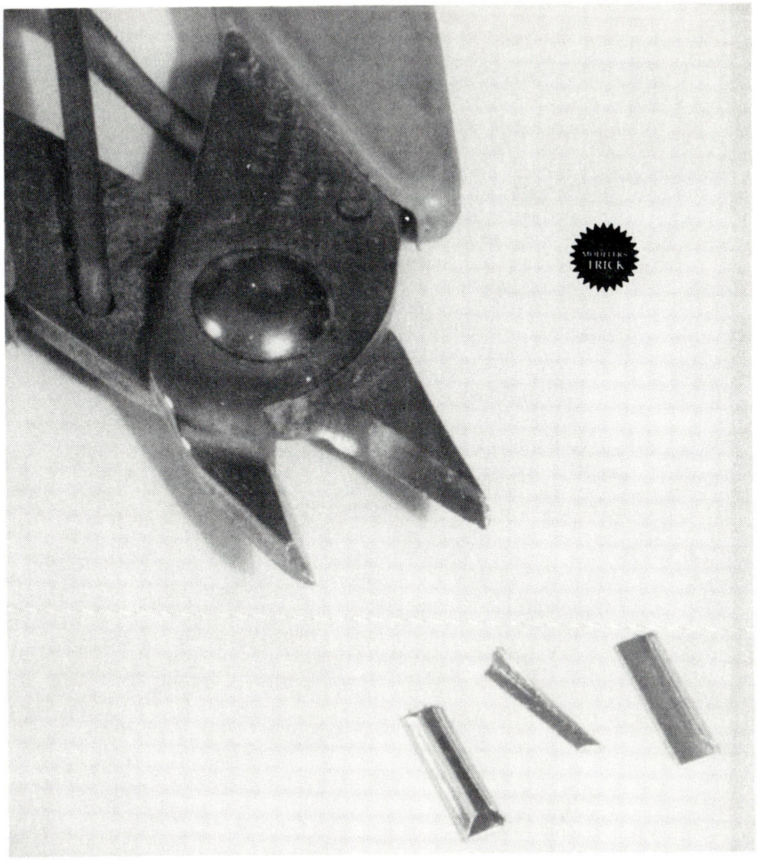

EXPANSION JOINTS: *If you solder all the rail joiners, you will need to make some gaps where the rails can expand and contract as the wood, Homosote and the rails themselves expand and contract with heat and humidity changes. Leave at least a $1/16$ inch gap in every 4 feet of track. Do NOT, repeat NOT, allow the insulated rail gaps to serve as expansion joints; any contraction will simply break the glue and there's no space available for expansion.*

All of the expansion joints are within a couple of inches of the joint between the two four foot modules.

Most of the joints can simply be cut in sections of flex track where there are enough plastic ties and spikes on each side of the joint (about four or more ties is enough) to hold the rail even when it expands. At one point, however, a true slip-joint type of rail joiner was needed. If you are not using Rivarossi-size flanges, you can simply leave one Railcraft rail joiner unsoldered to serve as an expansion joint. I needed one without any flange on the inside of the rail so I made it by cutting the flange off the rail joiner. I then used a piece of that cut off flange to solder inside the vertical web of the rail where the wheel flanges cannot reach it.

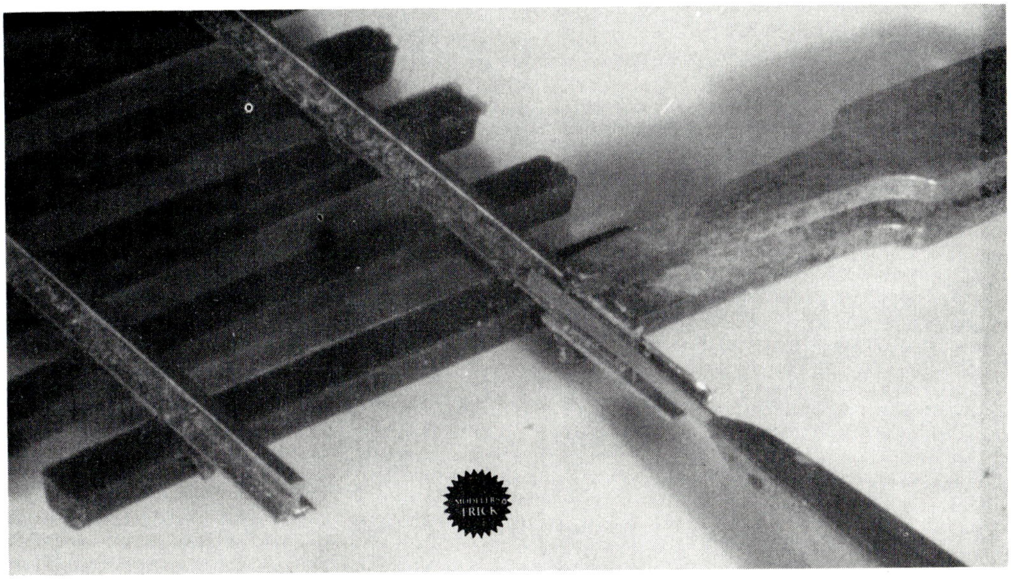

Hold the cut rail joiner to the bottom of the rail with aluminum tweezers (upper, right) and the cut-off rail joiner flange against the web of the rail with another pair of the tweezers (lower, right). When both are halfway onto the rail, solder them in place.

Solder a second cut rail joiner to the bottom of the opposite rail with that rail joiner's cut-off flange on the vertical inside web of that rail. Do not solder the joiner to the rail that will join it — this is a slip-joint to allow for expansion. Do double-check the operation of the wheel flanges on your locomotives — some of the Rivarossi flanges (which are among the largest, since they follow European toy train standards) will clear the Railcraft rail joiners right out of the package. I would still suggest you solder the joiners for positive rail alignment and perfect electrical current flow, but you might be able to skip the grinding step on the inside of the rail to clear the wheel flanges.

OPERATION-ORIENTED WIRING

State-of-the-art, today, is suppose to be the Carrier/Command-Control systems that were tested and reviewed in the Spring 1982 and Volume 13, Number 2 issues of **Model Railroading** magazine. These systems can avoid the need to divide some layouts into blocks because many locomotives can be operated, under independant control, in any given block. The fallacy with the seemingly less wiring idea is that it ignores the absolute need for NO SHORT CIRCUITS using two rail wiring.

Look at the wiring diagram for this track plan showing "Locations of Insulating Gaps in Rails and Wire Connections". Nearly all of those gaps and wires to the rails are necessary with ANY type of Carrier/Command-Control system to avoid short circuits. Why? Because there are turnouts with facing frogs and that situation demands gaps in the rails (as described in the Winter 1982 issue of **Model Railroading**).

If you are actually building this precise layout, you could skip the gaps and wires at blocks 6, 7, 8, 10 and 11 but ALL of those blocks will be needed if you ever intend (as I do) to expand this 8 foot layout into a larger system as shown in the previous plans in part I. Those gaps and wires will be needed with the larger layout regardless of the type of control so it's easier to get them in now to include them on the control panel. You will notice that the control panel includes those same turnouts and blocks on the right half that are not part of this layout — they are for future expansion, as are the "extra" blocks. Note that there are two wire-to-rail connections (1a and 1b; 5a and 5b) that are joined to avoid two unneccessary blocks.

Even if you are planning on using Carrier/Command-Control, you should install ALL of the power wires to the rails. These control systems are very sensitive to interruptions in the circuit at, for example, insulated frog turnouts. The turnouts on this layout are all of the live frog (all metal) variety and, as such, each of them also requires three wires to the rails that are NOT shown on the wiring diagram. The article in the Fall 1981 issue shows how to wire live frog turnouts to avoid either short circuits or dead spots.

Operating reliability was a prime consideration for this layout — again, those starting on their second (or twenty-second) layout understand the wisdom of eliminating derailments, locations of poor electrical flow (stalling) and short circuits at the CONSTRUCTION stage, rather than at the operating stage of building a model railroad. Hence, you've seen more pages, more "Modelers' Tricks" and more words devoted to building a model railroad BEFORE running the trains than have ever appeared in print before — the idea is to get it right once; the first time. This is why all the rail joints are soldered, why live frog turnouts are used and why even the expansion joints in the rails are spanned by electrical wires looped beneath the layout. The insulating gaps are staggered a scale 3 to 4 feet apart to make it less likely that a parked car or locomotive with metal wheels might span the gap to "open" a block that is supposed to be closed.

CARRIER/COMMAND-CONTROL WIRING:

Back to the Carrier/Command-Control systems: you could avoid running most of the wires from the tracks to the 11 D.P.D.T. center-off toggle switches I used for block A or block B selection with the new control systems. It would be wise to have at least four blocks just to help isolate any short circuits. Again, however, consider doing the wiring as shown. This method allows you the choice of operating locomotives either with conventional control (like Cab A) or with any type of Carrier/Command-Control (Cab B). The number of wires in the control cables will vary, depending on the type of Carrier/Command-Control systems but their location and connections to the layout would be as shown. Many of the more sophisticated power packs, like MRC's "Trainpower 5", have their own built-in walk-around control that is NOT Command/Carrier-Control — those power packs would also be wired to the layout as shown for Cab B.

For conventional power packs with separate walk-around throttles that need four wires (like the MRC Tech II and Cab 55 and Man Made SCR Add-On), the circuit in Cab A is needed. Cab A supplies both the 12-volt output from the hand-held walk-around control and the 18-volts of AC current needed by many of the brands of walk-around controllers. Be sure to follow the wiring diagrams and instructions furnished with any power pack, walk-around controller or Carrier/Command-Control system; these diagrams may NOT be suited to every imaginable brand or type.

All of the visible turnouts on this layout are controlled by the "Finger-Flickn'" manual control (with micro switches beneath each turnout). Only the four turnouts at the rear of the layout will be controlled by electric switch machines. Hence, there are only places for four toggle switches on the control panel. In truth, two of those toggles are wired to pairs of switch machines (2 toggles/4 turnouts) that lead to turnouts that always act as pairs or crossovers (like the pair between blocks 8 and 9). The pair between blocks 5 and 8 (closest to block 8) also act as crossovers. The two turnouts leading to the hidden passing siding (only the left turnout is actually on this layout) require an individual toggle for each turnout. I opted for spring-loaded (to off) S.P.D.T. toggles to actuate the switch machines; some modelers prefer a pair of push buttons to the S.P.D.T. toggle switch. I added a ¼ inch piece of surgical tubing over each switch machine toggle handle so I could tell by both sight and feel that it was not a block toggle. Further, the switch machine toggles are installed to operate the lever up and down. The D.P.D.T. center-off block toggles are installed to operate right and left with (obviously?) the lever pointing to the right when block B is selected. The four push buttons on the panel are to actuate the Kadee Magne-Electric uncoupling ramps.

I also installed a Capacitive Discharge kit from Train Tronics (Circuitron also makes one) to actuate the Rix (or any other brand) twin-coil switch machines. You will not need the Capacitive discharge unit if you use the Railway Engineering (or Circuitron or Mann-Made or GB) switch machines that have motors for power. All of the toggles, by the way, are heavy-duty products from Model Rectifier — I don't like the feel of (and I don't trust) slide switches.

The terminal strips are those series of pairs of screws you see in the photos. They give you the chance to make a mistake in connecting a wire without the need to replace the entire wire — usually, just a change from one screw-attached terminal to the other will do. The terminal strips also make it far easier to trackdown any short circuits: you can connect the lead wires from a test light to the screws to see if the fault is on the panel side of the circuit or on the layout side of the circuit — again, wisdom of hindsight (having not used them on a couple of previous layouts).

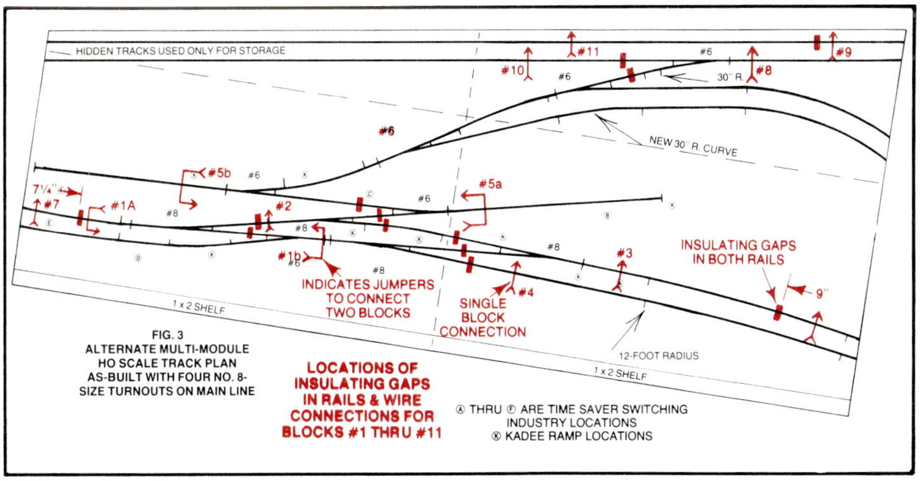

FIG. 3
ALTERNATE MULTI-MODULE
HO SCALE TRACK PLAN
AS-BUILT WITH FOUR NO. 8-
SIZE TURNOUTS ON MAIN LINE

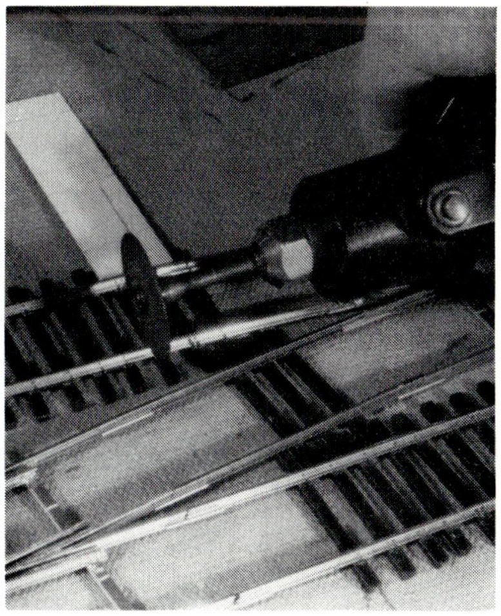

WIRING THE LAYOUT: *The wiring process begins by providing the insulating gaps that will prevent short circuits once the wiring is installed. While you're cutting them, you might as well cut the insulating gaps that allow the use of conventional power packs (as well as Carrier/Command-Control packs) for two-train operation (at blocks 6, 7, 10 and 11 on this plan). Use a cut-off disc in a motor tool (and wear eye protection — the discs can break) to cut the gaps through the rail. I marked a scale three feet on a scrap of plastic to help judge how much to offset the gaps. The three foot offset helps to prevent derailments caused by gaps directly opposite each other. The offset can also prevent some short circuits or gap-bridging by metal wheels. Look down into EVERY cut with a flashlight to see that all the metal really is gone — I found I needed to cut about 1/64 inch into the tie to clear away all the metal for a true insulating gap.*

I used pieces of .020 x .030 inch Evergreen plastic (with the .030 across the rails) to fill each insulating gap. Press in a drop of Super Jet or Super T thickened cyanoacrylate cement into the gap, then insert about 1/2 inch of the plastic strip. Let the cement dry overnight, then trim the plastic flush with a hobby knife. Finally, file the joint smooth with a jewelers' file and wash away any residue with a damp rag.

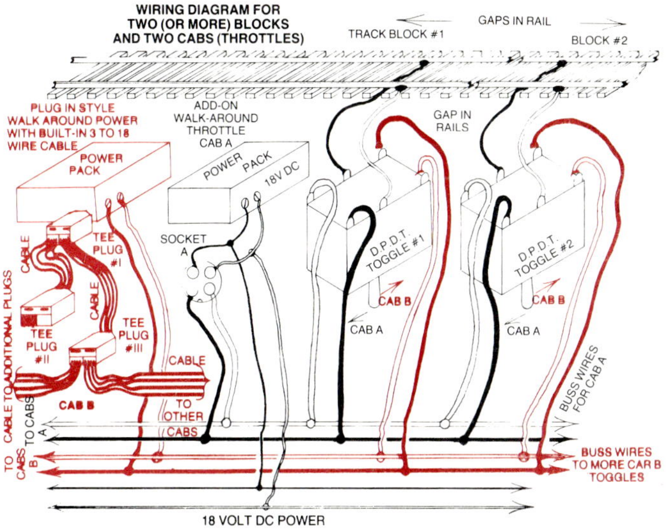

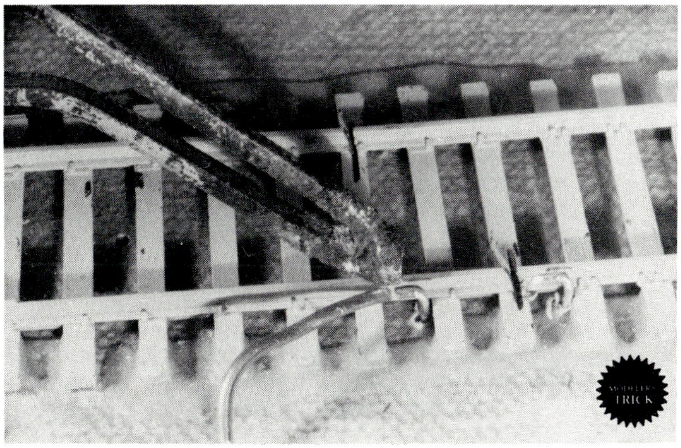

I used 30 gauge tinned solid copper wire to lead from the tracks through the tabletop. If you cannot find tinned, use magnet wire and scrape off the insulating paint. The insulated 24 gauge wires leading to the control panel are soldered to the dangling bare ends of the copper wire below the layout.

Drill 1/16 inch holes beside the outside of the rails and next to the ties. Bend a 1/16 inch hook in the 30 gauge wire and insert it into the hole. This is one of the expansion gaps, so there are two wires, one on either side of the gap. I was able to make four of these gap-spanning wire connections also serve as the connections to the D.P.D.T. block selector toggles to save a few wire connections.

Shove the 30 gauge wires tightly against the outside web of the rails and solder them in place. A tip (to save your back): solder the insulated #24 wires (that lead to the terminal strips) to the bare #30 wires before shoving the #30 wires up through the roadbed.

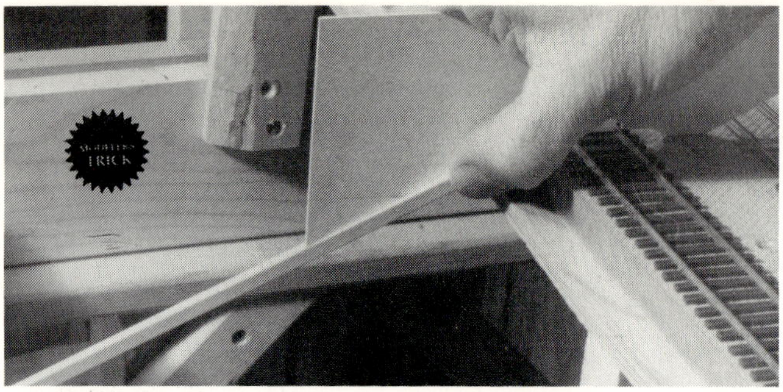

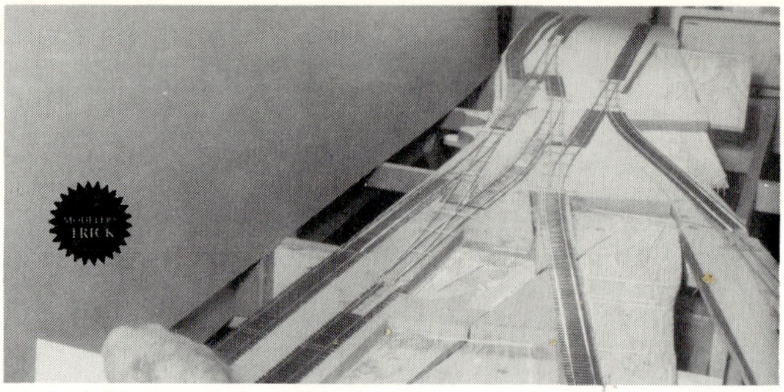

THE CONTROL PANEL: *It seems a bit early in the construction process to build a control panel, but you need someplace to connect those wires from the track. I made my panel part of the facia along the forward edge of the layout which means we need to skip ahead a bit to the scenery part of construction (another, of many reasons, why planning is a big help). The roadbed profile template will be used to shape the ballast shoulders and to be sure the simulated earth banks are not too steep. Here, I'm extending the slope of the bank down to the edge of the table. I held a piece of 1/8 inch thick Masonite hardboard against the back edge of the 1 x 2 "elbow rest" along the front of the layout. I marked the slope on the back of the Masonite.*

I already knew a river would flow about an inch below the track level. Whenever that marked slope was MORE than an inch below the track level, I knew the river was going to be very near the front if not actually flowing over the front of the layout. It was the contour of the bottom of the river, or its opposite bank that determined the shape of the 1/8 inch Masonite facia. A fine tooth blade in an electric saber saw was used to cut the Masonite.

I limited the size of the control panel to 20 inches, about the space between two of the open grid cross members. The 1/8 inch Masonite was supported on some 2 x 2 wood uprights screwed to the cross members. I cut the 20 inch (give or take) panel so there was at least an inch of the 2 x 2 on each vertical edge.

The size of the Model Rectifier D.P.D.T. center-off toggles used for block selector switches limited how close the track lines could be spaced on the panel. I painted the panel brown to blend with the dirt I was going to use for scenery. The lines for the tracks were then cut lightly into panel face about 3/8 inch apart for paralel tracks. The Model Rectifier S.P.D.T. switch with a spring-loaded centering to off (lower, left) was used to control the switch machines on the hidden turnouts.

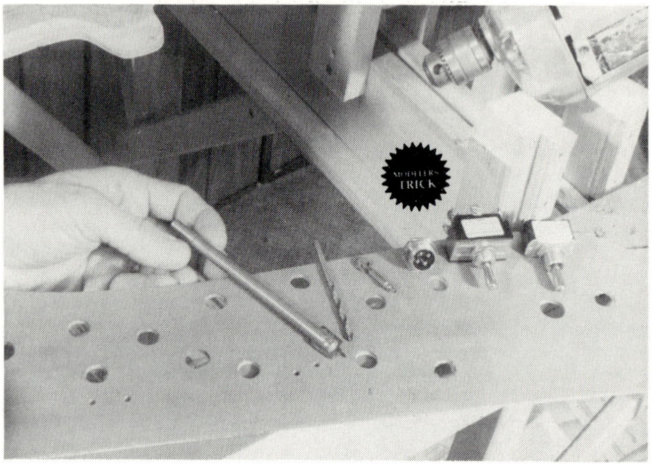

I used a 3/16 inch drill bit to bore the holes for the Kadee no. 160 push buttons. I also used that drill as a pilot drill for the larger holes. A wood screw countersink bit (left) was then used to drill the 1/2 inch holes for the sockets, D.P.D.T. and S.P.D.T. switches (upper, right) as shown in the photos. The diagram only shows positions for the D.P.D.T. switches and push buttons for those that might not want sockets for walk around throttles or turnout switches on their panels.

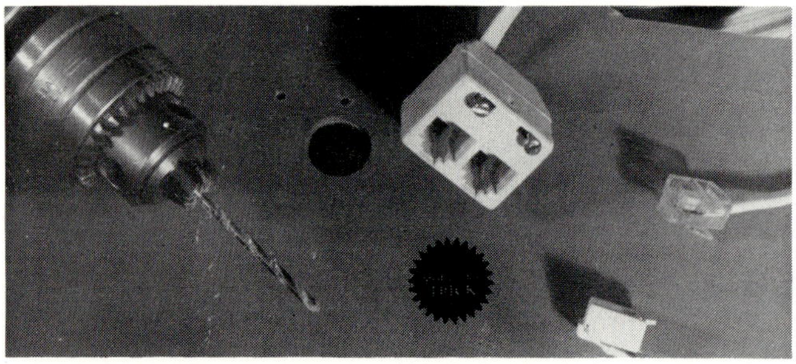

The Model Rectifier "Trainpower 5" furnished with telephone jacks or plugs and many modelers are connecting other types of walk-around throttles with these tiny plugs and sockets. Electronics hobby stores (like Radio Shack) sell a variety of plugs. This "Tee Plug" is available either to plug directly into a telephone or, as shown, on a extension cord. The two slots in the top are just wide enough to fit a 2-56 screw so the Tee Plug can be adapted to a compact panel socket (I couldn't find any sockets smaller than about 2 x 3 inches). Drill two 1/16 inch holes to position the tee plug behind a 1/2 inch hole in the panel as shown. Mount with two 1/2 inch 2-56 screws.

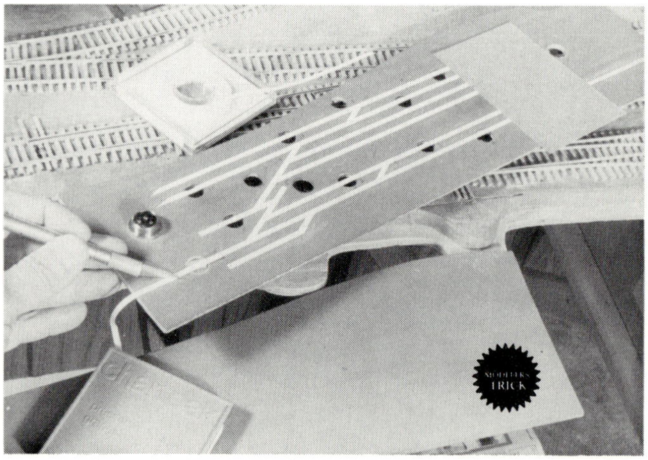

I used 1/8 inch wide drafting tape to mark the track diagram on the control panel face. I used yellow for the visible tracks and white for the tracks I knew would be hidden. Art supply stores sell the tape and a variety of number and letter stickers you can use to mark the face of the panel if you feel the need. The scrap of cardboard (upper, right) covers the portion of the panel that includes tracks for future expansion — only the visible tape duplicates tracks actually being built in this series.

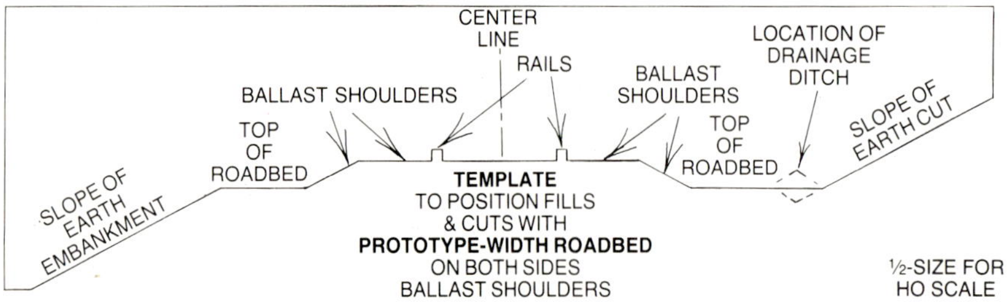

WIRING A CONTROL PANEL: *the back of even a simple panel like this will eventually be a maze of wires. Work systematically, one wire at a time, and the work will not be confusing. Also, use at least 8 different colors of wires so they'll be easier to trace if you need to locate a short or make a change later. Number 24 gauge wire is fine; I used a variety of wires from 16 to 24 gauge.*

Start with the wires that will connect to one of the throttles (Cab B) from the SAME CORNER of every one of the D.P.D.T. center-off block selector switches. You can simply loop the wire form one switch to the next, soldering each connection as you go (do NOT use the screw terminals — they are too inaccessible and unreliable). Here, the first wire is on and the 9-inch extension wandering off toggle switch number 4 (upper, right) will lead to the terminal strip and, hence, to the throttle. I marked the numbers on the back of the panel to avoid guesswork. Next, install the second wire that will lead from the adjacent corner terminals on all the D.P.D.T. switches to cab B. When that's done, install the two wires that lead to Cab A.

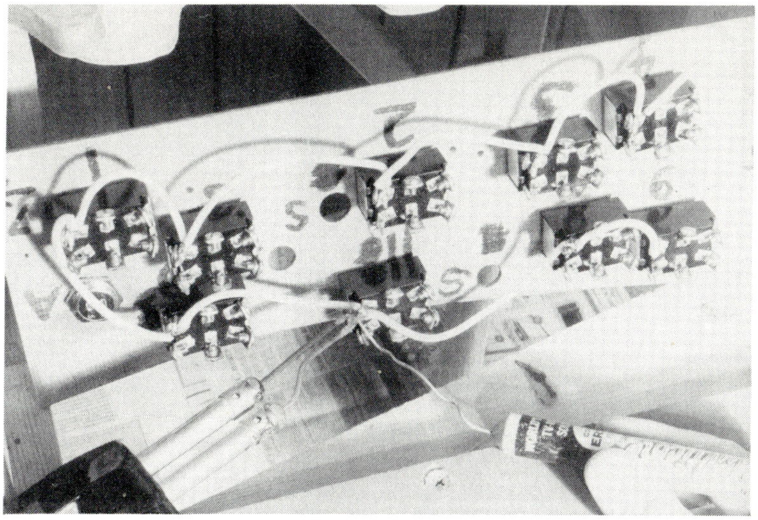

CONTROL PANEL SCHEMATIC

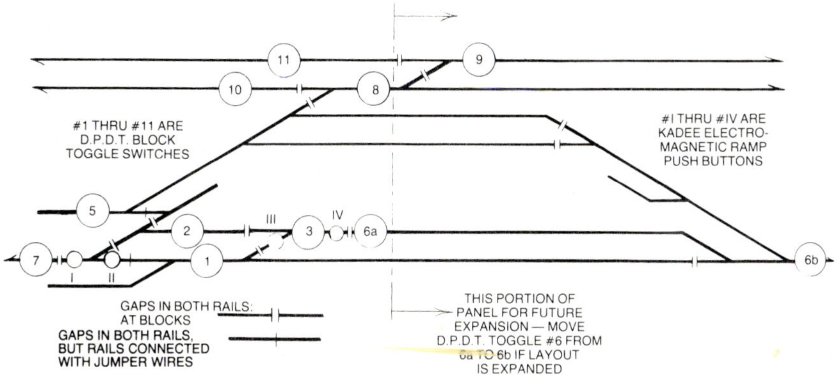

I did not actually cut off the strips of .020 x .030 plastic at the insulated rail gaps until AFTER I had wired the panel. The strips help to mark where the blocks are located at the rails so you can compare them to where the blocks are at the panel.

If you need a plug and socket for a throttle like MRC's Tech II (upper, left) walk-around, I recommend the "CB and Audio" 4-pin chassis mount socket (Radio Shack/Archer No. 274-002) and matching 4-pin connector (Radio Shack/Archer no. 274-001). They mount nicely, plug and unplug smoothly without shorts (like telephone jacks) and there's a screw cap connection if you want a semi-permanent tethered walk-around throttle connection.

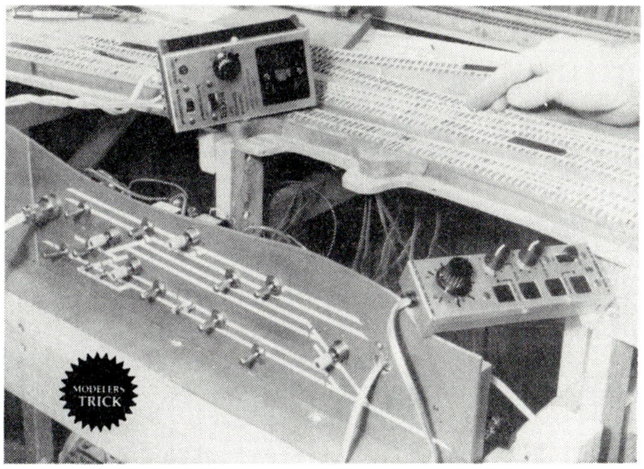

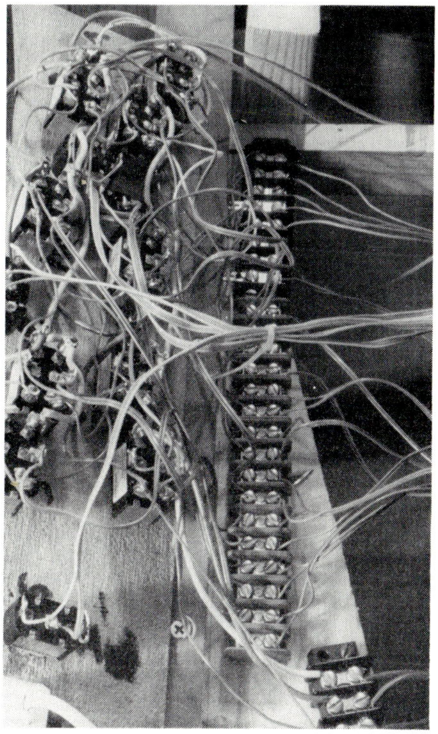

Take the wiring a step at a time, and this is what you'll achieve. There are three distinct circuits on the panel itself; the wires from each of 11 of the D.P.D.T. center-off switches, the wires from each of the 4 Kadee push buttons, and the wires from the S.P.D.T. spring-loaded to center-off switches that operate the hidden turnouts. Each one is illustrated with drawings on these pages. The complexity is due to the fact that there are so many circuits.

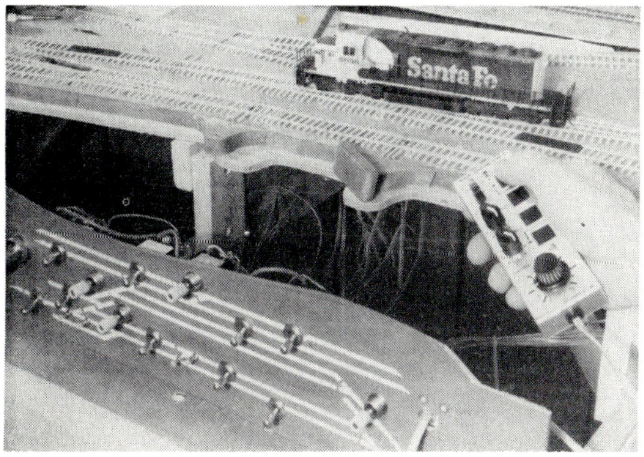

Connect the number 24 gauge wires at the rails to the proper center pair of terminals on the D.P.D.T. center-off switches on the panel (with the terminal strip in between). Connect the switch machine and uncoupling ramp wiring. Connect the walk around throttles and power packs. Smooth-off the rail joiners. Clean the rails with a "Bright Boy" abrasive rubber block (don't scrape them with a knife — the scratches oxidize more quickly than a smooth rail top). You are now ready to operate. Test run each size of locomotive to be sure one doesn't tend to derail somewhere.

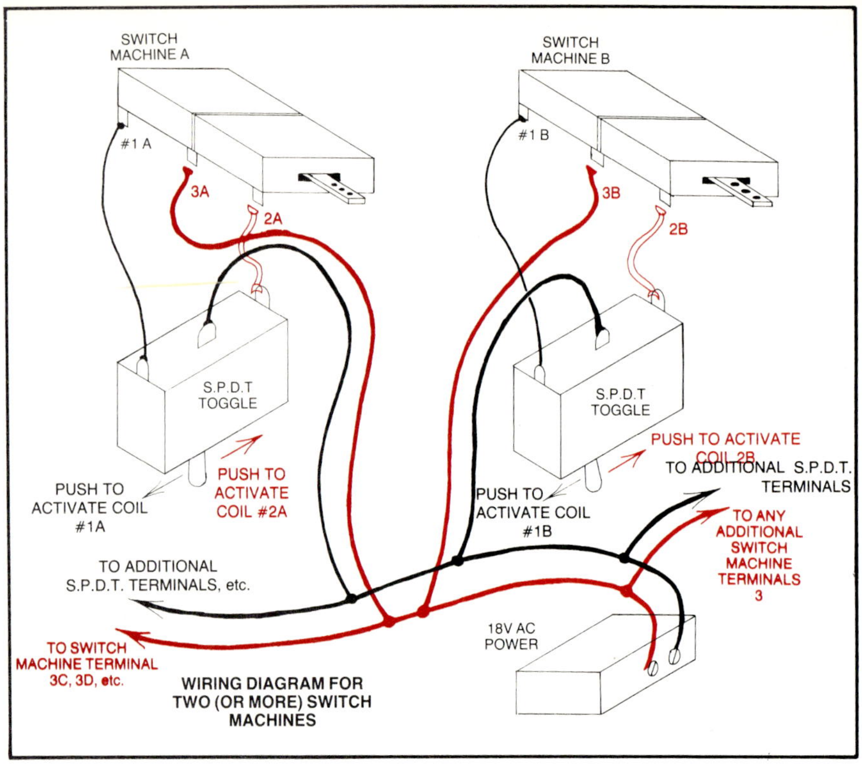

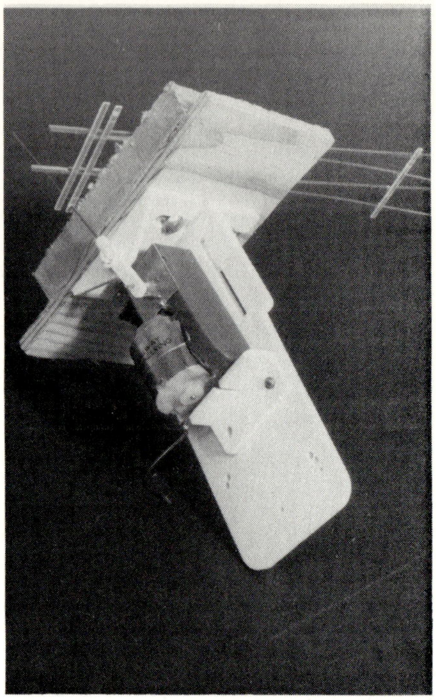

The Railway Engineering motor-driven switch machine is mounted on the Rix Rax number 628-1 and the rack mounted to the bottom of the layout. The Rix no. 628-6 is mounted beside the Rax as shown with the Y-shaped wire link (you made) connecting the rotating shaft of the switch machine to the pivoting wire leading to the turnout's throw bar.

The rubbing contacts on the Railway Engineering machine can be used for BOTH power to the frog and as contacts to automatically turn the motor in the machine on and off; a point not made clear by the instructions (that's why those three Railway Engineering wiring diagrams include diodes — to separate the switch machine power from the track power even through both use the same contacts at the switch machine).

SWITCH MACHINES: *even if you prefer to operate the turnouts by hand, you won't be able to do that with those that will later be hidden beneath the scenery. The most common method of operating turnouts is with a twin coil switch machine like this one by Rix. There are at least a dozen brands including NJ, Precision Scale, Lambert, Peco and Rix. An enclosed electrical magnet or "coil" at each end pulls an iron bar in one direction or the other to move the switch lever through linkage. There are usually three wires; a common center wire and one wire to each of the coils. The diagram shows how to wire them to an S.P.D.T. switch but be sure to get the type that is spring loaded to off — you only want to make a momentary contact to energize the coil. Most modelers also prefer to boost the effeciency of the action with a capacitive discharge unit between the 18 volts AC power pack and the switch machine circuit. Train Tronics and Circuitron sell the capacitive discharge systems.*

The least obtrusive way to move the turnout points (especially on visible trackage — looks don't matter much on hidden tracks) is with a vertical pivoting lever (a stiff wire) like this through the throwbar at the turnout points. Rix makes a dandy plastic mounting bracket called a "Rix Rack" (no. 628-1, shown) that includes all the mounting hardware. The two screws hold an angled piece of plastic that can be adjusted up or down to alter the amount of movement of the vertical wire to suit the turnout.

Most twin coil switch machines include at least one set of separate contacts (Rix has two sets) that can be used to supply track power to the live frog (as shown in the Fall 1981 issue of **Model Railroading magazine***).*

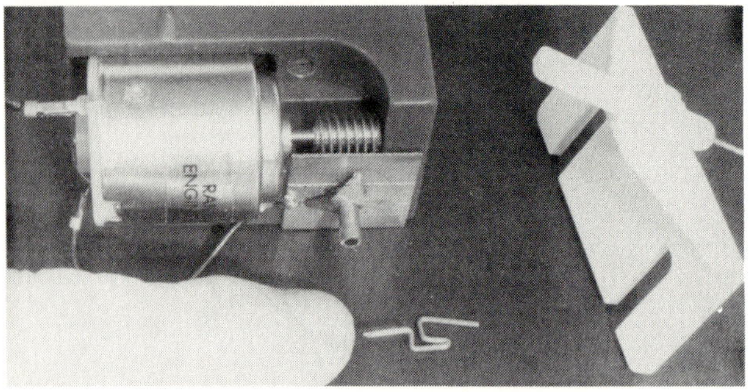

You can use the inexpensive Railway Engineering motor-driven switch machine with a vertical wire rather than the visible link shown in the machine's instructions. Bend a Y-shaped piece of the steel wire furnished with the machine as shown to connect the Railway Engineering pivoting post to the Rix number 628-6 "Pivoting Turnout Linkage" (right).

The final step in the installation of either the twin coil or Railway Engineering switch machines, is to cut the wire that moves the turnout throwbar. The wire is easier to slice if you use a cut-off disc in a motor tool (wear eye protection). Leave about 1/32 inch of the wire above the throwbar.

Positive-Action/Live-Frog Manual Switch Machines

The Ultimate "ground-throw" turnout control system?

New Modeling Techniques

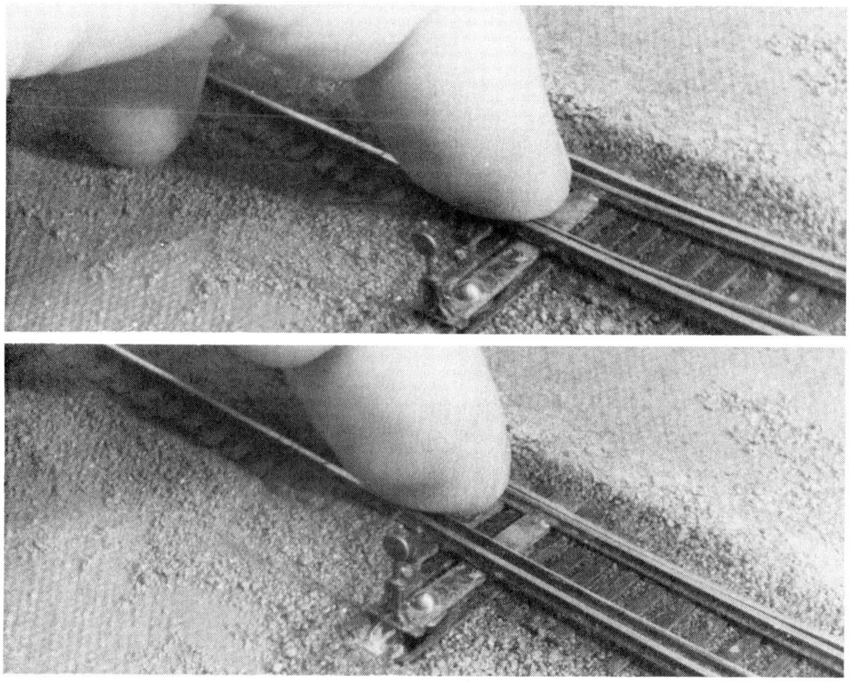

Finger-flickn' turnout control in action. This turnout control system allows you to simply push the turnout points to the proper route - the points automatically snap-close and electrical power flows automatically and reliably to the selected route - all for less than $2 per turnout.

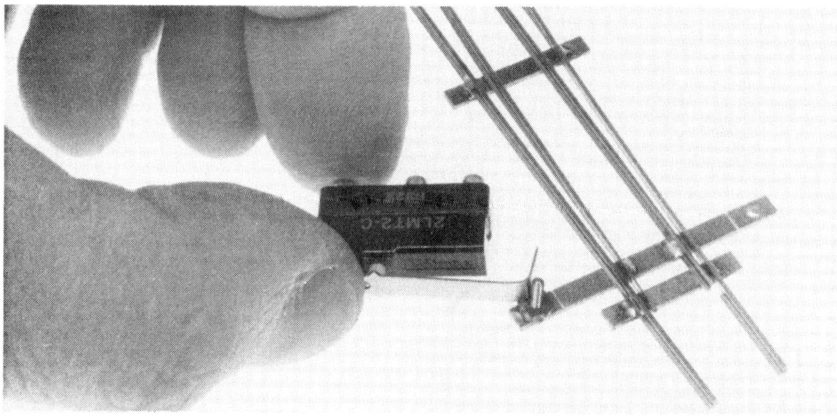

The basic Finger-Flickn' turnout control system uses an SPDT Micro Switch with a roller built-into the contact lever. The switch is positioned so the vertical 0-80 screw in the turnout throw bar flips the SPDT lever "on" as the screw rolls OVER the roller. Flicking the turnout points (by finger tip) the opposite direction forces the 0-80 screw back over the roller to allow the micro switch to flick off. Play with the system in a mock-up like this to understand how it works and the angle that the micro switch must be mounted before you install the switch permanently. The switch can be positioned beside the turnout (in this position) or under the table as depicted in the following photographs. The system will work for N scale (shown) as well as HO, HOn30, HOn3, and Sn3.

Now you can have the click-tight turnout movement, sealed-power electrical control AND use scale-size switch stands or ground throw levers

Robert Schleicher

The state-of-the-art model railroad is likely to be one built on a shelf around the walls of the room or as a "peninsula" rather than on the traditional island. Why? Because modelers have found, by the trial-and-error methods of building island-style layouts, that it's more realistic and more exciting to walk along beside the train than to stand at a fixed control panel. The follow-the-train scheme also means, of course, that some type of remote control throttle is needed; hence the hand-held throttles with wires or tethers to the control panel.

The walk-around operating scheme also effects the way people perform other model railroad control operations. Some modelers use small screwdrivers to manually lever the couplers apart (whether those couplers are NMRA-style HO scale horn-hooks, Rapido-style N scale hooks or Kadees). More and more modelers are opting for manually-actuated turnout controls rather than the remotecontrol type. When you are standing right beside the turnout, there's no reason to have a remote control - often, your throttle-holding hand is closer to the turnout than to the control panel that would contain the remote control turnout-actuating buttons. In practice, it is less realistic

Be sure, when the $1\frac{1}{2}$ inch diameter hole is cut in the plywood, that the hole is offset from the $\frac{1}{2}$ inch hole below the throwbar. Both operations MUST be performed with the turnout lifted up from the roadbed because the drill bit in the hole saw and the $\frac{1}{2}$ inch drill both penetrate the roadbed.

To use the Finger Flickn' system a $\frac{1}{2}$ inch long 0-80 screw (Walthers sells them) is threaded down through the center of the throwbar. It's possible to install those screws after the turnout is glued down, but it's a lot easier if you do it just before gluing it down. Use a compass point or ice pick to mark the center of the hole, then drill it with a number 55 size drill bit held in a pin vise.

Slip a $\frac{1}{16}$ 0-80 tap into the pin vise to thread the hole in the throwbar. The $\frac{1}{2}$ inch 0-80 screw goes in next, with an 0-80 nut locking it to the bottom of the throwbar. A $\frac{5}{8}$ inch long piece of $\frac{1}{16}$ K&S brass tubing is then glued around the thread of the screw. The tube rubs the roller on the micro switch to open and close the micro switch to provide power to the frog from the proper direction to match the way the turnout points are thrown.

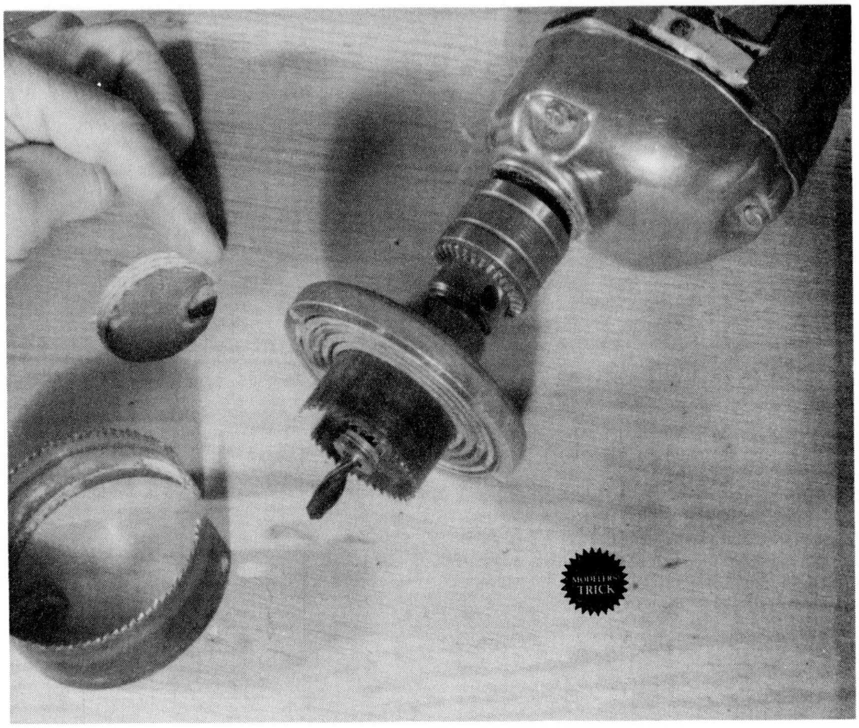

UNDER-THE-TABLE MOUNTING:

First, locate where the turnout will mount on the table and mark the center of the turnout throw bar. Drill a $\frac{1}{16}$-inch hole through that mark to locate the mounting beneath the table. If the turnout is already laid, you can drill between the throwbar and the next tie and be close enough. Use a hole saw to remove a 1 to $1\frac{1}{2}$-inch diameter "plug" from the wooden tabletop around that $\frac{1}{16}$-inch hole - the micro switch should be no MORE than $\frac{1}{2}$-inch below the turnout - mounting the micro switch too far below results in too much play in the 0-80 screw that actuates the roller.

Drill a $\frac{3}{8}$-inch diameter hole directly below the turnout (the location of that original $\frac{1}{16}$-inch hole is, again, close enough). If the turnout is already in place, mark the thickness of the roadbed on the drill with masking tape (as shown) so you don't drill up through the turnout itself. Note: all of these photos were taken from BELOW the tabletop looking up toward the bottom of the turnout.

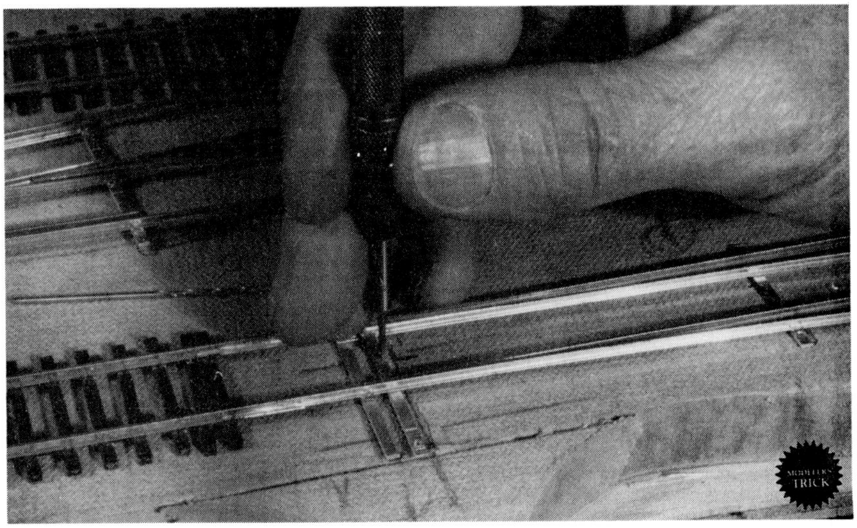

to reach for a control panel beside the layout than to reach onto the layout to the turnout itself. The modeler's mind is involved more in the scene, with walk-around control, and that illusion of "being there" is lost whenever you have to reach off the layout. It is really quite satisfying to simply reach down to the switch and turn it from main to siding (or vise versa); you really feel more like a scale model brakeman. In a photograph, that finger flicking the turnout looks ridiculous - when you're really running the trains and throwing the turnouts, however, the effect is completely the opposite; it feels ridiculous NOT to reach direclty for the turnout.

Modelers select manual turnout control for reasons of lower cost and more simplicity, as compared to the switch machines (electrical solenoid or motors) that control remote-control switches. Most of the ready-laid turnouts, with plastic ties, have some type of manual control built right into the turnout so the turnout points snap closed against the rails. You move a small pin on the Atlas, Model Power, and Bachmann turnouts, the points themselves can be moved on the Peco and on the Shinohara (imported by Lambert and ConCor) turnouts. Some modelers prefer a more positive locking on Peco or Shinohara turnouts, so they add a ground throw lever like those made by Caboose Industries for N scale and by Caboose, NJ International, Alexander, and LaBelle for HO scale. Those ground-throw levers are necessary for the manual (as opposed to remote-control) operation of the Railway Engineering and Railcraft turnouts, in both N and HO scale, that have the rails soldered to printed circuit board ties.

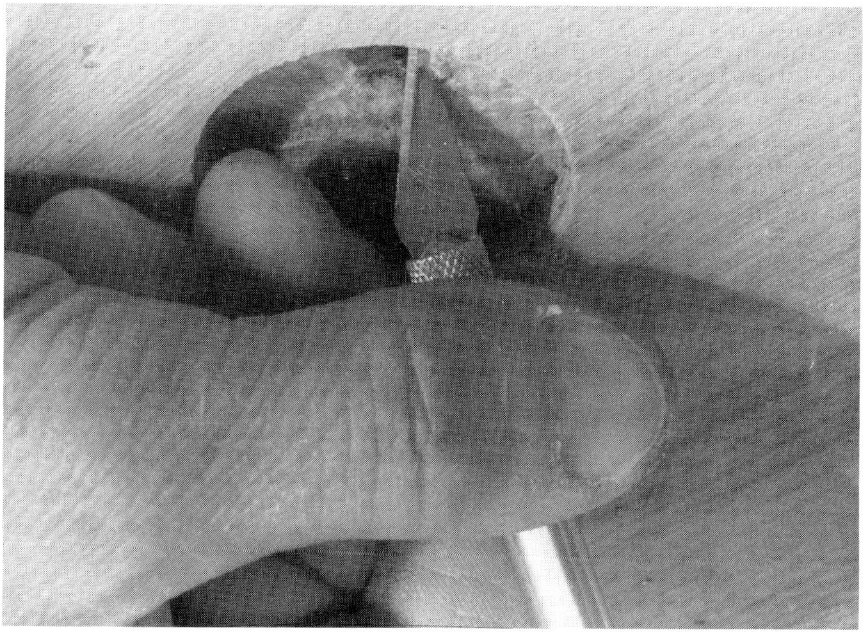

Use a hobby knife to clear-away any fuzz or slivers from both the top of that 3/8-inch hole (beneath the turnout throwbar) and the bottom (as shown). This roadbed is the cardboard-like Homosote wallboard.

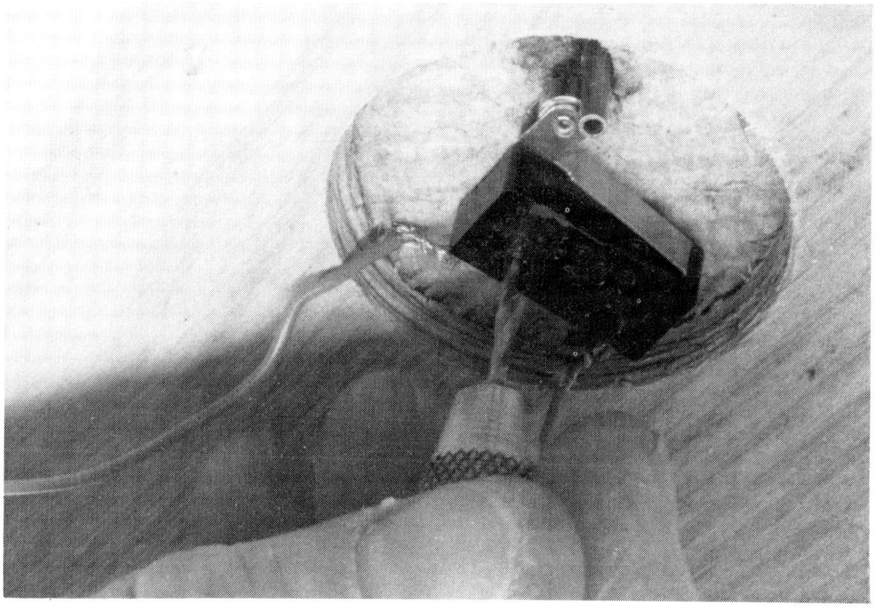

Install a 1/2-inch long 0-80 round head screw through the throwbar so the screw protrudes down through the roadbed. You'll need to drill a no. 55-size hole through the throwbar. Lock the screw in place with an 0-80 nut on the bottom of the throwbar (use needlenose pliers to hold the nut). Cut a piece of 3/32-inch (outside diameter) K&S-brand brass tubing long enough to extend from that 0-80 nut on the bottom of the throwbar, through the raodbed, and 1/4-inch beyond (with this 1/2-inch thick Homosote roadbed, my brass tube was 3/4-inch long). Attach brass tube to the threads of the 0-80 screw with either five-minute epoxy or thickened cyanoacrylate cement (like Super Jet). You are now ready to mount the micro switch.

Position the micro switch so it is turned-on when the turnout throw bar (and that 0-80 screw and brass tube) roll over the roller and so it turns off when the turnout throw bar is moved the opposite direction. To be sure, attach the wires to the three micro switch tabs with the wire to the turnout frog connected to tab "O" and one outside rail and its wire connected to one "on" tab and the other wire to the opposite "on" tab. Do NOT, yet, connect those three wires to the rails - connect them to a 12-volt light bulb so the micro switch is between the power pack and off (for test purposes). You can then adjust the micro switch accurately so it always turns that bulb on when the turnout is thrown one way and off when thrown the other AND so the roller on the micro switch keeps the turnout points snuggly against the outside rails in either "siding" or "mainline" positions. Once you're sure the micro switch is located accurately, drill number 55-size holes in the center of the two holes in the micro switch and up through the roadbed as shown in the photo. The 2-56 screw that will hold the micro switch is much smaller than the holes in the switch - that "play" will allow for slight adjustments.

So what is so great about the micro switch type of manual turnout control that you've seen in the photos on these pages? Two things: first, the micro switch provides an over-center type of spring action to positively lock the points against the rails in either "siding" or "main" turnout positions. That spring-shut action is helpful for all brands of turnouts and absolutely necessary with the Railway Engineering and Railcraft turnouts. The second advantage of the micro switch/manual turnout control will only be helpful to more experienced modelers; those who have decided that their turnouts should have electrically "live" or powered frogs, rather than completely insulated frogs. The Shinohara turnouts have live frogs; all of the other brands of turnouts with plastic ties (that are imported into America) have insulated frogs. The Atlas "Custom Line Mark 2" turnouts can also be converted to live-frog operation. The differences between the "live" and "dead" frogs and the extra wiring needed for ALL live frog turnouts are described in the Fall 1981 and Winter 1982 issues of **Model Railroading.**

The advantage of the live frog is simple; it eliminates a fairly long stretch of track that has no eletrical power at all. That insulated chunk of track is often just enough to make most locomotives stall over the frog. When **Model Railroading** magazine tests locomotives, one of those tests is the operation of the locomotive over an Atlas turnout with an insulated frog to determine how well the locomotive picks up power from the rails - to see if it can manage to get over that dead frog without stalling - it's far better, in the experience of most modelers, to get rid of those dead frogs in the first place. The live frog, however, does require the addition of three wires (even when converting those HO scale Atlas' . . . Mark 2 turnouts).

Briefly, the wires allow the electrical current flowing into the turnout from the single track route to flow ONLY into the siding or main route that is selected when the turnout points are thrown. Electrical insulating gaps are cut in the two rails leading to the frog to prevent short circuits - two of those three wires lead to the rails coming into the turnout, while the third wire connects to the all-metal frog. A contact switch allows current to flow ONLY from one of those two rail wires to the frog at a time. The contact switch is a simple petal-style switch

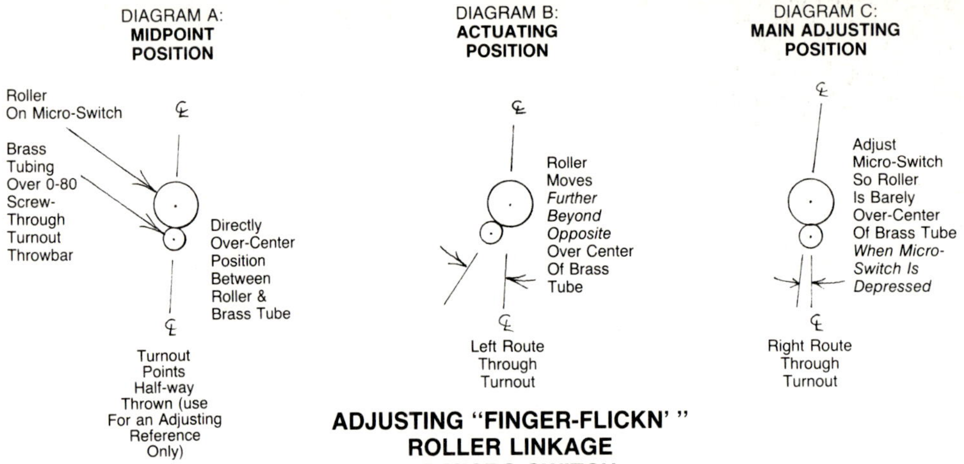

ADJUSTING "FINGER-FLICKN' " ROLLER LINKAGE AT MICRO-SWITCH AS VIEWED FROM BELOW

ADJUSTING THE MICRO SWITCH:

Move the turnout throwbar so the turnout is set for the right hand route with the 0-80 screw and $^{3}/_{32}$ brass tube in their furthest right position (Diagram C). Position the micro switch so its lever (and roller) are depressed just enough to click the switch "on" (this is where that test light circuit helps - you know precisely when the micro-switch is on whether you hear it click or not). The brass tube should be less than $^{1}/_{32}$-inch past dead center on the roller so the spring tension in the micro switch is barely holding the turnout points against the outside (stock) rail.

Next flick the turnout points passed dead center (Diagram A) to the farthest left position they will reach - this will set the turnout for the left hand route on the tabletop. The total travel of the throwbar on most N scale turnouts is about $^{1}/_{16}$-inch - most Shinohara HO turnouts only move $^{3}/_{32}$-inch. The goal is to have the micro switch snap-off (release) after the brass tube goes over-center on the micro switch roller. About $^{2}/_{3}$rds of that travel should occur on the "off" side of the action (Diagram B) for the most positive on-off action and to leave just enough right hand movement (Diagram C) to push the points against the rail.

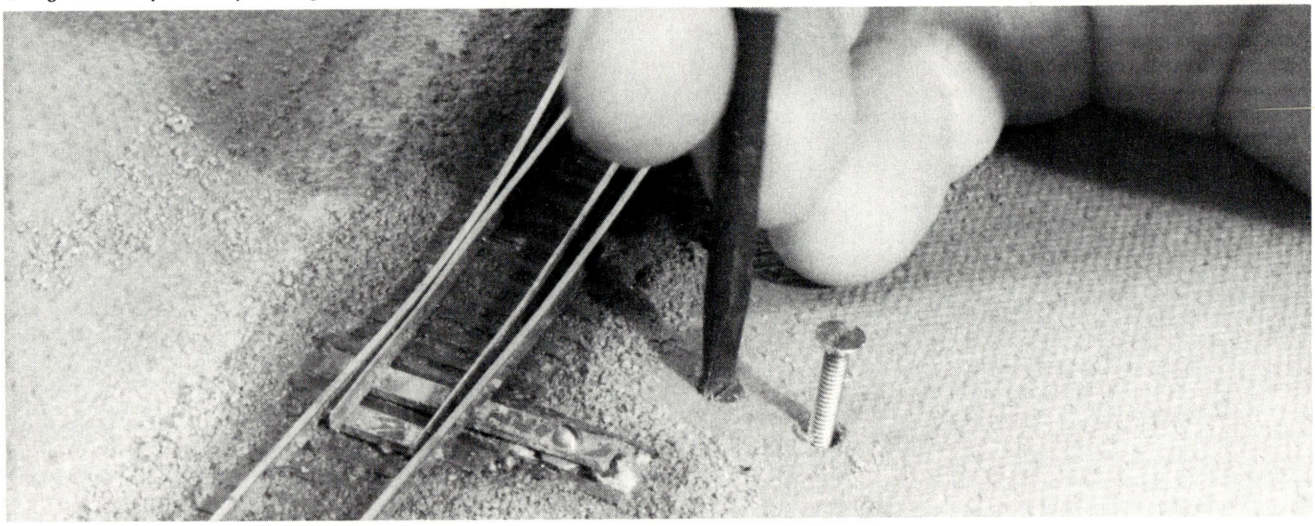

It is essential, with this system, that the micro switch be easily adjusted in a very small range AND that the 0-80 screw down through the throwbar be very rigid. You can mount the 0-80 screw through the end of the metal-faced throwbars on the Railway Engineering (shown) and Railcraft turnouts but the 0-80 should go through the center of the throwbar (between the points) on any turnouts with plastic throwbars.

The no. 947-1076 Walthers flat head 2-56 x $^{1}/_{2}$-inch screws actually thread into those no. 50-size holes from the TOP of the table. The screws, thus, become mounting STUDS for the micro switch.

built-into most of the solenoid style or motor-drive switch machines. Atlas sells a separate relay for this purpose, called a "Snap Relay" to use with their HO scale . . . Mark 2 turnouts. The small lever switches in the photographs on these pages perform the same power-routing function - all three types are what electricians call SPDT (Single Pole, Double Throw - one wire in, and the switch selects one of two wires out of the switch depending on how it is thrown).

The advantage of the lever switches in the photographs is that all the contacts are sealed inside so there is little chance they will corrode like the contacts on the petal-style switches. Electronics hobby shops sell the lever style switches as "Micro Switches" (a generic name), "Miniature Roller (or Lever)" or "Subminiature Roller Lever" switches. The switches are also available, at cheap prices, in electronic surplus stores. The least expensive new one seems to be Radio Shack's number 275-017 at about $1.50. The GC Electronics number 35-848 would be one alternate that is sold by other electronics shops, but the action is a bit stiffer (the spring is stronger) and the price is about $3.00. The GC switch is a bit too large for N scale - the Radio Shack switch will work for either N or HO. These two switches have small rollers that help smooth-out the over-center action used in this specific application.

This system of manual turnout actuation is so simple that I'm sure someone, somewhere, must have used it before. Fred Becker helped me develope a similar system for use with model aircraft control that appears in Volume III of THE MODEL RAILROADING HANDBOOK series (published by Chilton). Other articles have appeared that use the micro switch for power, but this is the first one that uses the micro switch both for power and to take advantage of the switch's built-in spring and roller to provide the positive - locking of the turnout points against the rails.

This system is most effective when the 0-80 brass screw and $^{3}/_{32}$-inch brass tubing are located directly below the center of the turnout throw bar and, thus, beneath the roadbed. It is also possible to mount the micro switch on the tabletop beside the turnout, by inserting the 0-80 screw in the end of the throwbar, but the slight amount of twist in most plastic throwbars makes the adjustment of the over center action difficult - for top of the table mounting, the metal throwbars in the Railway Engineering and Railcraft turnouts provide more positive action. The 0-80 x ½-inch round head brass screws are Walthers no. 947-1016, the nuts are no. 947-1251 and K&S makes the $^{3}/_{32}$-inch round brass tube. You should be able to get all this stuff at better hardware stores, although they may have steel rather than brass screws and nuts.

Walthers no. 947-1253 2-56 hex nuts are threaded over the protruding ends of those ½-inch screws. This "stud" and nut system allows the micro switch to be clamped more tightly, with less chance of misalignment, than if regular wood screws were used. A no. 947-1273 washer should be placed between the nut and the micro switch so the nut does not dig-into the switch and crack it. You'll need to readjust the micro switch a bit before tighting the nuts with pliers.

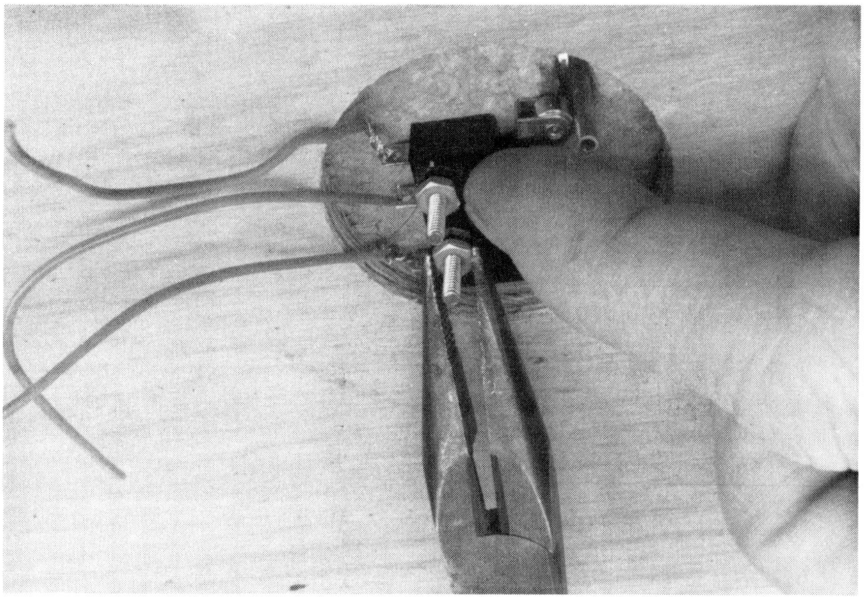

Drill $^{1}/_{16}$-inch holes from above the turnout, just beside the outside of the outer rails and beside the frog guard rails. Thread the wires from the micro switch up through the holes, strip-off ¼-inch of the insulation, and solder the wires to the outside of the rails. The wiring for live-frog turnouts is described in the Fall 1981 and Winter 1982 issues of* Model Railroading *magazine.

There is one more reason why I felt the need to devise a positive-lock manual turnout throw system with the built-in power-routing feature: Those Railway Engineering and Railcraft turnouts, with code 55 rail and Railcraft flex track with code 55 rail offer nearer-to-scale track for N scale modelers than any other system (the others use larger code 70 rail). That track system was described in the Volume 13, No. 3 issue of **Model Railroading** magazine. The use of Railway Engineering code 70 turnouts to allow operation of HO scale Rivarossi (and other plastic locomotives) with oversize wheel flanges was described in the Spring 1982 issue of **Model Railroading** magazine. You can use just about any brand or style of remote-control actuation for these turnouts and have built-in electrical switches (SPDT switches) for the power routing to the live frogs in these two brands. Now you have a system of manual, at-the turnout, actuation for these live frog turnouts that also includes that eletrical power-routing (SPDT) feature.

Super-Detailed Track & Roadbed

Truly detailed trackwork is easier and quicker to accomplish than applying decals to a freight car (and far more noticeable)

It's possible to disguise sectional track, with code 100 size rail, so it looks something like the real thing. It's no more difficult than weathering a Tyco or Life-Like freight car, complete with NMRA horn-hook couplers, so the car looks more realistic. If it's realism you are seeking, however, there are better ways to create realistic track and freight cars. . .

Track realism starts with the track itself. For HO scale, the rail size should be no larger than code 70 for yards, sidings and branchlines and no larger than code 83 for mainlines depicting 1940 or later real railroads. Shinohara makes turnouts with both code 70 and code 83 rail to match their flex track (as well as the Railcraft, Right-O'-Way and Precision Scale flex track), but the turnouts lack virtually all the small clamps and tie plates that are common to full size turnouts. Why Shinohara did not include those details, especially when they cut the new dies for code 83 turnouts, is shameful. They missed the chance to produce the only realistic HO scale turnout. If you want your turnouts to be as detailed as the rest of the cars and locomotives and structures, you'll have to do it yourself.

Right-O'-Way does make a line of cast turnout frogs, points and guard rails, in HO scale, as well as turnout kits that include those exquisite parts. You must, however, spike these components to wood ties. Send a stamped, self-addressed envelope, to Right-O'-Way, P.O. Box 25735, Dept. MRG, Los Angeles, CA 90025 for their price list. Their turnouts do not include the support plates shown in these photos. The turnouts in the photos do not, of course, include the nut and bolt head and rail support detail cast into the Right-O'-Way frogs and guard rails. Of the two types of details, the support plates (shown in these photos) are the more obvious.

We used the Railway Engineering ready-to-lay (after you add a few decorative ties) turnouts. You could also apply these details to any hand-spiked turnout or to the new Shinohara code 83 turnouts with their (relatively) small spike heads. The molded-in spike heads on the Shinohara code 70 and code 100 turnouts and the spike heads on Atlas turnouts are so huge that they are actually as large as these (simulated) support plates — in other words, it's not worth the trouble to add these details to turnouts with plastic ties and code 100 rail. The techniques for applying ballast and for weathering the track certainly are helpful with any brand of track.

There are two turnouts in the foreground, with their respective switch stands on the far right and left. The most obvious detail that's missing from most model railroad trackwork is those rail support plates that line the outside of the stock rails along the points. There are nine support plates on each rail of these turnouts (which are, probably, about a number 10 or larger size). For the number 8 turnouts on the model, I used 8 support plates (on 8 ties) per rail.

BALLASTING TRACK

The real secret to ballasting model railroad track lies in getting the ballast glued down without gluing the moving points as well. The ONLY way to be sure those points are not glued is to oil them before EVERY step in the track laying and ballasting procedure:

THE SURE WAY TO AVOID GLUED-SHUT TURNOUT POINTS:

1. Apply a drop of Labelle no. 107 plastic-compatible oil to every point where the tie bar rubs the bottoms of the outside rails and wherever the contacts or other parts need to rub or slide. Apply BEFORE painting the ties and turnout grey.
2. REPEAT Step 1, before gluing down the turnout with Matte Medium.
3. REPEAT Step 1 AFTER spreading the loose ballast (and after brushing the ballast from the points).
4. REPEAT Step 1 AGAIN, before misting on a mix of five parts water and one part Matte Medium over the loose ballast.
5. REPEAT Step 1, AGAIN, before brushing Roof Brown paint down the sides of the rails.
6. REPEAT Step 1, AGAIN, before weathering the ties and rails with an air brush.

It's necessary to move the points, every time you apply the oil, so you know the points are free before proceeding to the next step. Six applications of oil sounds like a lot, but it works. I know. I've tried to short-cut one or more of those applications of oil and discovered glued-tight switch points every time. Sometimes it is

Reprinted from September/October 1985 issue

The most noticeable detail on the frog area are those huge bolt heads protruding from the sides of the frog and from the sides of the guard rails. Note there are no support plates on the outside of the frogs or guard rails. Those bolts are cast into the frogs and guard rails sold by Right-O'-Way products — if you want them, that's the best way to get them, but you'll have to spike the turnout in place. The photos of the prototype for my railroad, the Colorado Midland, show rail support plates ONLY at the frogs and guard rails, with none at the points — that's the system I followed for the number 6 turnouts (on the theory that they were laid 20 years or more before the number 8's).

This is one of at least a dozen different styles of rail support plates that have been used over the last 100 years on real railroads. This one is simply spiked to the ties; some are bolted to the rails as well.

possible to free points glued solid with Matte Medium by using some solvent or lacquer thinner but that only works in some cases; some points stay gummy and move erratically no matter what you do (IF you forgot to apply that oil).

The contour tool used to shape the scenery and slopes helped to provide a proper shoulder for the ballast. I simply poured the ballast as carefully as I could to distribute it just to the tops of the ties, then brushed it very lightly with a medium-firm ½-inch wide paint brush to remove it from the tie tops and to shape the tops of the shoulders. I used Woodland Scenics fine-grade Cinders for the left half of the layout (where most of the turnouts are located) and the Rock Quarry's Finegrade Chama Red crushed rock for the double-track mainline on the left. The third segment of the layout is industrial sidings and they were ballasted with a mixture of Chama Red (to show traces of the original ballast) and the fine-sifted dirt I used for the hillsides. Later, I added some Green and Dead Grass colors of Heiki flocking to simulate areas where the industrial track was being engulfed with weeds.

After the ballast is spread precisely where you want it, use a soft number 1 or 2 flat brush (sable is a good choice) to brush every particle of ballast from the areas where the switch points must move, from the bottoms of the frogs and guard rails and from the inside edges of every inch of every rail. It is a lot easier to spend some time now, than to try to chisel the ballast away after you have applied and dried the Matte Medium.

Mix nine parts water with one part Matte Medium and a drop or two (no more) of detergent. Mist the solution over the ballast so it falls vertically onto the ballast. You do NOT want to blow that ballast back into the switch points and frog that you so carefully removed. A plant atomizer works fine and you can flush it out later with water to remove any traces of the Matte Medium so you can reuse the atomizer. Practice on some newspaper to learn the misting technique. Thoroughly soak the ballast — you must see water between every grain of ballast. Wait about five minutes to allow time for the water to soak in and repeat the wetting.

While the ballast is still wet, use a small ear syringe (available in drug stores) to flood the ballast with more Matte Medium — this time, though, mix just five parts water with one part Matte Medium and a single drop of detergent. The pre-soaked ballast should allow this mixture to penetrate without balling-up or running down the slopes in beads. Apply enough of the mixture so there is more white

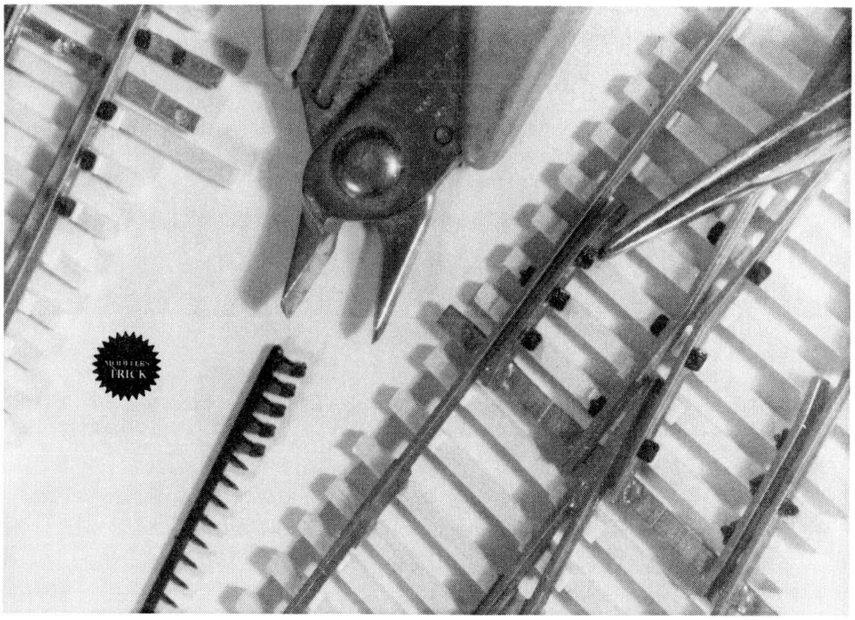

Since I wanted a "busy" looking detail, I opted for a bolt-style rail support. There are none available from any source I know of for HO scale model railroads. I used Grandt Line's number 5113 nut-bolt-washer castings. The pin on the back was cut almost flush with the back so the plate would lean easily against the web of the rail, with the opposite end resting on the top of the tie. I used Super T cyanoacrylate cement to hold the plastic castings. To match my prototype, I installed four castings per frog in the pattern shown. I used flush-cut diagonal cutters (from PBL, in Chama, New Mexico) to cut the parts off the sprue.

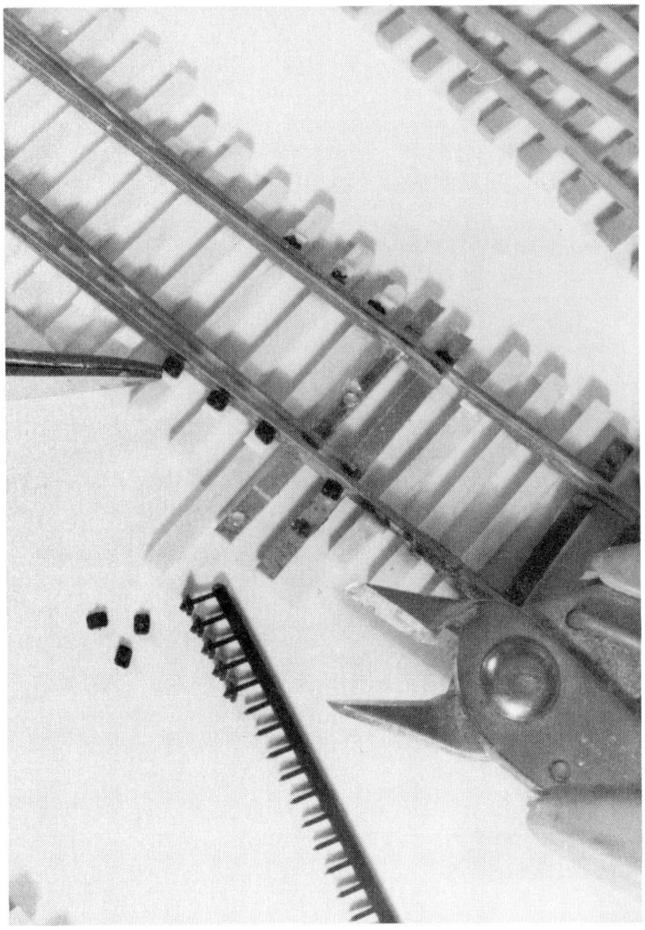

I mixed equal parts Polly S Dirt and water to "stain" the concrete grey ties (they were painted that grey color before the track was laid) for the industrial sidings. I wanted a darker color for the newer ties on the mainline, so I used Polly S "Flats" shade of Dark Earth mixed with an equal part water to stain those ties.

Four of the eight nut-bolt-washer castings are in place on each side of the stock rails. Another casting is added to the ties at the right of the points and three more to the ties at the left for a number 8 turnout (for a number 6 turnout, I'd just add three to the left of the tweezers).

Matte Medium visible than the ballast color — flood it.

After the Matte Medium dries for at least a week, you are ready to apply the final weathering. I brushed Floquil Polly S Roof Brown down the sides of the rails with a number 1-size paint brush. With practice, you can get the paint into the web of the rail so just $\frac{1}{32}$ inch or less rubs across the ties — that $\frac{1}{32}$ effectively simulates the rusted steel tie plates. Next, I applied a mix of equal parts water and Roof Brown with an air brush to blend the colors, followed by some shading and blending with a mix of water and the 1 part white, 10 parts Roof Brown that matched the dirt on the hillsides to simulate blown dust and mud. I mixed 1 part white with 9 parts Grimy Black and an equal part water. That mix was applied directly above the rails with an airbrush (so it didn't color the sides of the rails much — I wanted them to remain rust-colored). This simulates the grease and oil that dribbles from the locomotive and car bearings over time. The newer the track you are simulating, the less of this stain would appear. It also is stronger (as the color photo of the prototype turnouts shows) around turnouts where a lot of starting and stopping takes place and there is less stain on the mainline. A light streak of this same mix was applied down the center of the ties around the turnouts. I had pre-painted the track with regular Floquil Concrete Grey before laying it. That grey provided both a bleached undercoat and a primer that allowed me to use Polly S for all subsequent colors. I sprayed the Floquil grey outdoors and the Polly S indoors.

When the paint has dried overnight, rub the tops and inner corner of the rails (and the mating areas of the points) with a Bright Boy hard rubber eraser (Walthers sells them to dealers). This will remove the paint without scratching the rails. If you try to scrape the paint with a knife, the scratches that remain seem to attract more oxides and dirt to inhibt electrical contact. The final detail, the tall switch stands, will come much later.

There are some compromises that you must make if you expect to have an operating model railroad; one of them is switch points that are linked with something a bit more rugged than these tie bars. On most model railroads, the bar that moves the points is as big as a switch tie, not the two inch wide steel strap at the left of this photo. Grandt makes a throwbar like this one for On3 modelers, one reason why some prefer to model in a scale larger then HO. Right-O'-Way also makes O scale throw bars and "rail support plates".

Build-A-Railroad, step-by-step Part V: Scenery Shapes

Shaping the scenery, from not-SO-level ground to mountains-on-a-diet.

There are probably as many variations in the methods of making scenery as there are modelers. Anyone who has ever built a model railroad AND carried it to the completion of the scenery, has his or her own "best" methods. In my opinion, the methods you're looking at are the "best". These are certainly not my personal creations, but a weeding-out of techniques that just don't seem quite as good as these. Please, don't be offended if we didn't pick your favorite. If you like it that well, ignore these ideas and do it the way you know best.

There is a fear of the unkown when it comes to building scenery and, beleive me, I felt that fear as strongly as anyone. Scenery seems so permanent. Sure, I know you can rip it out and slap in something better, but that is not the kind of attitude that gets the scenery built in the first place. I do want you to know, however, that the main "modeler's trick" to creating scenery is to get started. . . . Do it now and worry later.

I wanted the scenery on this layout to be as lightweight as possible. The secondary criteria were a lack of both noxious fumes and ankle-deep mess. In other words; CLEAN DIRT. In truth, the actual dirt is actual dirt. The stuff that shapes that dirt, however, is about as lightweight and clean as fifty years of try-and-fail scenery construction can develop in this hobby.

For example: I selected the Mountains-in-Minutes brand foam rocks (over the cast-in-plaster types) because the rock walls contribute more to the weight of most scenery than any other component. Conversely, I feel that the thin-shell scenery (industrial-grade paper towels soaked in Hydrocal plaster) is at least as light as layers of insulating foam for the scenery shapes. I like the thin-shell method, too, because it allows you to shape the hills and valleys with easy-to-change

DRAINAGE DITCHES

Use the "Prototype-Width Roadbed" template from Part IV of this series to make a full-size scenery-shaping tool for your scale. The template will be used again and again to locate drainage ditches (here), to shape fills and to be sure your hills, mountains and valleys are not too steep. Use the dotted line marked "Drainage Ditch" to mark the centerline and both edges of the ditch on the Homosote.

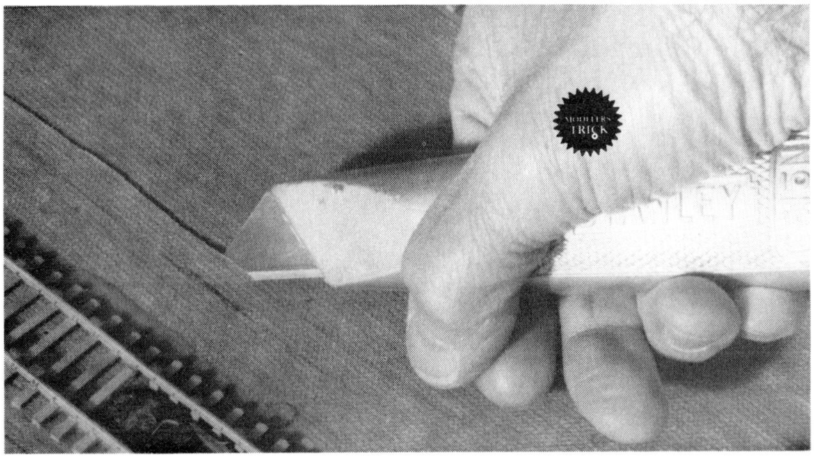

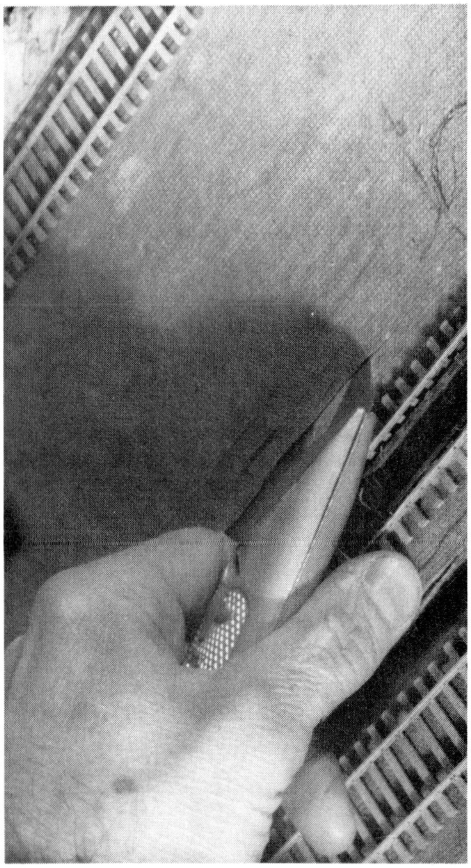

Use a hardware or utility knife to cut into the Homosote to shape the edges of the ditch. Make one light cut to guide the knife, then make three or four passes to cut deeper into the ditch.

wadded-up newspapers before you mix the plaster.

This combination of the foam rocks and plaster shapes, however, forces you to alter the sequence of scenery construction; building the cuts and cliffs first and shaping the hills last. It's a good method because it insures that you really do provide adequate clearance for your cars and locomotives (and, for that matter, enough room for structures) BEFORE you slap on the plaster.

I hesitate to list the actual rock castings used on the layout or even to tell you what colors were used on the rocks or plaster. You don't want to create someone else's model railroad (even if it is John Allen's); you want to recreate nature (that's another word for scenery). I matched the colors of my rocks as closely as I could to some in the Frying Pan River valley of Colorado because that is the area I wanted to duplicate. Go find your own rocks and dirt; please don't use mine (they've already been used). Even if you want to recreate this same valley, you will have a slightly different interpretation of the shapes of the rocks and the colors. If you copy mine, you're just one more step removed from the possible realism you could accomplish had you copied the real thing.

This technique and the basic ideas for shaping the scenery are as valid for a layout set in Florida's swamps as they are for one along the banks of the Mississippi or the edge of the Mojave — alter the shapes of the rocks and the colors and this Colorado valley can be relocated to just about anywhere.

Pry out the vee-shaped strip of Homosote to reveal the ditch. Remember, you can use this technique (and those on the next few pages) to make even a flat diorama or industrial area more interesting (and more realistic).

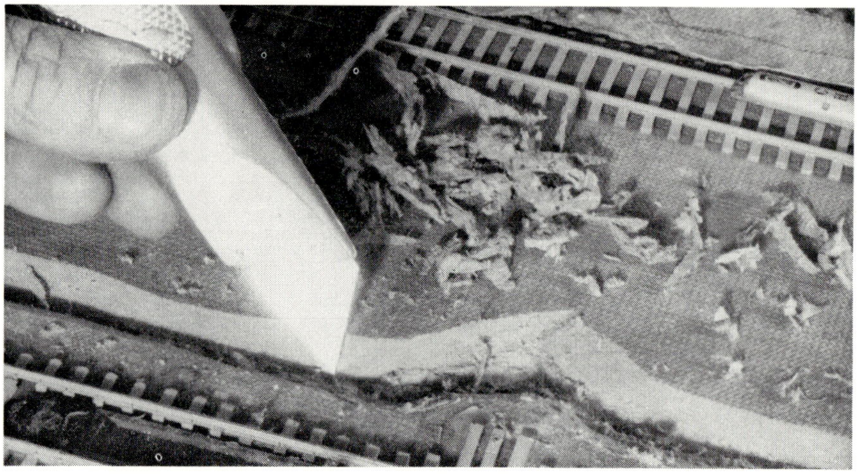

You'll probably leave some of the Homosote in the bottom of the ditch. Cut on down until the bottom of the ditch has a relatively sharp angle. We'll cover that surface, later, with real dirt to soften the contours.

BURYING THE TIES

The track in most industrial areas and in small yards is usually buried nearly to the tops of the ties. The easiest way to recreate that effect is to fill in the areas you want to look "industrial" with artists' illustration board that is between $\frac{1}{32}$ and $\frac{1}{16}$ inch thick — thick enough to match the thickness of the ties on whatever brand of track you are using. Lay the illustration board white side down and press firmly against it so the rails themselves will indent and mark the white surface — you can then use that line as your guide to cut the cardboard with scissors — move the actual cut about $\frac{1}{4}$ inch away from the rail-marked indentations so the cardboard rests against the ends of the ties, not the sides of the rail.

The artists' illustration board (fancy and expensive stiff cardboard) has been cut to fill the area from the edge of the drainage ditch to the ends of the ties (later, a loading ramp and team track dirt road will be located here). The cardboard in the lower right has been cut to rest against the sides of the rails to form a road crossing. A diamond-shaped piece of the cardboard rests between the rails where the future road will cross the track at an oblique angle.

This three-story brick factory is going to be used as the place where loaded cars and empty cars are interchanged. One of the plans shows a limestone kiln at this point but that's a scene that may (or may not) be added later. The factory is a combination of Pola/AHM/Tyco "Machine Shop" kits (also available in N scale) described in the Vol. 13, No. 1 issue of Model Railroading. *Now, I want the railroad cars to enter the building, so I cut the two end walls to fit a Grandt Line no. 5133 door. A cut-off disc, in a Dremel tool, works quickly enough to avoid shaking the whole model apart (do wear eye protection, though).*

ROADS AND RAIL/ROAD CROSSINGS

It's easiest to build the surfaces for any roads at the same time you are creating the rest of the scenery. Another reason why it's nice to plan the layout first. If you use illustration board that is between .040 and .060 thich ($^1/_{16}$ inch or less), you can cut it to fill in the area between the rails as well as the road surface leading up to the outside of the rails. I used TWO layers of the board (one to elevate the road to the tops of the ties; the second layer to elevate the road to the tops of the rails). Cut the pieces that go between the rails about $^1/_8$ inch less than the track gauge (rail spacing). The area next to the flangeway can then be filled with a strip of EverGreen 2 x 8 (on edge) to simulate a board or metal flangeway-clearance guide.

I used water-based acrylic contact cement to attach the cardboard. Hold the cardboard down with map pins pushed in at an angle, as shown, because the contact cement will try to warp the cardboard. I pressed the cardboard in place while the cement was still fluid so I could move it around slightly. The contact cement's slight flexibility makes it more suitable, here, than white glue or resin cement.

I also cut the surface for one stretch of dirt road that was to make a hairpin turn up into the hills. The cardboard is stapled to a 5-inch scrap of wood to be certain the roadway is well above the tracks beneath it. Later, the cardboard will be buried beneath the paper towels and plaster but it provides the location and shape. Most dirt road surfaces are a scale 13 to 15 feet wide, paved roads are 16 to 20 feet wide, even when they're two-lane country roads. I stapled the road surface to the Homosote and the 5 inch support block with a staple gun.

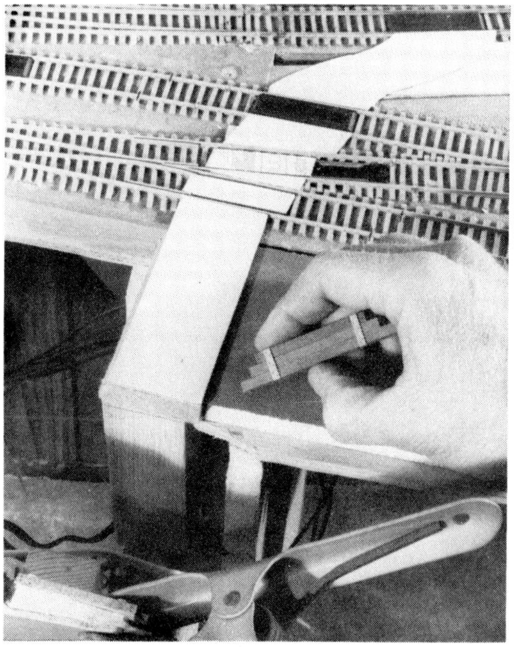

Here, the dirt road crosses the tracks and the stream at the front edge of the layout. I supported the road with 2 x 2 blocks glued to the benchwork. The bridge abutments are strips of Camino or Northeastern HO scale 12 x 12 to simulate timbers. The techniques for building a timber trestle are described in the March/April 1985 issue of Model Railroading. *I cemented the abutments to the vertical ends of the Homosote with contact cement.*

Seal all of the surfaces of the artists' illustration board (cardboard) with either Matte Medium (like that used to seal the Homosote) or acrylic paint. I used a reddish brown shade of Glidden Spred Satin called "Wild Turkey" that is a close match to the color of the rocks and dirt that will come later. There's a color chart (and a lot more scenery information) in the SCENERY & DIORAMAS book published by Chilton to provide some alternate colors for other geographic locales.

MOUNTAINS-IN-MINUTES POLYFOAM ROCKS

It's no longer necessary to make your own latex rubber molds for rocks over pieces of coal; Color-Rite has a choice of 13 different molds at prices ranging from $3.30 for this 5 x 3½ inch mold to $24.95 for a set of five 6 x 6 and larger molds. I used them for a few of the smaller rocks with Mountains-In-Minutes two part polyfoam. I used Armor—All for the mold release — Mountains-In-Minutes mold release is a better compound for this purpose.

Mountains-In-Minutes supplies a very complete and illustrated instruction sheet with their no. 900 casting kit (about $15.00). Two tips: use their mold release and be sure to pour the mixed fluids, as shown, so they cover every part of the mold. You can use this same process, with Color-Rite's molds and Armor-All or MIM's mold release, to make small rock castings from leftover plaster. I made a few very thin plaster castings to cover some of the slopes that were steeper than I had intended.

Most of the rock walls are made from the pre-molded Mountains-In-Minutes rocks. They use a pressure system that creates fewer air bubbles and produces a more usable product than molding your own. This is their no. 820 "Multi-Scale Embankment"; it provided most of the rock I needed.

Again, match the shapes of the rocks to the real world you are duplicating. Mountains-In-Minutes has five different styles of rock. All of them must, however, be painted to match "your" real world. I find that a combination of Pactra's "Authentic Scale Model" series (they used to call them "Military Flat") spray colors in Rust, Light Earth, Dark Earth, Camoflage Grey and Wood Tan can duplicate just about any rock I found. Experiment. I sprayed the darkest color from about a foot away, the lighter color tan from about two feet away and a final dust-on coat of grey and Light Earth from nearly three feet away. You can work outdoors (and should) to paint and dry all the rocks before bringing them to the layout room. The system works just as well with plaster rocks.

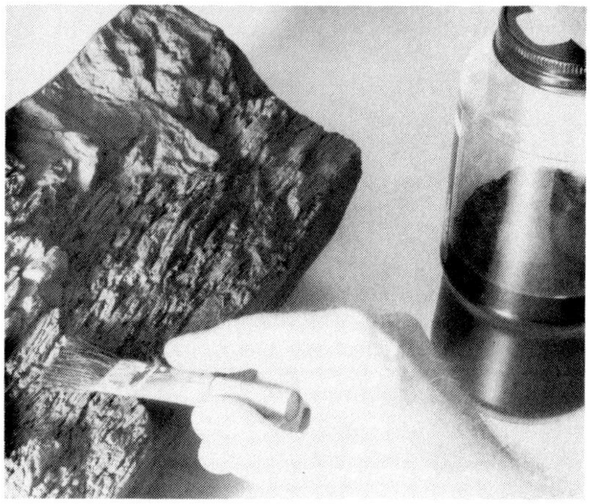

The final step in coloring the Mountains-In-Minutes pre-molded rocks (or rocks you mold yourself from either polyfoam or plaster) is to accent the cavities and crevices with black India ink. I mix the ink with about 4 parts water to one part ink plus four drops of liquid dish-washing detergent per quart (to make the stuff bead less). Brush the ink on, let it dry for about a half hour, then shake-off any excess ink.

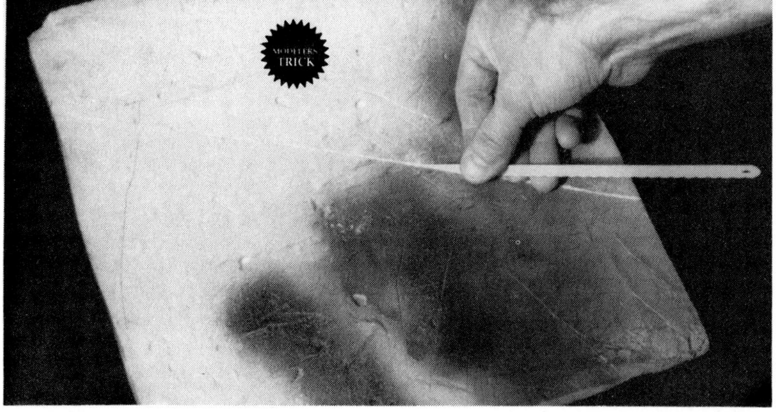

I used a hacksaw blade (but not the holder or handle) to cut the Mountains-In-Minutes polyfoam. You can guide the blade for straight cuts or twist it, as you cut, for wavy surfaces. Part of the "secret" of obtaining realism from the pre-molded rocks is cutting them so they rest at a slight angle to the horizon. I used a second pair of Mountains-In-Minutes rocks (no. 801 and an 802) and cut them on a diagonal as shown (after painting them).

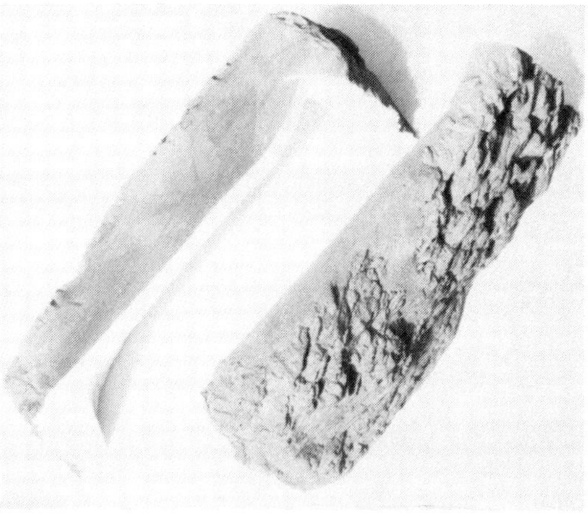

I cut the no. 820 Mountains-In-Minutes Embankment in half (it has rock details across both sides) as shown. I then cut the pieces of one side at a diagonal to match the other polyfoam parts. The thickness of the polyfoam is handy for this type of construction because the rock walls will rest (temporarily — they'll be pinned and glued in place later) on the layout to help in determining the various shapes of the hillsides. Slice the ends of any Polyfoam rocks at a 45 degree angle to form inside or outside corners.

SHAPING THE SCENERY

I wanted the rear edges of ALL the hills and valleys to stop about two full inches from the sky backdrop. Later, a light system will be installed beneath the scenery to create the "brighter horizon" effect that is seldom seen on model railroads (but common in TV and motion picture model work). The two inches will also prevent any trees or other details from casting shadows on the "sky". I merely clamped the Masonite hardboard that will be painted sky blue on two-inch wood blocks to space it away from its (eventual) 1 x 2 vertical supports. I then covered the surface with plastic dry cleaning bags to prevent the plaster from sticking to the backdrop.

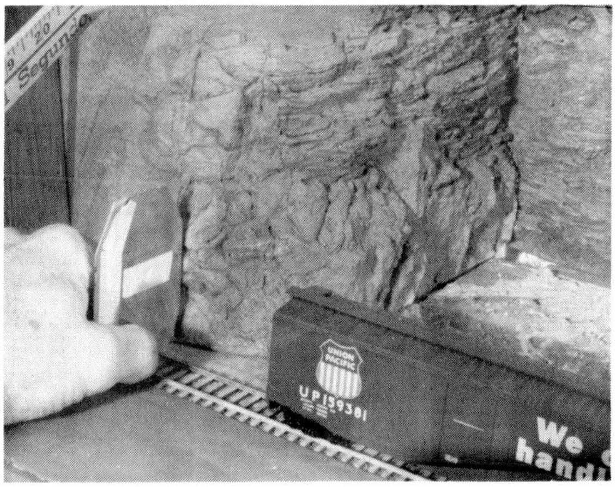

This is the time to determine if you have enough clearance along the sides of the cuts. I used TWO NMRA Standards gauges, taped side-by-side, to provide an extra half-inch of side clearance.

The bottom of the small creek that feeds the main river was a critical angle because it needed to rise enough to clear hidden track below. I used a scrap stick to determine the angle of what will become the bottom of this valley. The masking tape on the "Sky" was then pressed in place where the stick touched the "sky", with the angles matching the slopes of that "PROTOTYPE-WIDTH ROADBED" template, leading upslope from what will become the bottom of the valley.

This is how the angles on that ". . . ROADBED" template are extended. The template is placed over the rails and a ruler or straight scrap of wood held along the sloped edge of the template. The point where the ruler hits the sky is marked with a piece of masking tape — that is the absolute highest point any mountain could reach starting at the edge of the roadbed. Since the tracks extend well into that mountain, a cliff or cut or retaining wall would be needed to cut into the mountain. That cliff is shown here. I determined that I wanted a mountain peak at this corner so the slope will lead down from the point where the ruler meets the backdrop into a shallow valley on the backdrop. Again, a long strip of masking tape was stuck to the plastic cover on the backdrop (to match the angle of the ". . . ROADBED" template) leading downslope from this peak (the opposite procedure just used to locate the "valley" floor).

I added six 1 x 2 vertical supports from the benchwork to the level of the top of the Homosote to support the bottoms of the polyfoam cliffs. These two cliffs will be mounted on a removable scene site. 2 inch long finishing nails were then driven into the supports (or the scene site surface, here) and the Polyfoam was merely pushed down over the small heads of the nails. When you are completely sure the polyfoam is in the right place, it can be glued with white glue. The 45-degree bevel I cut into the backsides of the vertical joint between the "rocks" is also pinned with finishing nails and glued.

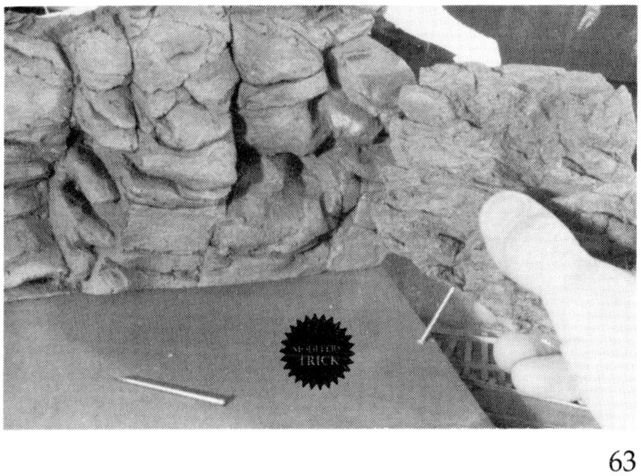

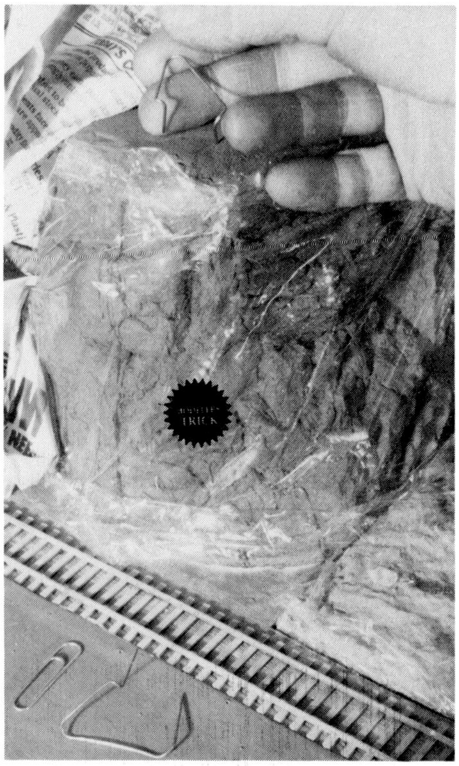

I bent the ends of paperclips to produce L-shaped wire clips. I pushed the longest ends into the polyfoam and left a loop protruding. The plaster and paper towels will be resting on these clips, at that stage of scenery construction, and the plaster will flow around the wire clips to bond the polyfoam to the plaster at the tops of the cliffs (the bottoms are glued to the 1 x 2 verticals and/or scene sites).

This is the time to locate any structures that you will place on the layout. If you don't have the structure completed, cut out a paper pattern to match its shape. The vertical rock walls can be moved (before they are glued in place) to provide the space needed for any structures.

The masking tape on the plastic-covered backdrop indicates where the peaks and valleys of the mountains should fall. The horizontal strips are the height of my eyes — that's the horizon for this model railroad "world". I wanted the hills to rise just slightly above horizon and the valleys to be just slightly below the horizon. Later, some background photomurals will be installed to fill any gaps in the horizon. That horizon line is a help because it makes it easier to see if your mountains are high enough (most modelers tend to make the peaks so high that no distant peaks can be seen and, worse, the too-high peaks produce too-steep slopes on the layout itself). Each mountain peak is supported by a vertical 1 x 2 board screwed to the benchwork cross braces.

Way back at the benchwork stage of construction, I suggested you allow at least 1/8 inch of space at each end for scenery profile boards. This is a scrap of 1/8 inch plywood wallboard. The slope leads up to another mountaintop and the angle is determined by (what else?) that "...ROADBED" template. I cut the board with an electric sabre saw and sliced a hole for the two hidden tracks. The profile board can end at the peak of the mountains (as this one does) or extend all the way back to the wall. You will need to insert a matching pair of similar 1/8 inch plywood profile boards where the two 4 foot sections of benchwork join, if you want the layout to separate in the middle.

Filament tape is used to provide a spiderweb of supports for the hills and valleys. Some modelers prefer to use 3 or 4 inch wide strips of corrugated cardboard attached to the edges of the roadbed and to the edges of the layout with a staple gun. I prefer the tape because I don't have to bang on the layout with a staplegun.

Wadded-up bunches of newspaper will be used to fill-out the humps and lumps in the scenery. The webbing merely supports them. When the Hydrocal plaster dries, the wadded-up newspapers and the filament tape web can be removed from beneath the layout.

I used masking tape to hold two or three layers of newspaper against the vertical sides of the roadbed. The papers will form the basic slope for the embankments downhill from the tracks and, as here, for the bottom and sides of the river channel. A short wooden trestle (the one that appears on pages 81 through 85) will be installed here. The tape helps to keep you from burying the bridge abutments in plaster.

Get the basic shapes of the scenery to your liking (those tape lines on the backdrop help). I taped a yardstick across one end of the layout at the "... ROADBED" angle to stop me from making the slopes too steep. The wadded paper is easier to work with if you spray it with water to get it barely damp.

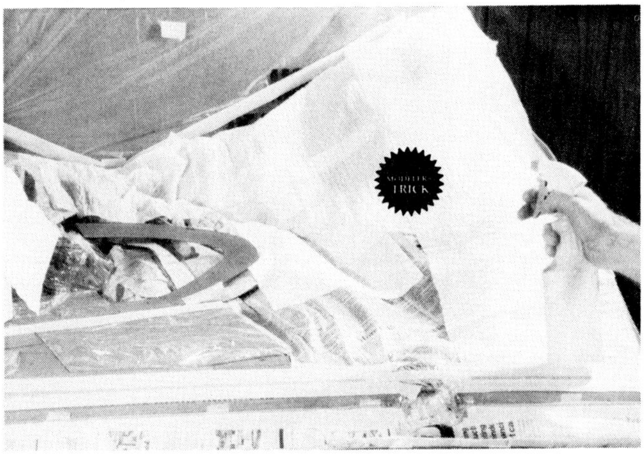

FULL-SIZE SCENERY MOCK-UPS

I used some cloth-reinforced industrial grade paper towels for the Hydrocal-soaked scenery as well as for the final layer of paper in mocking-up the shapes. The solid color (white) makes it easier to see the shapes. Again, the paper will form easier and not spring back if you spray it with a plant atomizer like this one. Don't be afraid to add more piles of wadded-up newspaper to make larger bulges or to press down on lumps you feel are too high. This is the final shaping before the plaster.

I lifted the removable scene sites (the bases for structures/dioramas) and wrapped each of them in plastic wrap. The plaster can then flow right to the edges of these sites and the plastic wrap will allow you to remove them after the plaster cures.

PROTECTING THE TRACK

From this stage on, there's a good chance you dribble plaster or too much water onto the track. I masked it off with some 1-inch wide masking tape. Keep the edge of the tape even with the ends of the ties. Press the tape down over the rail, as shown, so you can use the "... ROADBED" template later.

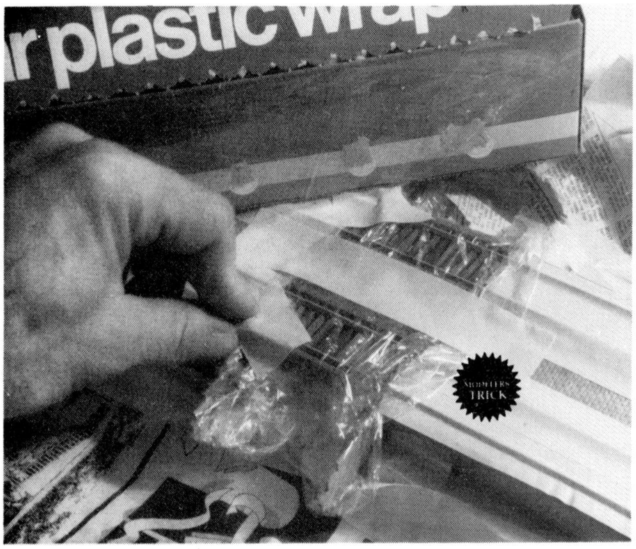

SELF-SUPPORTING PLASTER MOUNTAINS

This is the time to install any bridge abutments or, in this case, short trestles. I glued this timber trestle in place and, when the glue dried, covered the entire bridge with plastic sandwich wrapping (like Saran-wrap). Leave the bottom of the streambed and the backs of the abutments as clear as possible as you work the plaster and/or plaster-soaked paper towels around the bridge. Part of the plastic wrap will be embedded in the plaster but later texturing will hide any ragged edges of plaster or plastic that you could not remove.

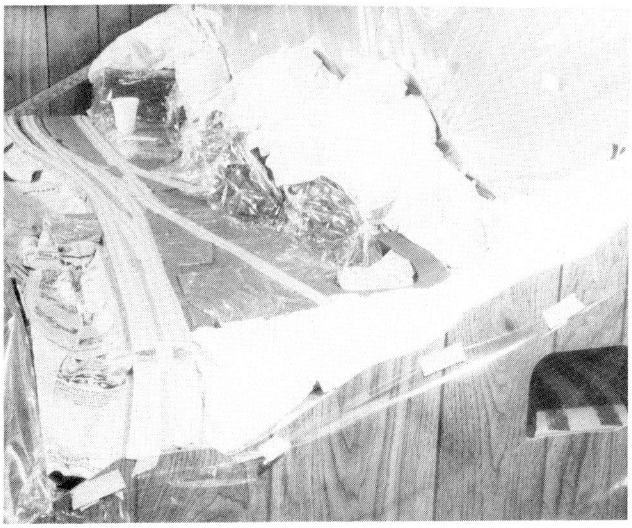

The track, structure sites (the scene sites), rock faces, the backdrop and the edges of the table are all protected with plastic and/or masking tape and the layout is ready for plaster.

PLASTER-MIX FORMULAE

48 ounces water
6 to 12 pounds of Hydrocal plaster
$\frac{1}{2}$ cup Rainbow dry plaster color

Large builders' supply firms stock Hydrocal. It's worth searching for because it is one of the only plasters that is hard enough to be self-supporting when reinforced with industrial grade paper towels. I use various combinations of Ochre, Van Dyke Brown and Brick Red in Rainbow-brand or Empire White-brand powdered colors (again, try a large lumberyard or hardware store). Mix the dry colors into the water and stir thoroughly before adding the plaster.

Reddish Brown: *$\frac{2}{3}$ Van Dyke Brown $\frac{1}{3}$ Brick Red.*
Pale Brown: *$\frac{2}{5}$ Van Dyke Brown $\frac{2}{5}$ Brick Red $\frac{1}{5}$ Ochre.*

The mountains are mostly "reddish-brown" and the stream bed is pale brown.

IMPORTANT! Add some color to the plaster as you mix it. If you do, there's no *chance to EVER see the bright white spots that ruin the appearance of so many miniature mountains. The colored plaster will also not show bright white if you accidentally chip it.*

I would suggest you mix no more than 48 ounces of water with the necessary amount of Hydrocal plaster (or Plaster of Paris). That's about all you can apply to the layout before the stuff begins to harden. Spray the inside of the plastic washtub (I used a Rubbermaid brand) with a light coat of Armor-All so the dried plaster won't stick.

Pour the Hydrocal plaster into the water just a few cups at a time and stir each batch vigorously to mix-out any lumps of plaster. Add just enough plaster to produce a creamy consistency that will color the paper towel when you dip the towel into the mixture. I used just about 5 pounds of plaster to 48 ounces of water, but that can vary depending on temperature and humidity.

Tear the paper towels into 6 inch wide strips. Dip the paper towels into the plaster mix and drape them over the layout wherever you want hillsides and mountains.

Cover every inch of the hillsides and slopes (right up to the edges of the rocks, ties, abutments and scene sites) with at least two layers of the Hydrocal-soaked paper towels. You can fold or push the towels to conform to the edges. Drape about $\frac{1}{4}$ inch of the towels over the edges of the profile boards at the sides and front of the layout to provide a mechanical bond at those points. I attached four vertical 2 x 2 boards to the layout with wood screws to mark the peaks of the mountains — those boards provide most of the vertical strength that supports the mountains so the dried Hydrocal-soaked paper towels will not be cantilevered from the edges of the track — the Hydrocal is self-supporting over a span of a couple of feet but it does need some support, especially along the rear of the layout where ***there are no profile boards or track roadbed edges.***

After the Hydrocal-soaked towels were in place, I mixed a *couple of batches more of the colored Hydrocal plaster to use for shaping the edges of the roadbed.*

I made a second "... ROADBED" template from .040 inch thick plastic. This second template only covers the two rails and the DOWNslope. I filled vee-shaped notches for the rails (to match the shape of the masking tape-covered rails). I did not have any UPslopes on this particular layout; if you do, make a third gauge and include the tops of the rails, the ditch beside the track on any upslope and the upslope (they're all on the original template). Apply just a bit more plaster than is needed and shape both the ballast and embankment angles by dragging the templates across the still-wet plaster as shown.

The plaster can take as long as a week to dry completely. The color will help *you determine when the plaster is dry because the color fades to a very pastel shade — you'll see the pastel shade on the lightest and smallest drops and dribbles of the plaster — when the darkest colors have bleached out to match the lightest, the plaster is dry. Mine (in a damp basement) took five full days. When the plaster is dry, remove the protection from the rock faces (but leave it in place on the track, bridges, abutments and scene sites until most of the dirt and texturing is installed).*

Build-A-Railroad, step-by-step Part VI: Ground Cover & Grass Textures

Super-detailing, as applied to scenery, is simple

One of the secrets of creating realistic scenery is to apply some type of texture to all the surfaces. When trees and bushes are added, at least part of that texture will be visible beneath them. Some modelers hope they can skip most of the texturing and merely cover the terrain with trees and bushes and, perhaps, a few patches of grass. It doesn't work.

Texture alone is certainly not the only way to achieve realism; the colors recreated by that texture must also be as close as possible to nature. That sounds simple enough, but how many of us have created scenery with GENERIC NATURE as the prototype for our scenes? I certainly have and the results looked like something, but nothing I'd actually seen. Secret number one, then, is to select a specific geographic area as the prototype for your model scenery. You certainly wouldn't model a "generic" box car, why try to model generic scenery?

There is absolutely no substitute for a visit to the area you are going to model. You will certainly want to see your prototype because, unlike steam locomotives and other items of history, the scenery doesn't change much. Take photographs, of course, with both color print film and color slide film. The colors are usually a bit closer to nature with the slides but the prints are easier to use — use one to cross-check the colors of the other. Take a few panorama shots for possible use, later, as sky backdrops. Most photo shops will make an 11 x 17 full color poster for less than $20.

The singularly most important reason for visiting the area you want to recreate is to obtain samples. There is no point in attempting to simulate the color or the texture of the soil or the ballast in the area when you can actually use the real thing. You will need to sift the samples through several sizes of strainers to obtain scale-size dirt and rocks and rubble. It takes about ten pounds or two gallons (in volume) of dirt to obtain dirt enough to texture a 16-square-foot area, so get plenty while you're there.

The track work is still covered with masking tape — leave it that way (the ballast is the last texture we'll add). Locate the edge of the ballast shoulders and scrape the rough plaster away from that area. The "prairie grass" will begin where the ballast stops but the grass is installed first. Vacuum the area to remove both plaster dust and small chunks of dry plaster.

The yellow/brown dirt I used came from one hillside near Basalt, Colorado (the opposite hillside was a much redder shade, but this particular scene does not portray that side of the valley). The Rock Quarry, makes fine, medium and coarse-size crushed rocks that includes about 20 shades of real rocks but none are quite this brown.

The Rock Quarry "Cumbres Brown" is close, but has more beige tone.

The Rock Quarry "Cumbres Brown" is close, but has more beige tone.

I used acrylic contact cement and I spread it with scraps of cardboard. I then sprayed it with water to help make the distribution more even. Try to keep pockets of white cement from collecting in the hollows in the scenery by pushing the cement out and onto the surrounding area. If you're covering patching plaster or plaster of Paris, the surface should first be sealed with Matte Medium and five parts water and allowed to dry.

I did use their fine grade of "Chama Red" for the ballast because it seemed to match the prototype Colorado Midland's ballast. Much of that real railroad (abandoned in the twenties, but the right-of-way is still there in some places) was ballasted with cinders. I used Woodland Scenics number 876 fine Cinders for the ballast on the left side of the railroad where most of the turnouts are concentrated (on the theory that the real railroad would have ballasted the turnouts first, the mainline second). The track to the rear is "ballasted" with the same sifted dirt (from Basalt) that covers the hillsides.

For HO scale, I find that three sizes of dirt/rock are adequate; the size that falls through a tea strainer is the smallest, the size that falls through a normal strainer (with screen the mesh size of a screen door) is the medium size and I sift the largest particles through a plastic strawberry basket with holes about $^{3}/_{16}$-inch square. The shifting process begins with the medium-size strainer; I scoop up about a third of the strainer full of dirt and shake the strainer over an empty coffee can. I dump what remains into the strawberry basket. What sifts through the basket's holes I save, the rest is discarded. The material that ran through the medium size strainer is used as-is for "dirt" on bare ground and hillsides. I sift about half of that through the tea strainer into a third container; that fine material is used for the surfaces of dirt roads and for adding "dirt" to the felt grass. The material that remains in the tea strainer is about right for O scale ballast; I use it for small streambed and rubble rocks in HO scale and keep it in a fourth can labeled "Medium". I also label the can with mixed medium and fine (that passed through the medium strainer) "mixed". For N scale dirt roads, I'd suggest a finer size yet; pour the stuff that made it through the tea strainer (the "fine") into an old pantyhose and tie-off the cloth to make a small bag. Tap the sides of the bag to loosen the "dust" or "extra fine" earth when you want to cover an N scale dirt road's surface. When the dust no longer flows, the remaining material can be put in yet another can and marked "sifted fine" — that dust-free or crushed rock is about the same size stuff you get when you buy "Fine" size ballast or rock from firms like the Rock Quarry or Woodland Scenics or John's. Once you have about a quart (or a couple of pounds) EACH of "fine," "medium," "mixed fine/medium" and "coarse" (plus "extra-fine", for N scale), you are ready to begin the texturing process.

Simulate prairie grass with 9 x 12-inch sheets of self-adhesive-backed **Presto-Felt.** *Mark the felt where it needs to be cut to conform to the edges of the ballast, rocks or other areas not to be covered with the "grass".*

Cut the felt with scissors before peeling away the paper backing. Stick the felt onto the contact cement covered scenery surfaces after the contact cement has dried just enough to no longer be white.

PRAIRIE GRASS

The July/August 1984 issue of **Model Railroading** was the first report, in an American magazine, on the use of felt to simulate grass. That basic technique has, however, been popular in England for many years. That felt "Prairie Grass" is the basis for any grassy area on this project layout. Now, however, there is an even better way to use felt: craft stores, including some of the large chains like Lee Wards, carry the "Presto Felt" made by the S.H. Kunin Felt Co. in Worchester, Massachusetts (they do NOT sell direct to consumers, however). This is simply felt with a self-adhesive back. It saves the step of coating the back of the felt with contact cement — a messy process. If you are covering a relatively flat surface, you can skip the application of the contact cement and just stick the Presto Felt in place. For rougher shapes, like the hillsides on a model railroad, I'd suggest applying acrylic-type contact cement to the plaster surfaces. In fact, the plaster itself should be pre-sealed with a mixture of 5 parts water to one part artist's Matte Medium (we'll use that stuff in a lot of steps). Hydrocal plaster surfaces are usually smooth enough so that no sealing coat is required, but wall plaster, patching plaster or plaster of Paris all need a sealing coat before the application of contact cement. Let the sealing coat dry for at least 48 hours and let the contact cement dry only until it loses its white color and begins to become clear.

Cut the felt so the edges match what you want to become the edge of the grass. I misjudged the edge of the ballast and needed to trim off a ¼-inch wide strip of the felt just before applying the ballast. The felt can be cut with scissors before it is stuck to the scenery; a utility or hobby knife will slice it after it is in place (if you need to correct mistakes). I would suggest you practice working with the felt because it sticks almost instantly to the contact cement. Use one hand to hold the felt away from the contact cement after peeling off the adhesive backing, while you push the felt down onto the contact cement with the opposite hand. If you do make a mistake, you can pull the entire sheet away but you will have to reapply (and dry) the contact cement and use a new sheet of felt.

The felt will stretch considerably if you pull it a bit, to conform to both concave and convex surfaces. Work the felt down like you would apply wallpaper or contact paper; starting in one corner and working your way across the sheet then down the sheet. Press one entire edge down, then try to get an adjoining edge pressed in place before working toward the middle and, finally, out toward the other two edges. The felt is sold in 9 x 12-inch sheets at most craft stores. If the felt folds and sticks to itself on a concave surface, just press the overlapping edges tightly together (as shown in the photos) then cut along the back and front of the overlap to trim the overlapping portion away. If you want to simulate really tall weeds, you can tease the felt with a brass brush (the type used for brushing suede is fine). I left it as-is.

The felt is available in a "Moss Green" that is nearly the shade of grass. It is very difficult to lighten the color, however, so I started with a tan color called "Flesh" that is very close to the shade of dead grass. With this color, any unpainted (not green) areas simply look like the underlying dead grass that is common in nature. You can paint the felt with just about any type of paint but I was working indoors and about a yard away from a furnace so I wanted water-based paints. The Badger *Air-Opaque* paints worked extremely well when thinned with one part of water to one part paint. I mixed 1 part Chrome Green, 1 part Lime Green, 1 part Brown and 3 parts Green for the grass. For trees and bushes, I left out the Brown. It might be possible to dab on the mixture with a paint brush or sponge but I wouldn't want to try it — use an air brush to apply the green as shown in the photos (you'll want to use that air brush to weather the track and rocks, later, just like you'd weather a box car, locomotive or structure).

Carefully hold the felt away from the scenery with one hand while you press one edge down onto the contact cement. Start by pressing one entire edge, then work across the sheet of felt in the same manner you would apply wallpaper or contact paper. If the felt does overlap, just push it down firmly and slice along the front and back (right and left) of the overlapped area.

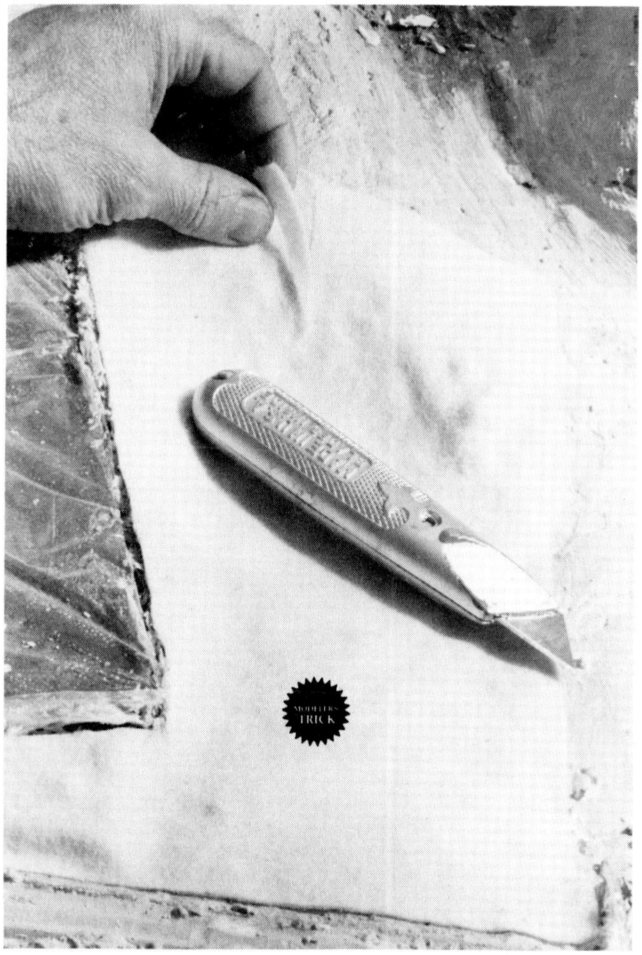

Peel off the area of overlapped felt to leave just a slight seam. The seams like this and seams between sheets of felt will be disguised, later, when the ground foam and flocking are added to complete the texturing process.

The real dirt is what makes the felt grass so realistic. After the green paint dries, simply sprinkle on some of the fine dirt, using the tea strainer to distribute the dirt where you want it. When it's on, brush it into the felt with a paint brush — the result is literally dirt with fibers (felt fibers) "growing" out of it. If you apply too much dirt, simply remove it with a vacuum cleaner.

When you are perfectly satisfied, spray the felt grass with a mixture of 5 parts water to one part artist's Matte Medium (and one drop or two of liquid detergent to make it flow easier) using one of the hand-pump plant atomizers. Spray until there is an even white cast to the area but not so much that the water actually runs down the slopes. Do about a square foot and, while the area is still wet, sprinkle on some fine ground foam (I used Woodland Scenics Green Grass color) and squeeze on some flocking to complete the texturing process.

When the Matte Medium has dried for about 48 hours, vacuum away any excess. If the scene is too bright or too green, just sift on a bit more dirt and spray again. If it's too dull, apply a bit more green paint, ground foam and flocking. Use a bit of restraint with the foam and flocking, so that at least half of the felt is still not covered with either flocking or ground foam.

The combination of the matted grass effect of the felt, the powdered dirt that looks like real earth, the fine particles of dirt that look like rocks, the ground foam (that looks like leafy weeds) and the flocking (that looks like taller weeds or grass) is incredible. It's also easy to do and, best of all, easy to change to a brighter or duller shade to achieve the results you wish.

FLOCKING

Flocking is another scenic technique that is popular in Europe but relatively little used in North America. The Noch brand flocking is sold (to dealers) by Walthers, and Portman Distributing in Peekskill, New York sells the Heiki brand flocking (also, to dealers). Both Heiki and Noch make electrostatic dispensers that are simply soft plastic bottles with holes in the lid. When you squeeze the bottle, the strands of flocking rub together to create static electricity so that, when they fly out the holes, they tend to stand up when they hit the Matte Medium (or glue) covered surface of the scenery. I used Heiki number 3350 Green flocking. Heiki has a new color that lends some incredible realism to any scene: "Dead Grass" number 3363. Vintage Reproductions also offers grass flocking and an applicator (both are described in the March/April 1984 issue).

After applying the green, I used a second applicator (I used Noch's applicators) to apply just enough of the tan colored Dead Grass to tone-down the green and impart a typical Prairie Grass variety of colors to the scene. After the Matte Medium dries, use a vacuum to remove any excess flocking. You can add flocking to a dirt-covered area and control the size of the patch of "weeds" by simply applying the solution of 5 parts water to one part Matte Medium with an eye dropper. Again, apply enough so a bit of white is visible and puff-on the flocking. Work with just 6 square inches or so at a time with this method so the Matte Medium doesn't dry — you want a watery surface to help keep those strands of electrostatically-charged flocking standing upright.

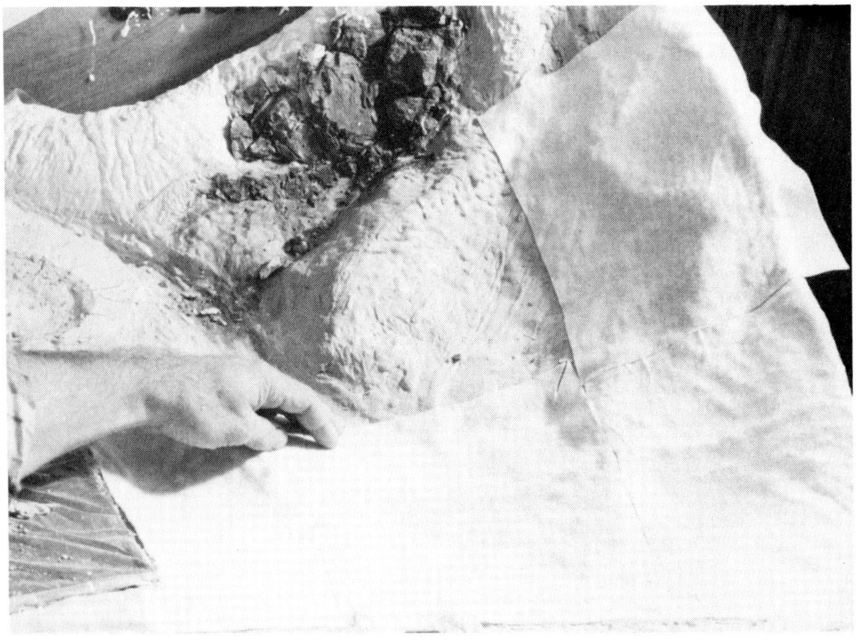

Four of the six sheets of felt used to cover this grassy valley are in place. When butting sheets together, apply the second sheet by pressing the first edge along that of the felt that is already in place.

The Kit That Makes Real Dirt!

That sounded pretty silly to me, too, until I actually tried the product. The Rock Quarry, P.O. Box 26372, Dept. MRG, Fair Park Station, Dallas, TX 75226-6372 makes nearly one hundred different colors and textures of earth colors. This stuff is real earth and then some. There is no dye used (it's all natural), it is non-magnetic and it is virtually dust free.

That "dust free" requires an explanation: too much dust, in some natural dirts, produces mud when you wet the stuff on the layout and that, in turn, looks like dried mud at best and cracked, dried, mud-colored glue, at worst.

Rock Quarry's "dust" is just that — you can use it for dusty weathering effects and as a final — dust-on — texturing for dirt roads and similar areas. Their "fine" is about equal to the dirt you would sift through a tea strainer (with the dust, then removed by sifting the remains through a pantyhose and keeping what remains in the pantyhose). Their "medium" is about equal, in size, to Woodland Scenics, John's and High Iron brands of "fine." The Rock Quarry medium and coarse sizes make fine rubble or talus. The medium is about the size of S or O scale ballast.

Send a stamped self-addressed envelope for their current product and price list.

There are six textures that make this scene so realistic: the predominant textures, left to right, are (1) the fine grade of Rocky Quarry-brand ballast on the track, (2) fine grind Woodland Scenics foam near the bridge abutment, (3) powdery real dirt, (4) small rocks (fine dirt after the dust has filtered into the felt), (5) felt (near the bottom edges of the ballast shoulder and (6) Heiki Green and Dead Grass colors of flocking.

All of the self-adhesive Presto-Felt *is in place. The basic light beige (they call it "Flesh") is about the color of dead grass. A mixture of* Badger's Air-Opaque *green and brown (see text) and water is applied with an air brush. So far, no other textures are in place, just bare plaster and felt.*

Real dirt is sifted onto the felt with a tea strainer. Work the dirt into the felt with a brush, brushing aside the larger pieces of dirt. Those larger particles can be brushed back to simulate random small rocks if that is what appears on the prototype terrain you are recreating.

I matched the brown dirt from Basalt with a mixture of equal parts Glidden-brand interior latex house paint "Wild Turkey" and "Seville" colors. The color is also very close to Floquil's Polly S "Roof Brown" with about 1 part white added to 10 parts Roof Brown. I added 1 part water to 5 parts paint and painted all the areas that were to be covered with rocks.

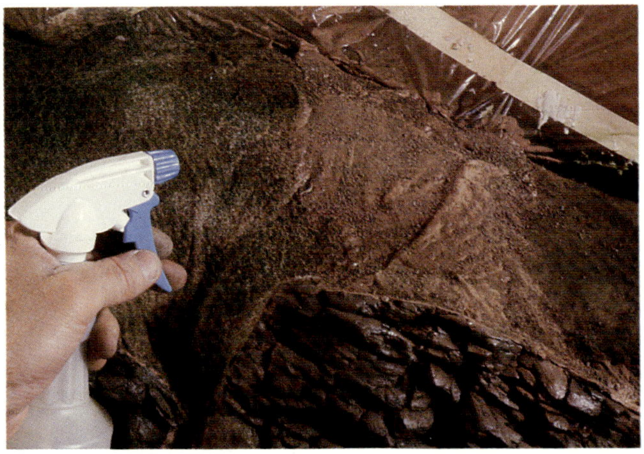

Spray the latex paint with a mist of water to prolong its drying time for a few more minutes. Work only with about a half of square foot area at a time.

Use the tea strainer to sprinkle on the dirt. Spray the dirt with a mixture of one part Matte Medium, five parts water and a drop or two of detergent.

Sprinkle the fine grind foam (Woodland Scenics' "Green Grass" Turf, here) over the still-wet Matte Medium. Apply only a few small patches of the foam to simulate clumps of leafy weeds.

The taller weeds are best simulated with flocking — large patches of low weeds or grass are simulated with the areas of felt. Spray the dirt and foam with another application of water and Matte Medium, then puff on the flocking with a Noch or Heiki dispenser. I used Heiki's green and Dead Grass colors.

When all the texturing is complete, it is finally time to remove the masking tape from the track — the tape protected it from accidental dribbles of Matte Medium and paints. Ballast is next. . .

Creating Streambeds & Streams

Realistic water looks wet, deep and like it is flowing.

Streams and other bodies of water are scenes that can greatly enhance the realism of any model railroad. There's also an obvious need for some type of water for bridges to span. If you plan your scenery, especially if it is matched to some prototype scene, the water can add some incredible realism.

There are three sizes of water that can dictate which is the best material to use to simulate water. For really large bodies of water, like an ocean shore or the banks of the Mississippi River, you will only want to model the bottom of the river for 20 or 30 scale feet from the banks; the rest of the area can be an inch or so of flat bottom. For smaller rivers and streams, up to about that inch of maximum depth, it's necessary to model the entire bottom surface. For the large bodies of water and these medium size streams, the best choice for "water" is decoupage resin. For the smallest streams, those less than an eighth inch deep, clear artists' acrylic varnish can be used. Both types of simulated water have virtually no odor.

The decoupage resin has replaced casting resin as the material of choice because the decoupage resin has little odor, does not give off the heat in curing that occurs with casting resin and is far more likely to have a hard, rather than tacky, surface. The decoupage resins are sold under a variety of brand names; I used Chemco's excellent *Ultra-Glo*. You can spot the decoupage products instantly because they include equal amounts of resin and hardener — the casting resin requires about 10 times more resin than catalyst or hardener — if the label doesn't state to mix equal amounts hardener (or catalyst) and resin, you've bought the wrong stuff.

The majority of the decoupage resins can be colored with the translucent dyes intended for casting resin. Again, I used Chemco's product: 3 drops of Blue, one drop of Green and one drop of Amber for each 10 ounces of mixed resin and hardener. Actually, the dye can (and should) be mixed at the same time you are mixing the resin with the hardener. All of these products are available at craft supply stores and chains like Lee Wards or Michaels. The only really tricky part about making water with decoupage resin is the mixing; you really must be certain the two parts are stirred completely (Chemco suggests you stir for at least two minutes). Chemco also sells a coated paper cup that holds up to 12 ounces and it is marked on the INSIDE where you need the markings. You must use a fresh container for each mix and I would not suggest you mix more than 10 ounces at a time (it's too hard to stir more than that). You can use any paper cups or old coffee cans, but use a measuring cup and water to mark precisely where 5 and 10 ounces rest (if you want to mix 10 ounce batches), then dry the container before mixing.

I sealed each corner of the layout where the "water" would pour off the table. A layer of plastic wrap, like Saranwrap™*, is next to the scenery so the water and Matte Medium won't stick to it, with a bead of foam rubber to act as a seal, followed by solid wood. At this end, I actually attached the wood, temporarily, to the benchwork with woodscrews.*

The decoupage resin is about the same thickness as honey but it will actually flow through holes and cracks just like water. Be certain, then, that all the holes and cracks are filled. I made dams for each end of the stream, where the "water" would have flowed off my modeled portion of reality and out into the real world. After those dams were in place, I poured a mixture of equal parts artists Matte Medium and water all along the streambed and especially along the seams where those dams contacted the layout. I then added the rocks and rubble that would form the bottom of the stream. I then sprayed the rocks and rubble with a mixture of 5 parts water to one part Matte Medium to seal-in any air bubbles and to cover any dust. I've found that step eliminates the crystalline appearance that sometimes occurs on the bottom of resin waterways.

The decoupage resin can be worked, just before it cures, to produce waves and ripples and water current patterns. I used an old dentist's pick, but a screwdriver would be fine. I worked loops and wavy lines through the resin about an hour after it was poured. It took nearly two more hours before all the resin hardened — during that time some areas were nearly rock hard while others were still as-poured. I simply went back to the water every 15 minutes or so and worked more waves and swirls into the resin where the old ones had vanished (because that part of the resin was still too fluid).

If you are pouring more than a half inch depth, I'd suggest you plan on making it a 48 hour project to leave two days for the first half inch of resin to harden before pouring the final half inch. For those really deep waters, paint the flat portion of the ocean or lake or massive river bottom with Polly S Grimy Black so the bare bottom is not visible — the thickness of resin, with the dyes I used, will be nearly opaque at that one inch depth. Do detail the bottom from that inch up the shoreline because it will become increasingly visible as the resin becomes shallow.

If you are modeling steep rapids or a waterfall, the decoupage can be mixed in very small batches and painted over the surface with disposable brushes. If possible, make the streambed removable so you can tilt it to maintain a level bottom while the resin hardens. With some practice, you might be able to let the resin begin to harden in the cup so you can spoon it out like a thick gelatin — the problem is, only part of the resin gets that hard at a time; the rest will still be fluid — it is a technique I intend to try because I did just that to move some resin from the deeper "still-water" areas of this stream to the rocky and rapids areas and it worked very well. Finally, touch the very tips of the rapids with some of the Pearl Colored Dye intended for the resin. I used a number 0-sized brush to be sure I applied just a trace of the pearl. You can do it after the resin dries.

You can use just about any type of clear paint that dries to a high gloss for those smaller streams, those less than an inch wide. I used the artists acrylic varnish because it had no odor and was not flammable. Just pour the fluid over the area that is to become the stream. Don't pour to more than about 1/16 inch of thickness, however, because the acrylic will run downhill and you might create a lake that is much larger than you intended. The edges of such an oversize body of water can, of course, be covered with Matte Medium, followed by dirt, ground foam and flocking to reduce the size of the shoreline. For a marsh effect, by the way, simply pour some of the acrylic varnish (or the decoupage resin) over a flat area with a heavy cover of ground foam and flocking — keep the "water" as shallow as possible and be ready to sprinkle a bit more ground foam over the top of the water — the flocking and the tips of the foam particles will protrude obove the level of the resin "water".

I used a C-clamp and an old electrical outlet box to hold the plastic wrap, foam and plywood dam at the left end of the layout. Some pieces of red duct tape sealed an inch or so of the end of the table.

I poured undiluted Matte Medium along the edges of the dams to be sure they were sealed. The Matte Medium must be allowed at least four days to dry in this area.

The bottoms of any streams or other waterways must be sealed completely so the fluid used to simulate water cannot soak into the plaster or leak through any holes. For this small stream, I painted the bottom with paint to match the surrounding dirt.

I sprinkled both fine and medium grades of dirt and crushed rock over the still-wet brown latex paint. I then poured a mixture of equal parts water and Matte Medium over just the area that would become the bottom of the stream. This seals any loose dirt and avoids air bubbles or crystal effects in the bottom of the resin or varnish used to simulate water.

I simply poured undiluted artist's acrylic varnish (the glossy form of Matte Medium) over the stream to simulate water. Yes, the white fluid will dry crystal clear and shiny in about 24 hours.

I used the same sealing and texturing techniques for the major river bottom. This area will be covered with a river made of decoupage resin to simulate water up to about a half inch deep.

The dirt and pebble-covered river bottom is sealed with that mix of equal parts water and Matte Medium, then more dirt is sifted onto the embankments, followed by a spray coating of a mixture of five parts water to one part Matte Medium, some fine grind green foam and flocking. Be sure to keep the foam and flocking away from the river bottom, however, as it can create air bubbles.

During the second hour of the hardening, I mixed and swirled the resin with a dentist's pick to create the effects of rapids and moving water currents.

I mixed three 10 ounce batches of Chemco's Ultra-Glo *decoupage resin (equal parts resin and hardener) with 3 drops blue, one drop green and one drop amber Chemco Resin dye in each batch. The first 10 ounces only covered this much area. I worked quickly so all three batches were mixed and poured in a half-hour, before the first batch could begin to harden.*

Set The Scene with photo mural backdrops

For maximum backdrop realism, a photo mural does the job but ONLY if you use it properly as a profile against a painted and seamless blue sky backdrop.

There is one cardinal rule that can help you decide whether it is worth the trouble to invest in photo murals for the background of your layout: can you elevate the model so the backdrop is slightly above eye level? If the backdrop does not come above eye level, any attempt at creating realism is lost. If, for example, you operate only with a modular layout group like NTRAK, your layout must be low enough so it matches all the other modules; the TOP of the sky backdrop is below your eye level. For those layouts, the printed backdrops from HO West: (now Walthers' Instant Horizons) and Details West are a worthwhile purchase.

If, however, you can build your layout so the backdrop really is at eye level, it will also coincide with the actual horizon in the real world for maximum realism. Then, it's worth the expense and trouble to do the best job possible. There are three basic sources of photo murals large enough for a model railroad: Walthers imports a no. 515 farm and hill scene and a no. 516 mountain scene made by Faller that is superb. Some of the photo murals intended to decorate walls are also suitable. The third alternative is the 11 x 17 inch full color poster prints that Kodak is currently selling for less than $20. I tried all three on this layout with mixed results.

The photo mural for the wall, sold by wall paper shops, was the least successful. It is visible in the right valley of layout scenes depicting Thomasville, Circa 1907 on the Colorado Midland. They look like snow-covered mountain profiles in the photos. The photo mural was simply too light in color for this application. Some are darker. You want something about one f stop to two (in photographers' terms) overexposed or washed out. The Faller backdrops are nearly perfect in this respect.

The only real problem with the Faller products is that they show too many of what are obviously European cottages and houses. You must cover them with trees actually on the layout for optimum realism. You can also cut and overlap the same scene to produce only farm covered hills so the second layer of hills covers houses on the first layer. The short pieces of backdrop needed for this layout did not present that problem. That solution, however, will allow you to use Faller's backdrops on a layout of any size.

I was most pleased with the photo mural Kodak made from my slide, but not until it was modified a bit. First, I mounted it on some stiff white poster board like the others as shown in the

Kodak will make an 11 x 17 photo mural for less than $20. I used two of them, but made the mistake of using a vertical format shot for one and, thus wasted a lot of expensive photo area. Tape them in place to see how much to trim from the bottom.

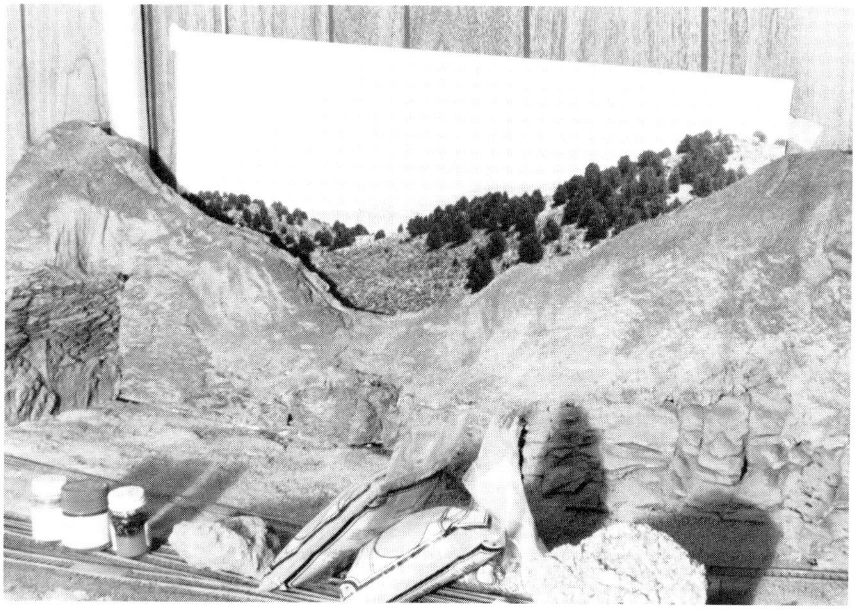

Trace the outline of the hilltops on a piece of white posterboard but cut about 1/16 inch below that mark so some of the mural paper protrudes above the top of the cardboard. I cemented the posters to the cardboard with 3M Spraymment cement.

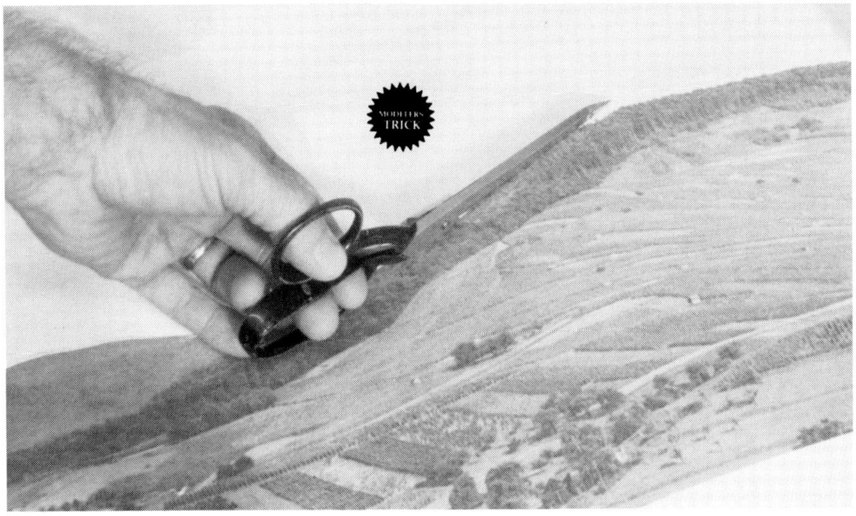

Trim the top of the hills or mountains to match the natural profiles. The murals are most credible if they depict relatively distant scenes. It should show groves of trees rather than individual trees or, worse, individual leaves.

Four of the photo murals used to transport this layout from the woods of the east (Faller's backdrops) to the mountains of Colorado photo murals bottom to the farmlands of the midwest (Faller's, again).

photographs. Since the photo was not only more realistic than the modeled scenery, but much brighter in its colors, it had the effect of making the photo mural seem like reality and the layout itself the background. To reverse that effect, I simply faded out the photo mural so it was just a bit whiter than the Faller backdrops. I used an air brush to apply a few coats of Polly S white mixed with 19 parts of water. I used three coats to be sure I did not get the photo mural faded too much. The results are visible in some of the scenes with the Colorado Midland equipment — the photo in this article shows the photo mural in its out-of-the-box brightness.

For this simple 8 foot layout, a piece of Masonite, smooth side out, served as the sky backdrop. For larger layouts, a seamless sky can be made using several pieces of plasterboard (with the recesses for wall tape) and plaster. They can be installed, just like on a wall, with tape to hide the seams. Another option would be to split a long piece of six foot wide linoleum to obtain a seamless sky backdrop.

There is a lot of disagreement about just how blue a sky might be. The best blue seems to be Dutch Boy brand number 36H Elite Blue or Glidden brand Cobalt blue. Those two are about the blue shade of the sky at 7000 feet where the real Thomasville was located. The degree of visible blue will vary however, depending on how much light you use for the layout. I used two pair of 4 foot fluorescent lights plus three small 75 watt indoor floodlamps and found the Cobalt blue to be about right. You can add as much white as you wish.

I installed a second set of two single-bulb fluorescent fixtures BEHIND the mountains and behind the photo mural cutouts. Those bulbs provided a bit of backlighting by bouncing some light off the blue sky. Frankly, I'm not yet sure it was worth the trouble to light the sky on a relatively shallow or shelf-style layout. If your layout is three feet deeper from the viewing edge of the benchwork, the sky backlighting should be worthwhile.

When I built the mountains, I made certain they were at least two inches from the sky to minimize the chances of shadows appearing on the "sky" — that technique is described in the scenery-building segment of this series.

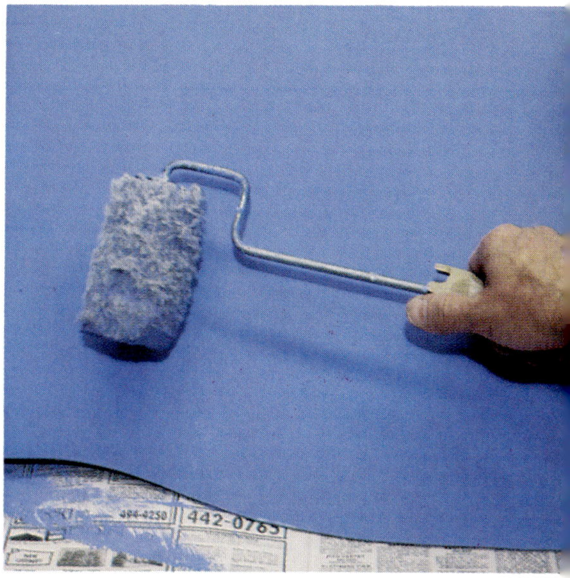

Glidden Cobalt blue, right from the can. You can blend in white with the roller to create a lighter horizon while the paint is still wet.

Before . . .

And After.

The sky adds depth and provides a contrast to the earth tones of the hills, trees and structures on the layout itself.

A pair of single bulb fluorescent lights provide illumination for the sky from behind the hills. The too-bright "hot" spots in the valleys will be hidden by the backdrop photo mural profiles.

The mountain photo murals in place but BEFORE both were faded to look like distant hills as shown in other photos of the layout.

Modelers Tricks With Ground Foam

Outdated scenic materials, like bottle brush pine trees and lichen can be upgraded to current standards of realism with a simple covering of ground foam from Woodland Scenics, Life-Like, Bachmann, Heiki, Faller, and Architectural Scale Models.

I spread most of the foam and Bachmann poly fibre mesh on scraps of newspaper, then sprayed them all with four slow passes of 3M Sprayment cement (stationery and art stores sell it). I then sprinkled on at least three brands of medium green fine foam. It's worth shopping for at least three of the four brands to get the subtle variations in color common in nature.

To make the sagebrushes for the mountain foothills and for the desert scenes, I spread fine grind Woodland Scenics "Burnt Grass" foam on waxed paper. I then sprayed them all with a heavy coat of Sprayment and, when dry, brushed the foam into small clumps. The Sprayment remains sticky enough to hold the clumps onto the hillsides, too.

Architectural Scale Models, Inc. (AMSI) was one of the first firms to offer ground foam for scenery. Dealers can order from AMSI at P.O. Box 3497, Dept. MRG, San Rafael, CA 94912. This is their fine grind "Conifer Green". The trees are Life Like bottle brush style, I mixed green latex house paint with an equal part water, to match the AMSI color. I then dipped each tree in the paint, then in a coffee can of foam.

Reprinted from March/April 1985 issue

Scratchbuilding: Timber Trestles In N, HO, S or O scales

For Experienced Modelers

More models based on narrow gauge practice that were also used on the standard gauge railroads.

The Colorado & Southern's Standard Timber Trestle was virtually the same bridge for the three-foot gauge lines and for the standard gauge lines.

Jim Cassidy

This "Wood Frame" trestle was probably built to standards similar to the C&S shown in the patterns on this page and in John Maxwell's copies of the standards. The photograph was taken in August of 1913 near Green Mountain Falls, Colorado on the Colorado Midland Railway. Note the rather sloppy construction and the very narrow (like the narrow gauge, even though the CM was standard gauge) width of embankment beneath the locomotives. Also note the lack of any guard rails inside the running rails. There appears to be some 8 x 8 inch square beams placed lengthwise over the tops of the three bents nearest the camera to act as sway bracing in place of the more common diagonal sway bracing.

The Nov/Dec 1983, March/April 1984 and May/June 1984 issues described the construction of the open platform wood passenger cars that match the second, third, fourth and fifth cars in this train. By the time this photo was taken, these cars had been rebuilt with enclosed vestibules in place of the original open platforms — we'll show you how to build these cars in a future issue. Photo courtesy Dick Kindig.

A more modern version of the Colorado & Southern trestles on the prototype C&S near Niwot, Colorado in the winter of 1985. Modern wood trestles usually have a steel deck beneath the ballast. This one has steel channels on top of each of the posts. There is a random mixture of square vertical posts and round vertical piles on the bents. Notice, too, that there are four more vertical bents and that the lengthwise stringers are both larger than the earlier standard and there are more of them (10). The dump bents or abutments at the extreme ends of the trestle are concrete cast in wooden forms that left wood grain in the surfaces.

There must be at least a dozen kits on the market to build HO scale trestles and another dozen for N, S and O scale trestles. Why, then, are we presenting yet another? Because this one happens to be different from any kit we know of and it follows the practices of the Colorado & Southern as applied to BOTH that road's narrow gauge and standard gauge trestles. You can use these plans and building tips to simply modify a Campbell (for example) kit or you can do as we did and build from scratch. There are some tips, on page 12, that relate directly to the Campbell kits.

This particular trestle is a very light duty design. The Santa Fe has a similar standard but it was intended mainly for "Unimportant Branch Line" operations. If you want a mainline type of trestle, the Campbell kits are the way to go for both N scale and HO scale. Crummy Products has a one-bent high trestle kit in O and S scales. The Colorado & Southern standard design that was the basis for these plans is available as part of a C&S set of 11 plans from John Maxwell, 3220 Balsam St., Dept.

MRG, Wheat Ridge, CO 80033 for $4.80 plus 75¢ postage.

The interesting aspect of these C&S wood trestle plans is that they show that the only difference between a trestle built for the three foot narrow gauge and one built for standard gauge lies in the spacing of the vertical bents — the size of all materials and ties are the same for both. The plans show just a single trestle bent with no indicated standards for higher trestles. There is also no drawing we know of for the abutments or, as the railroads called them, "dump bents" at the extreme ends of the trestle. We modified a Santa Fe standard design to arrive at the materials and shapes for these dump bent plans. The C&S standards Maxwell offers appear to be dated about 1912, so these standard gauge trestles are not 1860-era lightweights. Also, Maxwell has plans for the D&RG narrow gauge trestles and they are very similar except for the use of a slightly more upright pair of outer vertical piles.

You can use these plans to build a trestle of just about any size. For taller bents, simply add another panel with a top and bottom header and simulate the bolts that held such panels together with nut/bolt/washer castings. This is a 14 foot high bent; a trestle between about 17 and 28 feet high would have two bents (presumably the three feet below a 14 foot bent could be made up with cribbing for a 17 foot tall trestle). The angles of the outer vertical piles or posts would extend down to require longer top and bottom horizontal members and longer diagonal bracing for the lower bents of a two bent tall trestle.

We used the bent plans to make what really amounts to a trestle with no bents at all; just a pair of the end abutments or dump bents. For most such trestles, the dump bents were a maximum of 8 feet tall and were constructed like the other bents except that no cross or diagonal bracing was needed. The bents were bolted to the wooden cribbing that held back the earthen fill or roadbed. The plans are drawn so you can use them, as we did, to make a double-track pair of trestles that share a single cribbing. Again, on more modern trestles the trestle bent would extend all the way across and, in all likelihood, would have a timbered deck (like the modern C&S trestle) with ballasted ties. The Campbell kits can provide both plans and materials for those types of trestles.

Our plans show the material sizes that match the Colorado & Southern standards from Maxwell. Those standards appear to be for a "frame" trestle. Most real railroads referred to frame trestles when they were talking about ones with square vertical timbers. If the vertical timbers were round, the trestle was referred to as a "pile" trestle. In some rare cases (the D&RG was one) the piles really were

PREVIOUS ARTICLES IN THIS SERIES OF NARROW GAUGE STANDARDS:

Scratchbuilding: a complete index of previous articles on scratchbuilding appeared in the May/June f1984 issue.

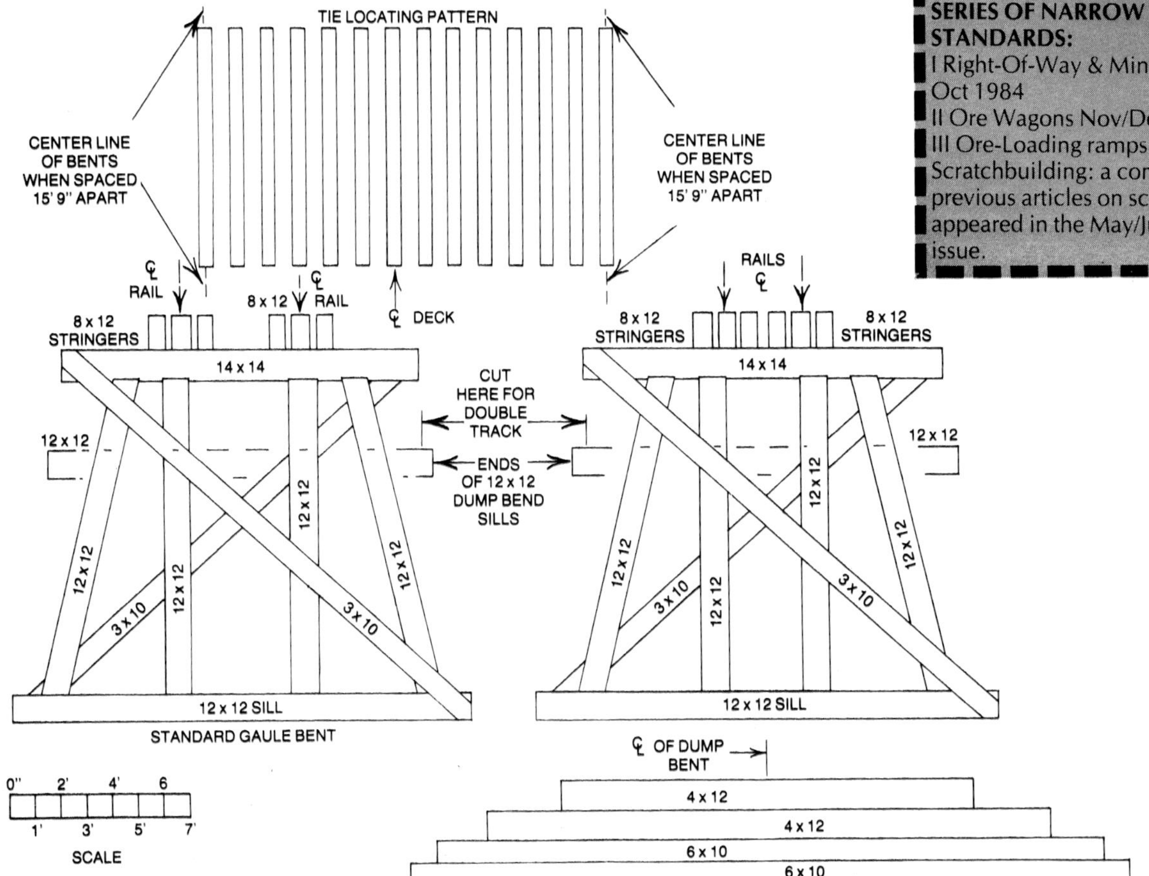

PATTERNS FOR SHORT TRESTLE BENTS & DUMP BENTS (ABUTMENTS) FOR NARROW & STANDARD GAUGE

CONVERSION CHART FOR ODD-SIZE TRESTLE TIMBERS IN HO SCALE

Full-Size beams	Nearest scale size wood for HO scale	Approx. scale size (error, if any)
3 x 10	Northeastern 1/3 x 1/8	3 x 10 7/8
8 x 16	Northeastern 3/32 x 3/16	7 x 16 1/2
14 x 14	Northeastern 5/32 x 5/32	14 x 14

The remaining 6 x 8, 6 x 10, 4 x 12 and 12 x 12 are standard scale lumber sizes offered by Kappler and Northeastern.

driven into the ground with a pile driver. More often (on the Santa Fe, for one) the pile trestle was constructed with a bottom horizontal beam just like a "timber" trestle. We opted for a pile trestle. You can use our materials to build from scratch or you can simply use our plans and the materials in a Campbell or Crummy kit. You will, however, need to buy the nut bolt washer castings for the Campbell kit.

You should spend some time determining just how much material your particular trestle will require. The horizontal spans of these trestles were most often about 16 feet which means the length of your trestle would be in multiples of 16 feet with any leftover length filled with a simulated earthen embankment.

If you are modeling in HO scale, you may need to know that the prototype piles range from about 12 to 18 inches in diameter. That's more than the common 1/8 inch diameter wood dowels. Clover House, however, and Northeastern have a 5/32 inch size which is about the equivalent of 14 inches in HO scale. The Campbell piles are closer to 17 scale inches; about right for a more modern mainline trestle. Also, the tie size on these C&S standard drawings is a bit different than that in the various kits and different from many other roads' trestles. These C&S ties are about 7 x 9 inches with the 9 inches the vertical dimension. The ties are about 9 scale feet long. The closest pre-cut ties I could find were Kappler's HO scale 7 x 9 inches by 8 foot 6 inches. You could, of course, cut the ties from the proper scale lumber size (5/64 x 3/32). Northeastern lumber would be closer to the proper size, in HO scale than the 6 x 8 inch scale strips in Kappler or Northeastern's scale lumber size range. There is a guard beam along the ends of the ties that is not shown on these drawings (but that does appear on Maxwell's copies) that I cut from HO scale 6 x 8 wood strip.

Maxwell's drawings show the locations of the bolt heads and even the nail heads. I used Grandt's number 5046 nut, bolt, washer castings with HO scale 1 3/4 inch square bolt heads. Those details are one of the most important parts of any wooden trestle — don't even think about skipping the step except, perhaps, to use a brown ink dot in N or Z scale to simulate the tiny bolts and washers. I used a brown ink dot to simulate the rust stains left by the nail heads on the tops of the top pieces and near the bases of the piles, again based on the nail locations shown on

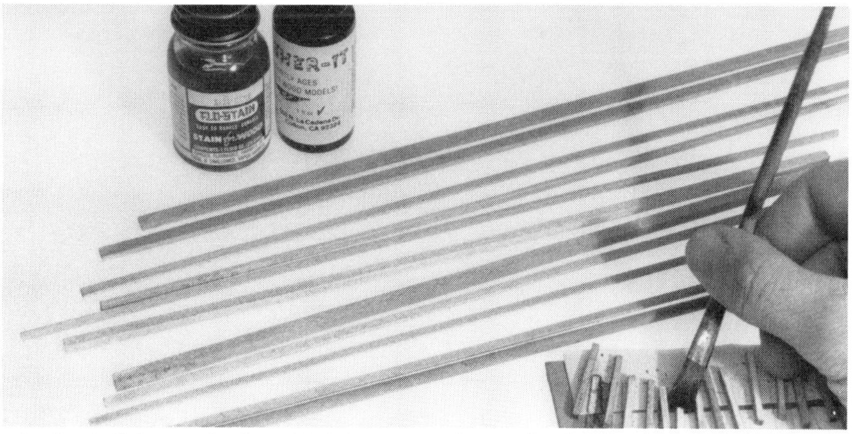

I stained all the wood strips with A-Wests "Weather-It", let that dry, then applied a coat of Floquil's Maple colored Flo-Stain. The colors that result are a close match for creosoted wood that has been outdoors for about a year or more.

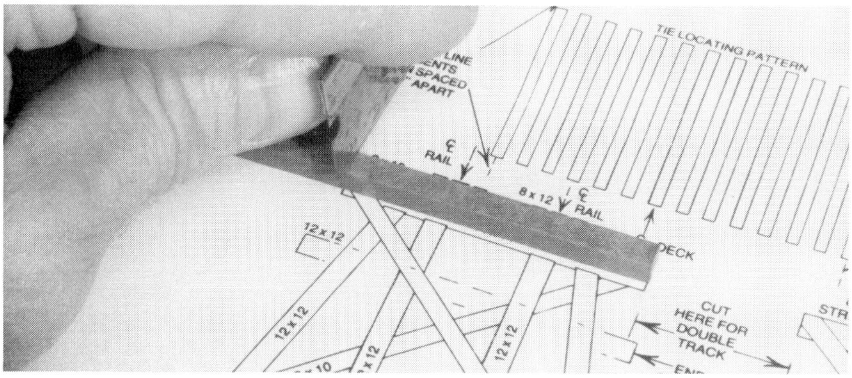

Have the HO scale plan enlarged or reduced by a photostat shop if you are not modeling in HO scale. You might also want to purchase John Maxwell's drawings as described in the text. Mark the length of the parts, from the plan, with a razor blade notch.

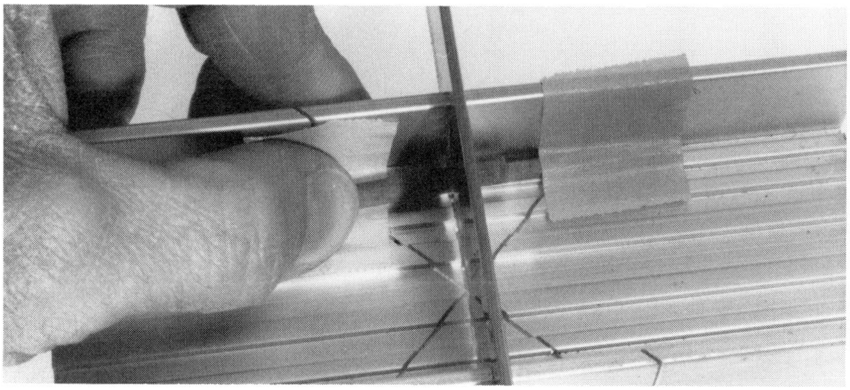

For parts larger than 1/8 inch across, cut with a razor saw rather than a razor blade or knife. I taped some scraps of wood inside this X-Acto miter box to make a jig for cutting the vertical pilings. A second block is taped to get the angle of the outside pilings.

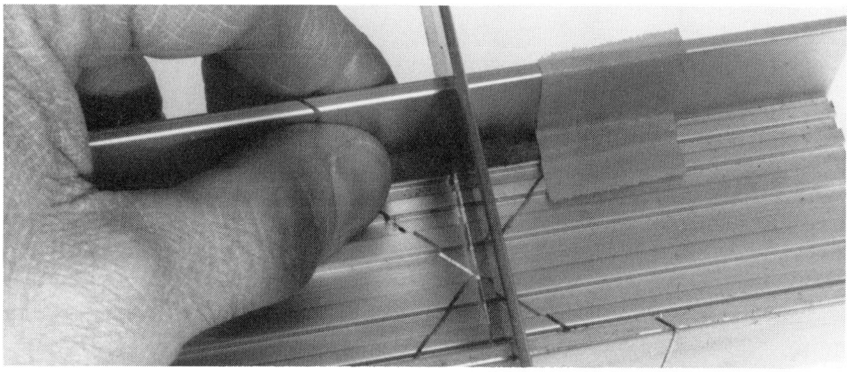

I removed the second block to cut the inside (perfectly vertical) pilings. That first block (right) provides a stop so that the angled and vertical pilings will all be the same length.

Maxwell's drawings. The drawing on this page is to HO scale and it shows only the important members so you can use it as a full-size assembly jig — the Maxwell drawings were photocopied from (according to the printing on the plans) ¼ inch = one foot originals, but the copies are approximately 20 percent smaller than S scale, so they must be photoreduced or enlarged if you are not modeling in HO scale. Remember, the plans are for either narrow or standard gauge so they are suitable for HO or HOn3.

Most mainline standard gauge railroads had an extra pair of rails spiked just inside the running rails of the track to act as guard rails. Most of the photos I've found of narrow gauge trestles and of earlier era standard gauge trestles that are 32 feet or shorter don't have those guard rails so you won't see them on the model of a 16 foot trestle in these photos.

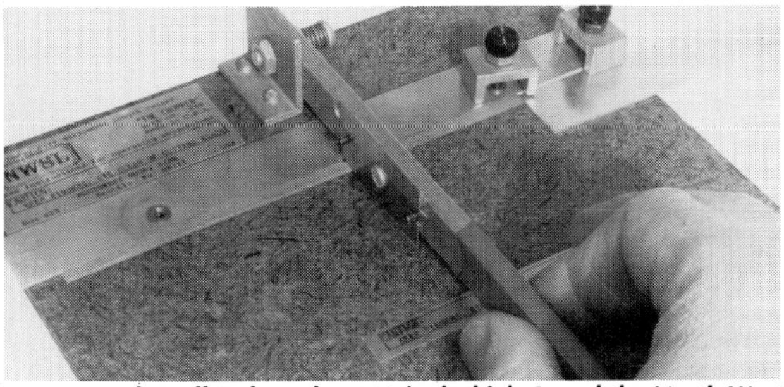

For wood smaller than about ⅛ inch thick, I used the North West Short Line "Chopper" to be sure all the parts were the same length. For thicker parts, you can make two cuts; one on each side of the wood.

I used only one copy of the plans for my jigs. If you are making a larger trestle, you might want to make several photocopies so you can build a half dozen bents and stringer units at a time to save delays waiting for the glue to dry. The width of the pins was just right to space the 8 x 12 stringers. I glued just the end ties in place, first, to hold the stringers together. When the glue dries, turn the unit over and place it over the tie drawing to add the rest of the ties.

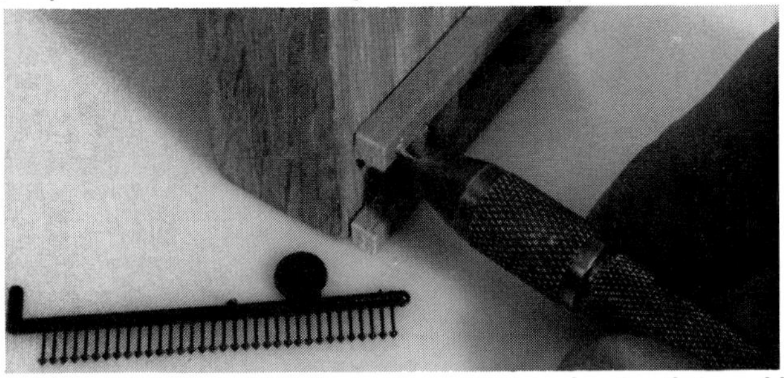

The only visible bolts in the bents are for cross bracing that would not be needed on these short dump bents (abutments). The bents would, however, be bolted to the wood that holds back the earthen fill. I used four nut, bolt, washer castings per bent.

I simulated the nail heads that hold the bottoms of the pilings to the horizontal beams with a dot of ink from a dark brown fine-tip felt-tipped pen. I also simulated a single nail head in each end of the top beam.

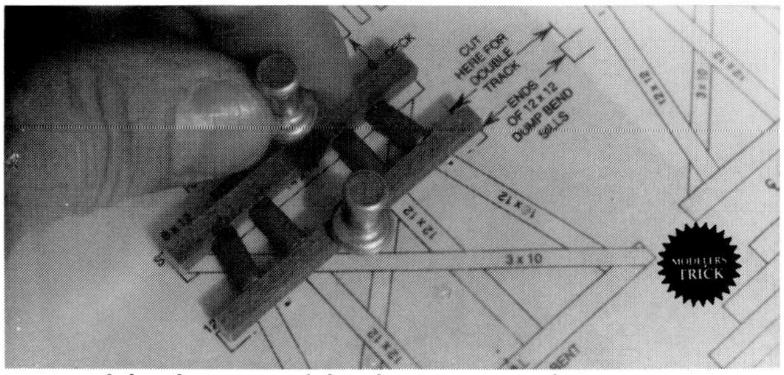

I taped the photocopy of the plan to a scrap of Homosote (Upsom board will also work). I covered the plan with waxed paper, then used metal map pins to hold the wood over the plan — the face of the pin, not the shaft, holds the wood. I used Super Jet cyanoacrylate cement because it dries quickly, but any wood glue will do.

The real secret of a realistic trestle lies in the profusion of bolt and nail marks. There are 8 bolts on each side of the stringer/tie units. I drilled number 74 size holes to fit the number 5046 Grandt nut, bolt, washer castings.

A pair of 6 x 8 inch boards run the length of the trestle to help cross brace the unit. Simulate the nuts, bolts and washers that hold these braces with the Grandt 5046 plastic castings, four per board. Some trestles have additional 2 x 6 boards beside these braces to serve as a walkway.

The dump bent board pattern has a centerline indicated. If you are building a double track trestle, like this one, add the center-to-center spacing of your double track to the length of the pieces at that centerline. I assembled the pieces over waxed paper on the plan and used a steel ruler and file to keep the parts straight. I cut the boards into random 8 to 16 foot lengths for this extra-wide dump bent; single lengths would be fine for a single track bent like the drawing.

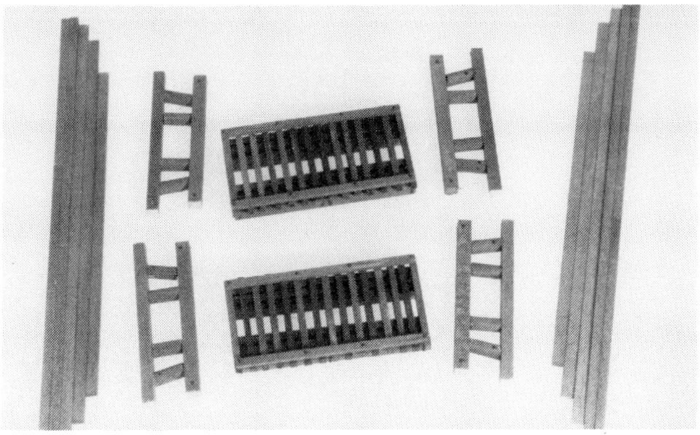

The parts for double track trestle just one span (16 scale feet) long. If you are building a double track trestle that is taller than about 8 feet, the bents must support both tracks. These low bents, however, would most likely be individual bents for each track, particularly in this lightweight C&S design.

This is what the assembled double track single span trestle would look like from the bottom. Do NOT, however, assemble the parts until you are ready to install them on the layout — this photo is here to show the construction more clearly than would be possible with the trestle in place.

Remove the plastic ties from the rails where they cross the bridge span. To assemble the trestle, clamp the tie units to the bottoms of the rails with clothespins and glue them down with Pliobond. Add the end bents and dump bent panels last with the tops of the dump bent panels just 3 scale inches below the tops of the ties.

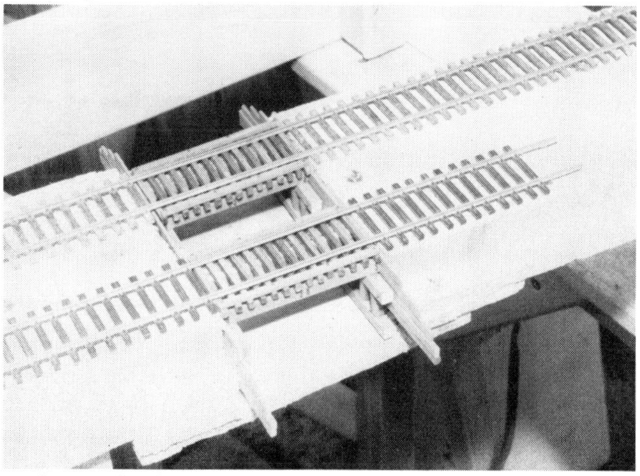

The completed trestle can now be touched up with Weather It and Maple stain on any areas that have bare wood.

Assembling Campbell's Trestle Kits

Basics For Beginners

ASSEMBLING CAMPBELL'S TRESTLE KITS:

Every step we've shown for the assembly of a scratchbuilt trestle would apply to the construction of a Campbell trestle kit. Campbell supplies the plans and pre-cuts many of the parts but you must still do some cutting. Follow the same sequence of pre-staining the parts and don't forget to add the nut, bolt, washer castings. The Campbell kits are replicas of stronger, more modern, trestles with six, rather than four, vertical pilings or beams. The angle of the extreme end pilings is also a bit different than this C&S Standard. You can use the parts of a Campbell kit with our plans to build a C&S Standard trestle, but some of the individual parts will be a bit larger. If you are going to build a ballasted deck trestle, the model will be more like the modern prototypes if you build it wider, with an extra pair of vertical pilings, to match the photos in this issue of the modern C&S trestle.

Setting The Scene

The hills and trees can stay much the same; just change the backdrops to match the terrain on the geographic-scene map and drop in the locomotive and rolling stock of the prototype that roamed that part of the country.

The concept of dropping in new structures and even complete diorama "scene sites" is part of the Thomasville layout concept. Just dropping in some B&O equipment doesn't set this scene in the east; the wooded backdrop and a few brick buildings also help to make it credibly eastern.

A cattle pen, a couple of timber/log houses in place of frame cottages and a mountain backdrop help transport the scene from the east to the rockies; from the fifties to the teens.

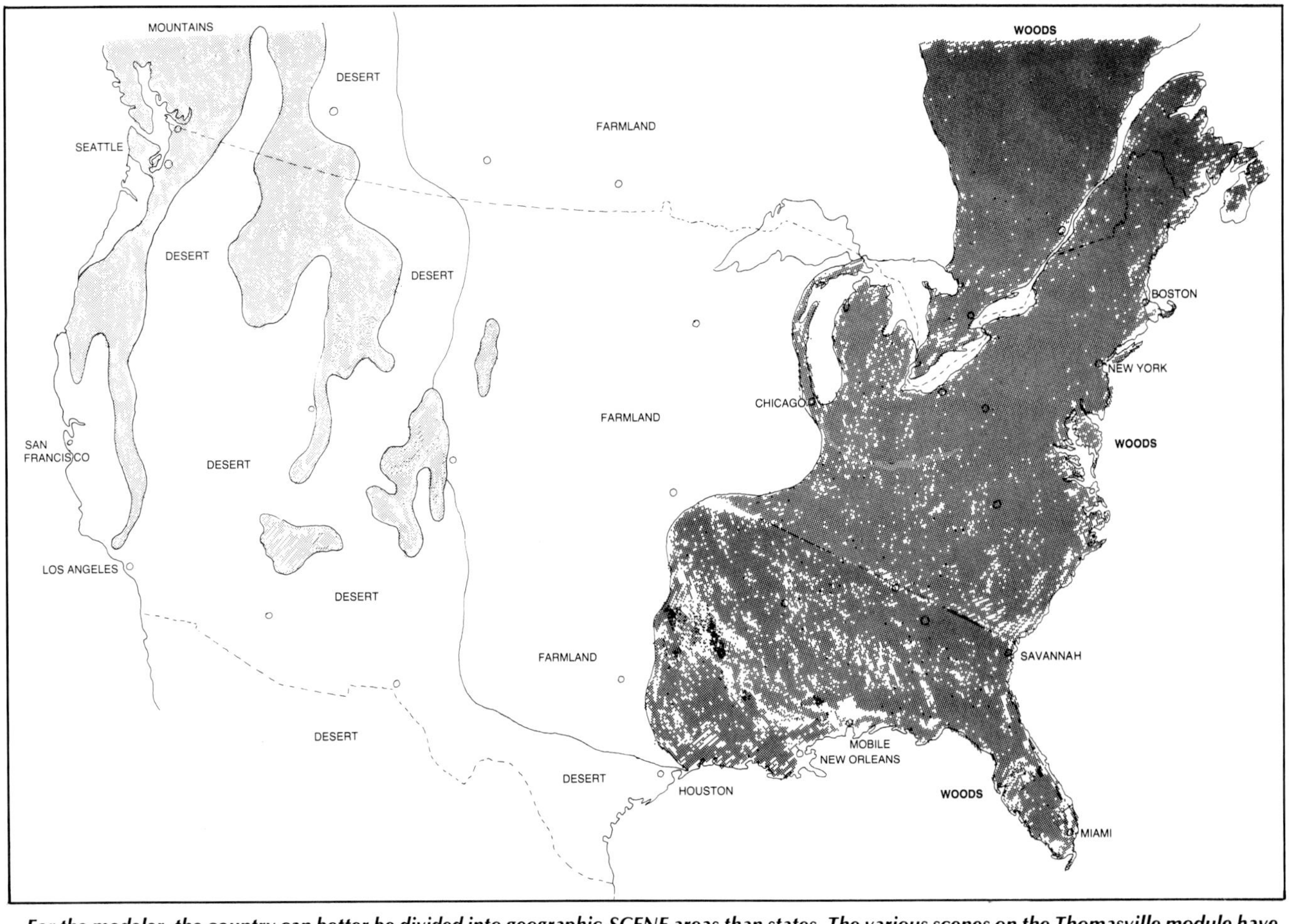

For the modeler, the country can better be divided into geographic-SCENE areas than states. The various scenes on the Thomasville module have been matched to the "Mountains", "Desert", Farmland" or "Woods" where the specific prototype operated. The Santa Fe, for instance traversed the farmlands and the mountains of Raton as well as the usual desert that is commonly identified with the ATSF.

Reprinted from November/December 1985 issue

A simple alteration in the colored sky backdrop can change the geographic locale. The far right end of Faller's number 515 backdrop used as-is to suggest the "WOODS" areas common to much of America.

The far left end of the Faller no. 515 backdrop includes enough FARMLAND to typify even Kansas along the river valleys.

A 11 x 17 inch photo-mural of the Roaring Fork Valley in Colorado was produced, by Kodak (any photo dealer can order one for you) from my slide. In the scenes of the completed Rocky Mountain (Colorado Midland), this backdrop has been faded with a thin coat of Polly S white and 19 parts water applied with an air brush.

A Library . . .

. . . of Buildings, Dioramas & Railroad Equipment for versatile, but prototype-satisfying modeling in less space.

THOMASVILLE, CIRCA 1907

The mountain-based industries included shipments of logs, hay, limestone, ore and cattle. Most of that stuff was simply piled into the cars by hand. Even the cattle pen was an option. Hence, there's a lot of bare ground scene sites in place with a couple of timber houses, a section house and, of course, outhouses for each. The locomotives are brass MEW imports from the Littletown Hobbies collection in Littleton, Colorado; both are collector's items.

MISSOURI, CIRCA 1959

Many of the structures and scene sites have been removed from the shelves to alter the geographic setting as well as the time period on the layout. The CM station happens to be painted in Union Pacific colors (accurate for both Colorado Midland and most eras of active UP passenger service). The cattle pen and station remain but the outhouses are gone. The grain elevator helps "place" the scene.

MIDWEST, CIRCA 1973

There are miles of Santa Fe mainline rolling through farmlands than through the desert so that geographic scene is certainly appropriate. This town is served by both the BN and ATSF. The grain elevator has expanded with extra silos, the station is gone, replaced by a couple of steel buildings. The cattle pen is also gone, replaced by a tilt-up concrete industry. The blue buildings are a prefab steel warehouse and a painted "stone" foundry.

We all make far too many decisions in our private and work lives. When it comes to our hobbies, we'd like to be able to kick back and avoid decision making in any form. But what if you like the Union Pacific as well as the Baltimore & Ohio, if you prefer a few 4-6-0 steam locomotives but simply love SD40-2 diesels? What if you like the wooden architecture of the midwest but want to model the B&O in Connecticut? If you're like most model railroaders, you simply mix in all that stuff on your decision-free layout.

What if, however, you want your model railroad to look like the real thing? Then that hodgepodge of railroads, geographic scenes and time periods just won't work. You're looking at the answer, of course; build one railroad with a few removable structures, a few removable dioramas and, perhaps, with even changeable backdrops. We did.

The concept of keeping a "library" of structures is one that is used by the Buhl Planetarium and Institute of Popular Science in Pittsburg. They completely rebuild their layout each year from just such a structure and scene library. The Buhl layout was featured in the January/February 1984 issue. Several later issues have also featured the concept. We call it "Scene Sites" because most folks consider a diorama to be a free-standing display, not a removable part of a model railroad layout.

Here you see the concept of a Scene Site Library at work. The wood grain elevator that was common in the east prior to the thirties appears only with the eastern-prototype Maryland & Pennsylvania equipment. When the era and the geographic scene change to the Union Pacific in the midwest, the grain elevator is swapped for a corrugated metal replica. Later, when the BN is portrayed in the seventies, the grain elevator is supplemented with three large grain silos. The mountain-based Colorado Midland, circa 1907, has no credible place for a grain elevator so its place is occupied by simple bare ground covered with weeds and bushes. Note, too that the backdrops are changed for the mountain scene and, in that one scene, even the trees are replaced with replicas of scrub pine seen beside the real CM right of way.

The point of all this is to show you don't have to make decisions in your modeling and you don't have to compromise realism. The scene site library, used with an appropriate mix of locomotives and rolling stock, can allow you to model a diverse array of prototypes on a single, small, model railroad layout.

The rolling stock and locomotives for eras NOT currently in use are stored in Proto Power West's "Train-Tote" corrugated boxes with foam dividers. They also offer a wood carrying case if you need to transport the equipment to a modular layout meeting. You can order direct from Proto Power West at 3432 Lucero Ave., Dept. MRG, LaVerne, CA 91750. You might also consider a glass front china cabinet (finish-it-yourself furniture stores sell them) to house the Scene Sites and structures rather than just a dusty metal shelf.

Corrections, Mistakes, blunders and ways to do it better *next* time

Nobody gets *everything* right the FIRST time.

The track planning, operation and construction techniques used to make this Thomasville model railroad have all been selected specifically to illustrate state-of-the-art in this hobby. The goal we established was to create a model railroad that could be as satisfying as possible both to operate and to view with stall-free operation and (relatively) simple wiring.

Part of the definition of state-of-the-art would be to include methods that avoided mistakes inherent in outmoded techniques. State-of-the-art does not, however, mean perfection. I don't know of any model railroader who has ever built the "perfect" model railroad. The process of building-it-better includes an awareness that there is something to be learned during the actual construction. I did learn. Here are some of my mistakes. You will probably make your own. You may even prefer to repeat my mistakes because you like the results of the "mistake" better than the "perfect" alternative.

The most noticeable changes are in the way the original Thomasville track plan was altered. First, to allow the use of four number 8 turnouts on the mainline in place of the original number 6 turnouts. The larger radius of the number 8s provided a much smoother appearance that better suited a mainline.

In a similar vein, the center-to-center track spacing on the mainline was changed from 2 inches to 2½ inches. The wider spacing allows articulated steam locomotives and/or 86 foot passenger cars and/or 89 foot Trailer Train flat cars to pass one another without sideswiping.

The three-dimensional aspect of a track plan is sometimes not apparent until you build it. The turnouts at the top and bottom of the siding © and "Loads-in/Empties-out" tracks were moved and the hidden tracks' curves altered so both were 30 inch radius. A crossover was built between the two tracks at the extreme rear of the layout but it does not appear on the plans. It will only be used if the railroad layout is extended to the right.

The angle of siding ® was altered to move it farther away from the station and to provide an extra couple of inches to increase its car-holding capacity.

I used white paper towels for the scenery, soaked in colored Hydrocal plaster. The coloring was wasted because any chips show up as bits of white paper. Next time I'll go back to brown industrial-grade paper towels so the chips will be brown.

Plaster of Paris was used to shape some of the hills. Another mistake. It is far too soft and powdery when colored. Hydrocal or, as Gordon Haack and others have suggested, U.S. Gypsum's Ultracal-30 would be a better choice. We sealed the plaster of Paris with Matte Medium and water to keep it from crumbling.

I'm not at all pleased with the concave shape of the mountain at the far right rear of the layout. More wadded-up newspaper should have been used to insure a convex shape to the hills. I'll wait to saw it off until the next segment of the layout is added.

I am, you can be sure, planning on extending the railroad up the hill beyond Thomasville (to the right). The extension will include a chunk of mountain, perhaps some snowsheds and a wye/reverse loop to increase the scope of operations.

It's more difficult to create a finely-textured model railroad scene like this than you might imagine. The texturing is no problem but keeping the switch points moving and the flangeways clear is difficult. The liberal use of oil on the switch points, as listed in the "Super-Detailed Track and Roadbed" segment (wherein the track was ballasted) MUST be followed. Also, the layout must be thoroughly vacuumed at least five times: before pinning down the track on the bare Homosote, (2) after installing the Kadee ramps, (3) after pulling up the masking tape that protected the track during plaster-application, (4) after you have applied the textures and ballast and (5) after rubbing the tops of the rails with a Bright Boy eraser AND digging-out any clogged flangeways at turnouts or road crossings AND scraping the dirt road surfaces with the Bright Boy to simulate tire-worn dirt.

The wiring diagram illustrates the old-fashioned buss wire method of connecting power to the layout. I used it bacause I find it easier to be sure I have a common ground. If you understand model railroad electronics well use the common rail wiring method. A sample is on page 46 of the Winter 1981 issue of **Model Railroading** showing a typical wiring diagram for common rail. The carrier/command-control systems can be wired using the common rail system or the buss wire system. The common rail system uses less wire but you must be absulutely certain to make the same rail "common"; a point I personally find confusing. The Spring 1982 and the Vol. 13, No. 2 issues of **Model Railroading** contain test reports on all fine popular brands of carrier/command-control systems.

Again, if this is your "next" model railroad, don't try to make it perfect because you probably cannot accomplish that goal. Do the best you can to avoid the mistakes you made on the first layout and the mistakes I made on this one. If you're not really having fun, you're taking the hobby too seriously. For me, building this layout was fun.